Contents

Acknowledgements

The authors wish to acknowledge Jay Slater and Nick Grant, for their adventurousness and imagination in commissioning *The Devil's History Book*.

We would also specifically like to thank the following individuals regarding their contributions to *God's Assassins*:

Dr Farhad Daftary, for speaking with authority and erudition on behalf of the Institute of Ismaili Studies.

Ken Hollings, for his imaginative input and cerebral stimulation.

Abandon reason, all ye who enter.

This is the first volume of *The Devil's History Book*, and the authors make no apologies for the subjective views of the distant past and contemporary society that you are about to read.

In marrying the arcane with popular culture, we are entering areas where no reputable historian would stray. It is only fitting, therefore, that we should begin with the subject of Hasan-i-Sabbah and the Assassins.

To subvert the words oft attributed to Hasan:

Everything is true. Everything is permitted . . .

Introduction

As the sepia-brown mist descends over the twilight mountain, the old man's knowing eyes gaze through narrowed slits. Eyes that have known the bloodshed of the ages and the inner peace of godliness. From his fortress vantage point he sees all: how the doctrines of true faith and commitment have been written in blood.

He sees the phantoms that bestride the centuries. The diligent killers who await their moment to step out of the anonymous crowd and into history. The political zealots who extol the bomb over the ballot box. The cyber-guerrillas who wage war through the medium of electronic communications . . .

The word 'assassin' was bequeathed to us via Hasan-i-Sabbah (or Hassan bin-Sabah – make your choice; choose your reality) and his mysterious campaign in the eleventh and twelfth centuries. Today, the word evokes a rogue's gallery of killers for hire or drug-crazed thugs, or perhaps lonely little men who long to usurp the status of the bigger men they plan to kill.

The 'Hashishim' (as history sometimes terms them) were made of more substantial stuff. Trained by Hasan to defend the Nizari sub-sect of Islam (now known as the Ismailis) against the might of the Sunni majority, their stealth and ruthlessness were matched only by their courage and fervent belief. Representing a small minority within the Shi'a faith, in their targeted murders (or assassinations) they were fighting for the survival of their creed. In our modern world they might be termed 'terrorists' or 'freedom fighters', depending on which side of the blade you stand.

So we invite the reader to submit to the homicidal raptures of faith, and to follow the progress through history of the *Assassin* (the follower of Hasan Sabbah) and the *assassin* (whose existence is defined by an act of targeted murder) alike. In our retelling of ancient history we perceive the medieval Middle East via the sensibilities of the fascinated Westerners that we are. And so we tell our tale in Western shorthand: for followers of the Nizari or Ismaili faith, read 'Assassin'; when we speak of them collectively we may refer to them as the 'Hashishim'. Where history infers that these clandestine religious hitmen were pious abstainers, we will acknowledge it; where legend depicts them as inspired to acts of homicidal bravery by hallucinogenic drugs, we will follow the suggestion to its ultimate conclusion.

In exploring such shadowy legends, myth becomes as real and as potent as empirically-provable history. Ancient and modern times collide and collapse into each other; the roots of political and theological terrorism intertwine and interconnect. The self-sacrificing Assassin and the suicide bomber are not one, but they are bound by a distant vision of Paradise which becomes the mnemonic to murder. Modern 'asymmetric wars' are fought with the adapted tools of consumer technology, yet they have their roots in events depicted in this book, in the epic bloodshed and internecine rivalries of the medieval Crusades.

In seeking to act as historians, we have sometimes behaved as pulp-fiction writers. In trying to establish the truth about a murkily obscure period of history, we have become enmeshed in mythology. For the Old Man of the Mountain – as Hasan, and one of his successors as Grand Master of the Assassins, has become known – maintains a shadowy presence in the culture in his mythic form. The pious patriarch of Ismaili history becomes the ghostly subversive imagined by dystopian visionary author William Burroughs.

Both are one. The mythology can no longer be extricated from the reality. *Nothing is true. Everything is permitted.*

I

BETWEEN THE BROADSWORD AND THE SCIMITAR

It is the year 1291 in the mighty walled city of Acre, a Crusader port in the ancient land of Syria. Surrounding the city on all three sides is the mighty host of the Sultan Qalawun, tens of thousands of Mamluk shock troops, Nubian archers and Muslim militia, among them many volunteers whose kin have been butchered by the Crusaders. They now bay for Christian blood.

Only the harbour provides a vital link to the open sea for Acre's beleaguered Christian defenders. All attempts to dislodge the attackers have failed; surprise counterattacks have been bloodily repulsed, naval assaults scattered by storms. Many citizens have already left by sea, a growing flood of refugees that began in January when the rumours of Muslim attack became certainty, and the few remaining picket troops were pulled back from outlying garrisons to man the walls of Acre. Now only the desperate and insanely stubborn remain, those with nothing to lose, committed by sacred oath or crazed determination to stem the Saracen tide or perish.

Just as the defences of Acre are pitted with gaping holes and crumbling at the foundations, so a month of siege has left its mark on faces hollow with exhaustion and fear. Towering war machines that the Mamluks call Fury and Victory hurl rocks the size of tables at the city, creating a ceaseless barrage that shakes the ground, as dozens of sister engines rain crude explosives and Greek fire, the dreaded incendiary that turns any unfortunate human target into a living torch.

Day by day, inch by inch, the Sultan's frontlines draw closer to Acre's outer walls, sheltered by wooden barricades and wicker screens, supported by trenches dug by industrious siege engineers. The stones launched by Crusader counterbatteries bounce off the Saracen's mobile defences, while the carabohas fire keeps the Christian crossbowmen off the walls. The defenders have learned to dread this Turkish war engine which launches large iron bolts with startling speed and accuracy, punching through shields and wooden defences.

Throughout the second week of May, Acre's formidable defences gradually disintegrate. First the King's Tower implodes in a plume of dust, rubble and smoke, then the English Tower, the Tower of the Countess of Blois and those flanking St Anthony's Gate crumble, as Mamluk engineers patiently dig tunnels to weaken their foundations. By 17 May, the Accursed Tower has become the linchpin of the Crusader defences, a final desperate bulwark against the furious swell of Mamluk fire and steel now engulfing Acre. That day the docks are alive with the last refugees fleeing the ultimate assault. Dazed women and children too tired for tearful farewells fight for space with defiant merchants and nobles, their attachment to their former lives finally overcome by the miasma of hopelessness, black as the pall of smoke and dust that hangs over the doomed city. Only the damned remain.

Had the Roman Catholic or Greek Orthodox Churches required images of Hell to terrify their congregations, they need have looked no further than the morning of 18 May 1291 in Acre.

Before dawn a terrible tattoo begins from a huge drum to signal the final assault, soon joined by 300 camels carrying drummers and trumpeters, and a deafening cacophony that echoes through the skull like a maddening pulse. The shower of rocks, grenades and Greek fire intensifies and then, after a strange silence, the attack truly begins.

The air within the walls is soon so thick with sulphur and smoke that the defenders can scarcely see beyond their shields. From out of this stinging mist comes an iron hail of arrows, javelins and bolts. An agonised choir screams and hurls oaths in many different European tongues, augmenting the unholy percussion of the Mamluk drums as the metal downpour takes its lethal toll. The wise warrior lays low, weapon clasped in his sweat-slicked palm, awaiting the moment to take again to his feet.

Seconds seem to telescope into hours before the unmistakable sound of steel striking shield. The Crusaders give out their battle-cry, as the bloodthirsty havoc of mêlée engulfs the walls. Amid the chaos, the mail-clad warrior monks of the Military Orders stand in their distinctive liveries – the red cross on white of the Templars, the white on black of the Hospitaller Order of St John, the black on white of the Teutonic Knights. Every sword-bearing brother fights with bloodthirsty determination, bellowing encouragement to their fellow defenders, berating any that turn to run.

But it is not enough. The Mamluk horde is implacable, a heaving tide of edged steel and battle-maddened eyes that laps around the walls, surging over ruined masonry and human casualties, carrying all before it. Knots of warrior monks stem the tide, but then they fall. Resistance melts, fight turns to panic as Acre's defenders try to flee toward the docks or to one of the stoutly fortified buildings providing a last line of defence within the walls of Acre.

Of these, only the house of the Knights Templar endures, though those within witness a soul-searing display as the Mamluk army, gorged on glory, vent their vengeful anger. Few buildings escape the torch. Almost none of the inhabitants are spared. Soldiers and priests alike are butchered like so many cattle, their pleas of surrender ignored; women are raped repeatedly – some, it will later be said, have mutilated their own faces with knives in the hope of avoiding sexual assault.

The Templars can only look on impotently from the arrow-slits of their headquarters until the enemy's fury is glutted. Then a second siege begins, as Sultan Qalawun directs his attentions to the handful of warrior monks and civilians who took shelter in their fortified stronghold. Days turn into weeks as the Mamluk siege engineers patiently tunnel their way inside the Templars' walls.

Meanwhile, the Sultan sends envoys to the gate. The siege has gone on long enough, they say, enough blood has been spilt. If the Templars will surrender their final foothold in Acre, then they and those under their protection will be free to leave unmolested, their property and honour intact.

The garrison, exhausted and short of supplies, agrees. The bolts are drawn back and the heavy gates creak open, allowing entry to a dazzling sunset and a stream of heavily-armed Mamluk warriors. The air is stifling with tension as Saracen eyes adjust to the gloom of the Templar courtyard. Women and children huddle by the walls, as the Templars observe their conquerors striding into the inner sanctum with gritted teeth.

The Mamluks' broad grins turn to triumphant laughter. One stoops towards a girl crouched closest to the gate; he reaches out and yanks her filthy dress from her shoulders to a sound of tearing cloth. With that comes a sudden explosion of violence. Templars, outraged at the betrayal, fall upon the Mamluk contingent with a flurry of heavy blows. Shoulders are put to the gates, closing them fast behind those members of the Saracen contingent who survive the first attack.

None will survive the second. Outside, the Mamluks watch with horror as the broken bodies of their comrades cascade from the upper windows of the Templar headquarters.

The following morning sees more Saracen envoys at the gates. The previous day's events were unfortunate, they say, but it was nobody's intention. Nothing has changed, the Sultan's offer still stands and, to confirm his good faith, he will meet with a contingent of the Knights of the Temple.

Internal discussion among the brotherhood reaches fever-pitch. Eventually, those who see nothing to lose in negotiation, when things are becoming more desperate by the day, prevail. A party of Templars, led by the most senior surviving brother, emerge from the gates, blinking in the morning sun. They have walked only a few paces before the Sultan's envoy confronts them, barking for them to kneel. The command is soon backed by action; Mamluk guards surround the Templars, forcing them to their knees. Then, with shocking suddenness, blades began to fall. They catch the sunlight before hacking into bared necks, sending crimson geysers arcing into the air as the Templars' heads tumble from their limp bodies.

If the atmosphere within the Templar headquarters had previously been that of the condemned cell, it is now that of a tomb. The only palatable prospect for the grim survivors is that they take as many of their foes to the grave with them as possible. If any such silent prayer is mouthed during those unbearable final days, then it will be answered.

A messenger informs Sultan Qalawun that their mines have finally reached beneath the foundations. The engineers have only to set fire to the props holding up the roof of the mine and the walls of the Templar fortification above will surely crumble. The Mamluk horde assembles; the drummers and trumpeters begin their menacing din; at the Sultan's signal, the assault begins. Battering rams thunder against the gates as the defenders hurl everything they can find from the fortification's upper windows. The building itself seems to shudder, then one of its walls gives way from the bottom. Bloodthirsty Mamluks pour through the breach, overwhelming the solitary knight who turns to face them.

In moments every Templar will face a dozen opponents, fighting back-to-back against impossible odds. For each Mamluk that falls, three more force their way into each chamber and courtyard. The building echoes with shouts, cries and the clatter of steel upon steel. Soon there is barely room to swing a sword, as a surge of Saracen warriors step up to take part in the final triumph over the hated Crusaders. The building shudders once more as another wall falls and masonry begins to cascade down upon Crusader and Saracen alike. Then there is a rumble like approaching thunder from the very bowels of the building and, with a juddering crash, the entire structure falls in on itself. The Mamluk engineers have done their job too well. Arches collapse, roofs tumble, walls disintegrate in a whirlwind of dust and debris, forming an instant tomb for all within, defender and attacker alike.

***

The rumble of Acre's final collapse could be felt as far afield as Europe. The mighty walled city of Acre was the last Crusader stronghold in the Middle East. When it fell to the Mamluk army, it left the Western dream of Outremer – a Christian kingdom in the Middle East, ruled from the holy city of Jerusalem – in smouldering ruins. The Mamluks – elite Islamic warrior-slaves, bought in boyhood to be trained as soldiers, earning their freedom through military service – were now in the ascendant. Facing them were the cream of the Christian forces, the fanatics of the Military Orders who served God by slaying unbelievers. Combining the lifelong training at arms of the knight with the fanatical dedication of a monk, the orders were the medieval Church's foreshadow of the Nazi SS (indeed, the SS would be partially modelled on orders like those of the Templars and the Teutonic Knights). Horrific stories had abounded among the besieged Muslims of Jerusalem that the infidel orders had impaled and eaten Arab children. Today they read like a myth to rival the Jewish blood libels – except that some of the Crusaders' own military logs concur with these descriptions of cannibal terrorism.

The Assassins represent the third of these military elites of the Medieval Middle East, the most effective 'black ops' or secret service units of the era, with a record that at least rivals the most effective modern organisations like the CIA or Mossad. 'Assassin' is a controversial title for members of a revolutionary religious sect which developed into a small nation-state of sorts, but it describes the act for which they became infamous in their day – sufficiently so to leave its mark on history as the semantic origin of the modern word.

Some historians prefer to refer to the sect as Ismailis or, earlier in their history, Nizaris, in reference to the specific religious factions to which they belonged. They reject 'Assassin' and the Arabic terms from which it derived, with all of their overtones of drug consumption, as politically-incorrect libels. While conceding that the term 'Assassin' may well have been one more commonly used by Europeans than the natives of the Middle East, and quite possibly based upon negative views of the sect broadcast by their Islamic rivals, nobody denies that they were masters of the art of political murder. And so, for us, they will be termed 'Assassins'. (The etymology of the word 'Assassin' is much disputed – it may have originated from 'Hashishim' or else, as Dr Farhad Daftary suggests, have merely been shorthand for 'follower of Hasan'.)

So, were the Assassins present at the climactic clash between the Military Orders and Mamluks in 1291? It is very possible. Assassin agents are recorded as having successfully infiltrated Christian courts (including Acre) and Islamic armies (including the Mamluk forces), both as overt envoys for the sect and as covert enemy operatives – what we might today call 'sleeper agents'. But if any such undercover agents were present then they would remain 'sleepers' for ever, awaiting the secret command to action in vain. For unless we believe some of the more exotic conspiracy theories (of which more later), then Assassin power was broken by this time, its leaders dead, its strongholds destroyed. If this heretical medieval sect survived as a credible force at all, it was as hired murderers at the beck and call of the Mamluk Sultans – a mere shadow of the glory days when the cult's very name struck terror into the hearts of caliphs and kings, Christians and Muslims, alike.

***

The history of the Assassins occupies an almost identical period to that of the Crusades. Alamut, the fortress in what is now modern Iran that would become the sect's stronghold, fell to their legendary founder Hasan Sabbah in 1090 by a combination of conversion and cunning. Just five years later but thousands of miles distant, the Christian holy man Pope Urban II's preaching would launch the European invasion that struck deep into Muslim territory, and later become known as the First Crusade. 'A race alien to God has invaded the land of Christians,' ran Urban's rousing of the faithful, 'has reduced the people with sword, rapine and flame.' His bizarre description of the satanic Saracens (for which read Muslims) smearing the blood of their circumcised foreskins on Christian altars pre-dated the more extreme Christian 'blood libel' against the Jews in the twelfth century. (The accusation that Jews slaughtered Christian children to use their blood in religious rites later provoked a violent attack on the Jewish delegation at the coronation of Richard the Lionheart, bloodstained British hero of the Crusades.)

There were eight subsequent Crusades, before the fall of Acre in 1291 effectively ended Christendom's ambitions. Assassin dreams of power and influence ended at much the same time, in much the same way. In around 1275, a small force of the faithful managed to recapture the Assassins' fortress stronghold of Alamut in Persia, but were driven out within the year – from whence they disappear from the history books, into the realms of rumour and legend. Some continue to claim, however, as we shall see, that the Assassins survive underground and are still with us to this day.

In the Western popular imagination the central characters in the drama of the Crusades have always been the English Crusader king, Richard I, who first captured the city of Acre for the Christians in 1192, and his Kurdish nemesis, Saladin, Muslim Sultan of Syria and Egypt. Though they exchanged gifts in the spirit of worthy foes, contrary to popular mythology the two never actually met face-to-face. The idea that they did derives primarily from a book by the Scottish author Sir Walter Scott entitled *The Talisman*, one of a number of popular European novels of the 1800s that romanticised the brutality of the Middle Ages. In *The Talisman*, when Scott has the two foes meet to parlay, Richard tries to impress Saladin by severing an iron bar in two with a single stroke of his broadsword. In response, the Saracen deftly slices a silk pillow in half with his razor-sharp scimitar, something Richard's powerful but blunt blade could never achieve. While the entire episode is fiction, it also captures a certain essence of the conflict.

For a pattern had emerged during the battles of the Crusades. The essential Christian soldier was the mounted knight; heavily armoured and highly trained, his favoured tactic was to hit the opponent with a charge. The full force of a trained warhorse at full gallop, concentrated into the tip of a lance, could shatter any shield, armour, flesh or bone that it connected with head-on. By way of contrast, Christian commentators were stunned by the skill and speed with which lightly-armoured mounted Muslim warriors could approach their opponents, loosing a deadly salvo of arrows while deftly evading pursuit. But if the Crusaders could successfully land the deadly hammer blow of a cavalry charge, they could generally carry the day.

In other circumstances, fatigue and attrition often took their toll. Records of the Crusades state that it was not uncommon to see a knight continuing to advance while peppered with arrows like a porcupine. The same armour that protected him from the arrowheads was cripplingly heavy under any conditions; under the heat of a Middle Eastern sun it could be a potentially fatal encumbrance as, blinded by sweat and weakened by dehydration, he fell easy prey to a more nimble opponent. This same contest between force and flexibility – the raw power of the broadsword versus the fluid sharpness of the scimitar – characterises many aspects of the Crusades.

If the Christian invaders can be characterised by a broadsword and the forces of orthodox Islam as a scimitar, the emblem of the Assassins is the knife. While Hasan Sabbah did field regular armies on occasion, his principle strategic weapon was the lone killer who struck a single opponent by surprise, far from the chaos of the battlefield. Death dealt by the Assassin's blade was up close and personal, often taking place in public.

The agents Hasan employed against his deadly adversaries in Sunni Islam were expressly forbidden from using conventional weapons of war, such as swords or bows, which might allow some hope of escape or a fighting chance. It was considered the greatest of honours for the agent to give his life in the course of an assassination, and use of the knife demanded that he get close to his target with no thought for his own survival. The Assassin's knife became a weapon of psychological warfare, sometimes simply left on a sleeping opponent's pillow to remind him that he would never be safe, a vivid warning to those leaders and religious scholars who opposed the sect.

Osama ibn Murshid ibn Munqidh, probably the most important personal chronicler of the Crusades from an Islamic perspective, records a contest between Saracen steel and the Assassin's blade:

> 'I had a fight with an Assassin who had a dagger in his hand while I had my sword. He rushed at me with the dagger and I hit him in the middle of his forearm as he was grasping the hilt of the dagger and holding the blade close to his forearm. My blow cut about four inches off the dagger-blade and severed his forearm in two. The mark of the edge of the dagger was left on the edge of my sword. A craftsman in our town, on seeing it, said: "I can remove this dent." But I said: "Leave it as it is. It is the best thing on my sword." The mark is there to this day.'

Osama had both personal and religious reasons for his antipathy towards the Assassins, and has a habit of making himself the hero of the many fascinating episodes he records. While evidently proud of overcoming his foe with an Arabic blade, it would be interesting to know just how easily he slept after the event.

The curved cavalry sabre, reminiscent of the Saracens, would become the commonest sword seen on the battlefield in ensuing centuries. During the Crusades, straight weapons had been slowly replaced by the scimitar among Muslim warriors while many Christian foot soldiers favoured a curbed sword called a falchion.

Similarly to both of these weapons, the Assassin's dagger would be gradually made obsolete in subsequent centuries by firearms and explosives – the weapons of choice for the lone killer on a mission. However, the 1954 CIA training manual *A Study of Assassination*, compiled for local death squads operating in South America as part of Operation PBSCUCCESS, condemns guns as 'consistently overrated', and cautions that bombs are 'highly unreliable'. Weapons like knives have the advantage of easy local availability and 'apparent innocence' until employed, though 'a certain minimum anatomical knowledge is needed for reliability'. These same advantages also applied to the knife for the

Assassins, while more primitive medical science meant that 'anatomical knowledge' was less of an issue – a number of their targets died of their wounds days after the attack. In a disturbing moment of levity, the manual observes that 'the obviously lethal machinegun failed to kill Trotsky where an item of sporting equipment (an ice pick) succeeded'.

Both Richard and Saladin had direct dealings with the Assassins which illustrate the relationship between the rival kingdoms and factions. Niccolò Machiavelli in *The Prince*, his notoriously cynical 1513 guide to practical statesmanship, considers whether it is better to be feared or loved, a question that has occupied leaders throughout history. 'The answer is of course, that it would be best to be both loved and feared,' concludes Machiavelli. 'But since the two rarely come together, anyone compelled to choose will find greater security in being feared than in being loved.' This same dilemma was played out over and over throughout the Crusades.

While Richard seldom hesitated to employ the power of fear, Saladin understood the long-term benefits of mercy and tolerance. History has largely been kind to the reputation of Richard. In addition to retaining his romantic title of 'Lionheart' – an honour shared by only a handful of English monarchs – he survives in fictions like Scott's *The Talisman* and the legends of Robin Hood as a dashing and chivalrous knight, captured in triumphant bronze outside the Palace of Westminster in London. His reputation during his own lifetime was ambivalent. For the king spoke little English, spent almost no time in England and famously declared that he would happily sell London if it would help finance his military ambitions abroad.

Richard was a member of the Angevin dynasty, originally French aristocrats from the district of Anjou, who legend insisted were originally descended from the daughter of Satan himself. (According to local lore, the mythical Melusine married one of the Counts of Anjou, bearing him several sons before flying off into the distance upon discovery of her demonic identity.) 'What wonder if we lack the natural affections of mankind – we come from the Devil, and must needs go back to the Devil,' he once joked in reference to this popular myth. While none could deny that he was a brilliant warlord, Richard was infamously ruthless. 'Never have we had to face a bolder or more subtle opponent,' conceded one Muslim chronicler in a rare deviation from standard descriptions of the Crusaders as primitive pigs. Acre had surrendered to Richard in 1192 on condition he guaranteed its Turkish garrison safe passage. Once the city was in Christian hands, however, the 2,700 Turks were taken out in front of the city walls and systematically beheaded by fanatics among Richard's army – a savage business entailing hours of bloodshed beneath the merciless Middle Eastern sun. According to some Islamic chroniclers, it also puts into context the savage treatment meted out to Acre's Christian defenders by the Muslims exactly 100 years later.

Apologists for Richard have claimed Saladin was too slow in honouring the rest of the surrender terms, though this savage act of treachery probably reflected his reluctance to allow so many enemy troops to rejoin the Sultan's ranks. If it was part of a deliberate policy of terror then it bore fruit. Ascalon was the next citadel in Richard's path, but Saladin could not convince any of his troops to defend it after the atrocity at Acre. He had to content himself with demolishing its fortifications.

Saladin was also capable of brutality. In response to Richard's massacre at Acre, the Sultan had all of his Christian prisoners put to death. Most infamously, in the wake of his victory at Hattin in 1187, Saladin separated the members of the elite monastic fighting orders of the Templars and Hospitallers from the rest of his Crusader prisoners, offering them the choice of conversion or death. Those that refused to embrace Islam were passed to the holy men and scholars in his army for execution. Much to the amusement of Saladin and his men, these eager but weak and inexpert executioners struggled messily to complete their task. It leant an air of grim slapstick to the proceedings. As the wide-eyed Muslims fumbled with the swords they were given, struggling to cut through the sinewy necks of their captives, their slender arms unused to physical labour, the groans and screams of the condemned mingled hideously with the guffaws of Saladin's hardened soldiers.

But this episode is generally regarded as an exception to the rule, and stories of the Sultan's compassion and forgiveness far outweigh any reputation for ruthlessness. After he captured Jerusalem from the Crusaders in 1187, Saladin presided over a propaganda triumph. In contrast to the brutal Christian capture of the Holy City in 1099, when the streets literally ran with innocent blood, no harm was done to the garrison or the inhabitants. The Sultan even paid for the release of thousands of the poorer prisoners from his own pocket.

In Europe, Saladin was regarded as a paragon of chivalry, celebrated as one of the greatest knights of history despite his Islamic faith. More recently, he was paid the unusual compliment of having a British armoured car named after him in the 1950s. (The British armed forces had also previously fielded a tank christened the Crusader.) His reputation is more ambivalent in the Middle East, often overshadowed by that of his more ruthless Mamluk successor Sultan Baibars (1223-77), and by enduring suspicion of the clemency he showed towards the infidel – alongside the racist prejudices of some Arabs about Saladin's comparatively humble Kurdish origins. Despite this, however, modern-day Iraq issued a postage stamp showing President Saddam Hussein, mass murderer of the Kurds, standing shoulder to shoulder with the immortal hero Saladin.

Both Saladin and Richard are said to have had direct dealings with the Assassins. Richard is reputed to have secured their services to murder Marquis Conrad of Montferrat, the Christian King of Jerusalem, who was stabbed to death by men dressed as monks in 1192. Certainly, the Assassin who survived the assassination confessed to as much under torture. (Of course, he may have simply been saying what he thought his torturers wanted him to say, or may have been told to make the confession by his superiors to sow dissent among the Crusaders.) By way of contrast, Saladin found himself the target of the Assassins, with attempts on his life in late 1174 or early 1175 and the spring of 1176. He was wounded in the second attack, and sufficiently shaken to take to sleeping in a special wooden tower while on campaign, refusing to see anyone he did not know personally.

With such precautions in place Saladin set out to avenge himself, laying siege to the Assassins' Syrian stronghold of Masyaf in August 1176. He soon lifted the siege, according to contemporary Assassin accounts, out of awe at the supernatural powers of their legendary Syrian leader, Sinan. Other stories tell of Saladin awaking to find a pastry of a kind only baked by the Assassins on his pillow, still warm, with a note proclaiming, 'You are in our power.' Whatever the circumstances, a truce was made. Saladin never attacked the Assassins again and was never again the subject of an Assassin plot. Other stories exist explaining the arrangement reached between Saladin and Sinan which are more revealing of the sect's fearsome reputation and its favoured *modus operandi*.

***

The encampment of the mighty Sultan Saladin stretches as far as the eye can see, surrounding the fortress of Masyaf and engulfing the settlement at its foot. Dozens of war engines, sleeping monsters of wood, rope and iron, currently lie silent. Beneath the star-studded sky, silk and canvas tents are punctuated by torches and campfires that keep the worst chills of the nocturnal desert winds at bay. Huddled around them are clumps of soldiers and camp-followers, some laughing, singing or eating, more looking warily around them, uncomfortably aware that they are now deep in enemy territory. Saladin has promised them victory. None can best him on the battlefield, and his battle-hardened host is many times the size of any army his foe can muster. But the Assassin sect can strike at any place and at any time, before disappearing back into their lofty fortresses like unholy spectres. Even Saladin's veteran warriors feel a little chill that cannot be accounted for by the desert night alone.

Then a ripple of whispers breaks across the camp. At its centre is a lone, unarmed figure in white. The soldiers snatch up their weapons before stepping aside, rather than impeding his progress. He picks a slow, steady route towards the centre of the encampment, where the Sultan himself holds court. By the time he reaches Saladin's tent a knot of guards surrounds him, their senior members stepping to block his path at the silken antechamber to the cavernous tent in which the Sultan holds counsel of war.

'I bring a message for your Lord Salah al-Din Yusuf ibn Ayyub from my master, Sinan ibn Salman ibn Muhammed,' says the Assassin, bowing low. 'I will pass your message on to the Sultan,' offers the captain of the guard, holding out a nervous hand to receive it. The Assassin shakes his head. 'My orders are explicit, my master's words are for the Sultan's ears alone.'

Within the yawning tent all is silence. At the centre sits Saladin. He is, upon first sight, a slight, even small figure, with an impeccably trimmed beard and modest if exquisitely detailed attire. But his commanding bearing, even sat cross-legged, and his quick, intelligent eyes leave little doubt as to who is in command here. Seated around the turbaned Sultan are his generals and advisers, religious and secular, tended by servants and slaves, flanked by soldiers still armed as for battle. On the opulent cushions and rugs that carpet the floor a plan of the fortifications is spread, illuminated by the dancing light of brass oil lamps. 'Search our guest . . .' says the Sultan, his face a mask of calm, pausing to emphasise, '. . . thoroughly. Then bring him in and we shall see what terms these heretics will offer us for their lives.'

Silence rules once more, with all eyes but the Sultan's dipped towards the map of Masyaf until the Assassin enters the tent. Bowed, he approaches. 'Have I the honour to address Salah al-Din Yusuf ibn Ayyub?'

'You have,' responds Saladin, eyeing the heavily-bearded messenger with the intent gaze of one examining an intriguing but dangerous reptile.

'I bring word from my master, Lord of the Persian Nizaris, Captain of Masyaf and Qadmus, of Khariba . . .'

'We know who sent you, Ismaili,' interrupts the Sultan, 'now tell us what he wants.'

'That I can tell only you,' says the Assassin, now looking straight at Saladin, 'and you alone. Your men have searched me in every detail and found no weapon.'

The Sultan's expressive eyes betray curiosity and indignation in equal measure. He motions for those around him to leave with two sweeps of his hand. The generals, counsellors, slaves, soldiers and imams file out in silence, except for two tall, battle-scarred figures in full armour, hands resting upon scimitar hilts, standing motionless at the left and right shoulders of the seated Saladin.

'Now give me your message,' orders the Sultan. 'The message is for you and you alone, my lord,' responds the Assassin calmly.

'These two men never leave my side,' Saladin booms impatiently, 'so deliver your message, or leave now while I still extend to you the benefits of hospitality.'

'But why will you not send these two men away when you have dismissed all of your other companions?' persists the Assassin.

'I regard these men as my own sons, and they and I are as one,' responds Saladin.

With that, the Assassin's gaze turns up from the seated Sultan to the two powerfully-built Mamluk warriors beside him. 'If I ordered you to kill the Sultan in the name of my master, would you do so?' he asks, with chilling serenity.

Saladin's face pales visibly as he hears the unmistakable sound of two swords being drawn at each side. 'Command us as you wish,' reply the Mamluks ominously, while the messenger fixes the horror-struck Sultan with a brief, baleful glare. His message is delivered: no foe of his master is ever truly safe. The Assassin leaves the tent, flanked now by the two Mamluk bodyguards, leaving the Sultan to consider his next move.

The following morning, Saladin secretly sues for peace. A fearless soldier on the battlefield, he has no stomach to fight a foe whose reach is seemingly limitless, a force that can hide behind castle walls, using stealth and murder just as other lords fielded mighty armies to defend their people . . .

***

The Assassins never employed fear in the same way Richard, or indeed Saladin, did. There are no massacres in the sect's history to rival those after Richard's capture of Acre or Saladin's victory at Hattin. But fear was their primary political weapon, focused like the point of a knife. Their other principal tactic was that of religious conversion, but their hostile contemporaries, Christian and Muslim alike, routinely depicted the Assassins as evil incarnate. But is targeted assassination really worse than the mayhem of open warfare? Before we consider such a moral dilemma, let us look at the history of the Assassins, their methods and legacy.

The era of the Crusades is one of fanatical idealism and breathtaking cynicism, where alliances shift and reverse with bewildering speed. It was not a simplistic battle of Christian Crusaders versus Islamic Saracens. Divisions within these faiths, of ideology, culture and geography, played a pivotal role in feeding the fire of conflict. Both sides were riven by bitter internal conflict that led to rivalries between brothers, fathers and sons. Just as the Christians were divided between Orthodox and Catholic denominations, so Muslims were split into Shiite and Sunni, with further subdivisions separating the religion yet further. It was a volatile, unpredictable arena that would look depressingly familiar to students of the modern Middle East.

The touch paper of the Crusades was essentially lit in Byzantium (modern-day Istanbul), a political player oft-overlooked in the more simplistic overviews. With an empire stretching from Greece and Central Europe to the Near East, the Byzantines saw themselves as guardians of the intellectual and cultural heritage of the Roman Empire. Certainly they had done a better job of it than the Western Europeans, who had descended into the factionalism and intellectual decay of the Dark Ages.

The Byzantine Empire remained a beacon of art and culture, yet they too had their problems. By the eleventh century aggressive new competitors, the Seljuq Turks, were beginning to encroach upon their eastern borders and the Normans were steadily eroding their remaining southern Italian territories. In 1071 the Byzantines suffered a catastrophic defeat at Manzikert (Malazgirt in modern Turkey) at the hands of the Seljuqs, which sent shockwaves through the empire.

In 1095 the Byzantine Emperor Alexis I sent envoys to Pope Urban II in Rome, asking for assistance against the Muslim threat from the east. He had expected a few units of their devastating heavy cavalry to supplement his overstretched forces. What he got was a fully-fledged invasion force. The Pope took the opportunity of Alexis's entreaties to begin an international campaign of raising an army to march east, with the ultimate intention of capturing the far-off holy city of Jerusalem. Those that answered the call were promised plentiful booty and absolution from sin, a two-for-one offer that proved irresistible to many ambitious princes and warlords. By 1096, forces totalling some 30,000 took up arms in the service of the cross.

It was not just the powerful and their retinues that were inspired by this call to holy war. In a sort of unofficial prequel, a charismatic holy man named Peter the Hermit led what later became known as the People's Crusade eastward, consisting of a huge, unruly mob of miscellaneous armed opportunists and rootless religious fanatics.

They progressed across Eastern Europe like medieval football hooligans, fighting and looting indiscriminately as they went. Alexis was obliged to provide them with an escort, like police shadowing drunken sports fans, and no doubt heaved a sigh of relief when he shipped them over the River Bosporus into enemy territory in Anatolia. There Peter the Hermit's holy thugs continued their murderous campaign of indiscriminate looting and pillaging, until they met their first serious resistance in the shape of a Seljuq army. The Seljuqs butchered their undisciplined Christian quarry like cattle. Their easy victory confirmed Islamic assumptions about the military incompetence of the Western barbarians, but such complacency would ultimately prove a disastrous mistake.

Alexis felt even greater reservations about the 'official' First Crusade fast converging on Byzantium. Many of the leaders were Normans, and while in theory they were fellow Christians they were of the Catholic faith, unlike the Orthodox Byzantines, and might forget their Christian brotherhood when tempted by the conspicuous wealth of the Byzantine Empire. (Such fears would prove well-founded when the Fourth Crusade diverted from its purpose and sacked Byzantium in 1204.) With deft diplomacy, Alexis shipped each contingent of the Crusade over the Bosporus before the next could arrive, ensuring that the combined force could never converge and turn on their hosts. Once in Asia, the Crusade began its long march east. Crossing hostile territory, in alien conditions, with starvation and disease as constant companions, constantly harassed by an aggressive enemy and plagued by factional rivalry, in the summer of 1099, against all odds, the Crusaders reached the walls of Jerusalem.

Their subsequent capture of the Holy City was followed by an episode of merciless brutality that remains a stain on the Christian conscience to this day. In the words of the Christian chronicler Fulcher of Chartres, the Crusaders

> 'joyfully rushed into the city to pursue and kill the nefarious enemies, as their comrades were already doing. Some Saracens, Arabs, and Ethiopians took refuge in the tower of David, others fled to the temples of the Lord and of Solomon. A great fight took place in the court and porch of the temples, where they were unable to escape from our gladiators. Many fled to the roof of the temple of Solomon, and were shot with arrows, so that they fell to the ground dead. In this temple almost ten thousand were killed.

Indeed, if you had been there you would have seen our feet coloured to our ankles with the blood of the slain. But what more shall I relate? None of them were left alive; neither women nor children were spared.'

Leaving aside the hideous aftermath of the capture of Jerusalem, in terms of military achievement, the term 'miraculous' is not inappropriate. As the army had made its progress east, fortified towns and castles had to be taken, both to provide vital supply lines and suitable booty for the soldiers and princes. A crucial turning point came in October of 1097 when they reached the formidable walls of Antioch, a city with a strong Christian tradition. Stalemate swiftly ensued; the undermanned Seljuq garrison lacked the force to break the siege, their Christian foes unable to storm the defences. Hunger took its toll on both sides – many knights were forced to eat their horses, while the remnants of Peter the Hermit's Crusade now accompanying the army reputedly turned to cannibalism, devouring the corpses of fallen Saracens.

By the summer of 1098, things looked increasingly bleak for the Crusaders as word reached them that the Seljuqs had despatched a powerful army to relieve the city. The impasse was broken in the nick of time by treachery. An armourer within the city had a grudge against his commanding officer – rumour says the superior was sleeping with his wife – and, in return for a bribe, agreed to open a gate. Once within the walls, the Crusaders ran riot, making short work of the surprised garrison in an orgy of bloodshed.

The Crusaders awoke to a new situation – an overwhelming enemy army was fast approaching, and they were still desperately short of supplies without hope of reinforcement. The besiegers became the besieged, and by rights the First Crusade should have ended there. How the Christian defenders managed to turn certain defeat into a surprise victory is a matter of some debate, and one which says something about all of the conflicts in this era. On 28 June, the tattered, starving remnants of the Crusader army emerged from the gates of Antioch and charged headlong into the numerically superior, well-prepared Seljuq army. The Saracens showered them with arrows, set fire to the grass beneath the enemy's feet, hesitated and then broke, panic spreading like a contagion through their ranks as the mounted Crusaders ploughed through the retreating army like avenging angels, bellowing religious exhortations as they felled their fleeing foes.

For some this was divine deliverance. Two weeks before, a wild-eyed

Christian holy man had claimed to have a vision, revealing to him the location of a holy lance buried in Antioch Cathedral, which subsequent excavation unearthed. It was this weapon that had been brandished at the head of the charge, and some Crusaders swore they saw a host of angelic warriors joining the attack as they slammed into their heathen foe with devastating effect. Other witnesses, including many Christians, dismissed this as delirium brought on by an excess of religious fervour and a dearth of food and water.

In fact, the Saracen commander had made a critical tactical mistake brought on by complacency, splitting his force then showing fatal indecisiveness at the crucial moment. Historians have also subsequently highlighted political factors that fatally compromised the Saracen forces, where leaders were often as fearful of betrayal by Islamic allies, casting a jealous eye over their territory, as they were of any Christian invader. The Seljuq army was far from united and there were even contingents who would rather their commander did not capture Antioch, as it would have strengthened his position enough to threaten their own influence in the region.

Whatever the truth, all these factors – religious zeal, tactical dynamics, factional intrigue – are the core of the history of the Assassins. The capture of Jerusalem was a high watermark for the Crusaders. They would establish the kingdoms of Outremer in surrounding territories, and Crusader fortunes in the Holy Lands would ebb and flow. But ultimately the story of the eight subsequent Crusades was one of diminishing returns, of a kingdom under siege, under constant sentence of death should the Muslims achieve unity and expel the Christian invader – as they finally did at Acre in 1291.

Islamic unity threatened not only the Crusader kingdoms but other minorities in the Middle East. At the same time that the First Crusade was carving its way westward from Byzantium, in the region of Persia a heretical Islamic sect was establishing itself which many Muslim princes regarded with greater dread than they did the brutal Christian barbarians from the West. The web of murderous intrigue spun by the Assassins in their struggle to survive would shatter Islamic unity for centuries, entangling the Middle East throughout the era of the Crusades and creating an explosive impact still felt to this day. For Islamist rhetoric continues to dwell on the Middle Ages, while self-sacrificing fanatics still destabilise the region using targeted political violence.

When, in the wake of the 9/11 attacks, President George W. Bush announced, 'This crusade – this war on terrorism – is going to take a while,' his unfortunate choice of phrase would reinforce the belief of many Muslims that the holy wars of the early Middle Ages were still being fought. It could only lend credence to claims by the extreme Islamists of al-Qaeda that all Western soldiers were 'Crusaders' and that every conflict between the infidel and an Islamic nation was a continuation of the campaign launched in the eleventh century by Pope Urban II.

II

BACKSTABBING FOR FUN AND PROFIT

If legend is to be believed (legend and history being sometimes inextricable), Hasan Sabbah's words had the power to propel the most fanatical of the Assassins to their deaths. At his command, it is claimed, they would leap to assured destruction from the battlements of El Alamut. All this, it seems, in order to impress watchful outsiders with the strength of their devotion.

It seems like a dubious strategy. The Ismailis were a minority heretical sect, and their militant wing, the Assassins, were fewer still in number. Taking a headlong dive into splinter-skulled oblivion suggests nothing more than wilful extinction, both of the individual devotee and the group.

But let us not forget the essence of terrorism: the terrorist's strength lies not in numbers, but in the extremes that he or she is willing to go to in order to wage asymmetric warfare. 'We have no choice but to transform ourselves into human bombs and pursue the Israeli enemy everywhere in the interior and overseas,' claimed a spokesman for the Popular Front for the Liberation of Palestine in 2002, seeking to justify suicide bombing against the heavily armed Israelis.

In reality, it seems a matter of bad faith for any activist to claim 'no choice' but one course of action, even for as marginalised and desperate a people as the Palestinians. Perhaps only the promise of Paradise – as briefly glimpsed by Hasan's Assassins, so legend tells us – allows young Arabs to steel themselves for the act that may reduce them and any hapless bystander to bleeding meat.

Still, the blood-soaked principle remains the same. Where political or military might may be overwhelming, it is with grand, almost theatrical acts of violence that the perpetrators hope to shift the political balance of power.

***

Political assassination had been around for a very long time before the legend of the Assassins lent it its title. When Shakespeare claimed that Senator Caius Cassius cried, 'Speak now! Hands for me!' before drawing his dagger with fellow conspirators and reducing the Roman general Caesar to a 'bloodstained piece of earth', he was claiming artistic licence for what was actually a more sordid affair.

According to the Bard, the 44 BC assassination (pre-dating the actual birth of Christ by about 41 years, due to the vagaries of the early Roman Catholic calendar, and that of Muhammad by approximately 615 years) was a matter of anguished principle. In the best known of his Roman Plays, Cassius heads a small cabal of former supporters and conspirators alarmed that Julius Caesar, the 'colossus that doth bestride the world', is about to overturn the principles of the Roman Republic to be crowned emperor. Foremost among these is Marcus Brutus, a younger member of the senate beloved by Caesar whose recruitment to the assassins has come after much soul-searching.

According to Plutarch, however, the Roman historian who provided Shakespeare's source material, Cassius Longinus (note how the Bard changed the conspirator's name – our most legendary playwright taking as many liberties as any sword-and-sandal movie) and Brutus were among a whole plethora of senators who plunged the knife in, leaving Rome's all-conquering hero like a deflated blood balloon. Even the classic dying murmour of betrayal, '*Et tu, Brute?*' ('You too, Brutus?'), is apparently artistic licence, Caesar's original words reputedly being the Greek form of, 'You too, my child?' (Like many a powerful man, Caesar is said to have had trouble keeping it in his toga, and there are suggestions that Brutus was his illegitimate son.)

Assassination, as we recognise it now, was almost a standard means of career furtherance and settling disputes during the Roman Empire that followed Caesar. While Shakespeare depicts him as struck down before the status of emperor could be bestowed, the historical model died after powers granted by the Senate had effectively made him a dictator. Of those who plunged their blades in, it seems just as many may have been motivated by envy of his power as by republican principles.

Caesar's own ruthlessness may have set the template for his vicious end. Shakespeare makes much mention of Pompey, the great general who was both Caesar's contemporary and his rival. Allusions to Pompey's downfall, however, downplay the fact that he was assassinated and decapitated by two of Caesar's soldiers while seeking refuge in Egypt, fearful of reprisals by his former comrade.

By the time Caesar's descendants and in-laws began to ascend to the now hereditary title of emperor (or 'Caesar'), the internecine killings and familial warfare make Robert Graves' historical novels of the era (*I, Claudius* and *Claudius the God*) read like bizarre Mafia prototypes. The Emperor Caligula, Caesar's great-nephew and infamous polymorphous pervert, would be murdered by disgruntled members of the Praetorian guard along with his wife and little daughter.

After a long line of interfamilial murders, political assassination returned to Rome at the end of the first century AD. The Emperor Domitian, though less is known of him than of his forebears, seems to have taken the despotic behaviour, random murder and sexual sadism of Caligula and Nero to the furthest extreme. The citizenry can only have felt relief when a disloyal manservant granted access to an assassin posing as a messenger. Though his attackers numbered only one, Domitian truly died like a Caesar, with multiple dagger blows puncturing much of his body.

After a period of relative stability, when the title of 'Caesar' passed from the hereditary line to a series of soldiers-turned-politicians, Rome was granted one of its most bizarre emperors in Heliogabalus, during the third century. An early transsexual who opted for castration and competed with Rome's whores in giving male pleasure, he can scarcely have been worse than his mass-murdering counterparts. However, his military guard eventually tired of his antics and stabbed him to death, rather comically, in the toilet in 222 AD.

Though political murder was part of the grain of Imperial Roman life, the killers of the various emperors were not 'assassins' in the way we would interpret the word today. Neither idealists who believed the ends justified the means nor detached professional killers offering their services for a fee, they were merely participating in the cut and thrust of everyday court and senate life. Their casual brutality was mirrored and oft-surpassed by the Caesars themselves, their bloody actions a matter of expediency or switched loyalties. For its time and place, this was merely business as usual. In the centuries that followed, such internecine homicide would become a standard means of conducting affairs in royal courts across Europe.

By contrast, the Sicarii, a sect of early political and religious assassins named after their weapon (the 'sica'), conducted a guerrilla campaign against their Roman occupiers in first-century Judea. Devout believers in a single god, they bristled under their country's servitude to the decadent, pagan and altogether more cosmopolitan Romans.

Direct cultural antecedents of the Assassins, 'Sicarii' translates literally as the more brutal 'knifemen' or 'dagger-men'. Not long after the time of the heretical lay rabbi Jeshua, this group of Jewish rebels proved the modern adage that one man's freedom fighter is another man's terrorist.

In many ways they were close cousins of the Zealots – an earlier Judean grouping resistant to Roman occupation, whose number included a feared killer named Saul. After becoming a follower of Jeshua – or 'Jesus', as we now know him by his Romanised name – Saul became 'Paul' (later Saint Paul), proselytising for his rabbi's new creed after Jesus was crucified for heresy at the insistence of the High Priests. Thus was born Christianity.

Meanwhile, the Sicarii remained committed to the traditional Jewish faith and direct political action, targeting their Roman enemy by stealth, attacking suddenly with knives or targeting their homes for arson. Their co-religionists were not immune from their attentions, victims including the High Priest Jonathan, assassinated for his accommodation of the Roman governors.

At the pilgrimage to the Holy Temple Mount, other reputed Jewish collaborators were targeted for their treachery – foreshadowing both the tactics of modern terrorism, and one of the modern flashpoints of the Middle East, where fundamentalist Israeli Jews and Islamist groups clash over the shared historical location of the Temple Mount/Al Aqsa Mosque. (In its dual identity as the mosque, it would witness the massacre of 3,000 in the Crusades that began over a thousand years later.)

In the years immediately following the crushed Jewish revolt in Jerusalem of 66AD and the destruction of the sacred Temple, one of the Sicarii leaders, Eleazar ben Jair, made his retreat along with a number of Zealots to the desert fortress of Masada, originally built as a refuge for Herod the Great. According to the Jewish-Roman historian Josephus, 960 Jews committed mutual knifepoint suicide at Masada rather than surrender to the besieging Romans. The details of the event are disputed up to the present day – like the history of the Assassins, many historians claim they are shrouded in myth.

But hybrids of history, legend and myth carry a heavy potency, and Masada looms large in the folklore of modern Israel's Jews. Its embodiment of the beleaguered siege mentality continues to echo through the history of the tormented Middle East.

***

Distinct from the realm of theological rivalry and religious fanaticism, political assassination has recurred continually over the three millennia. It was in the nineteenth century – by which time the word 'assassin' was a well-established part of contemporary vernacular – that the political assassin took centre stage, and assassination was viewed as a legitimate tool by latter-day zealots.

On Good Friday of 1865, just five days after the Southern Confederacy surrendered to the Union, marking the end of the American Civil War, President Abraham Lincoln was seated in a box at Ford's Theatre in Washington. His companions were the Union Army's Major Henry Rathbone and both of their wives. The night's entertainment was a light comedy called *Our American Cousin*, performed at a time when the United States of America was just being born. The President would never see the play's conclusion, leading to the oft-told off-colour joke: 'Yes, but apart from *that*, Mrs Lincoln, how was the theatre?'

When John Wilkes Booth, himself a locally recognised stage actor, entered the presidential box, he fired a ball from a single-shot Derringer pistol (its antique design based on the old muskets) into the back of Lincoln's head. With such rudimentary weaponry, the President was denied the instant oblivion that would deliver him today. Instead he lingered on, suffering all night, the ball lodged in his brain behind his right eye. He would not give up the ghost until after 7am the next morning.

During the course of the Civil War (still North America's hugest conflict in terms of lives lost, both World Wars included), Lincoln had granted emancipation to America's black slaves. This was the hub around which the whole conflagration coalesced, with most members of the Southern Confederate states (including dirt-poor farmers with little to lose) prepared to go to war as a stand against this blow to their region's economy and against the principle of interference by the Yankee North.

It is for this reason that Lincoln is remembered as a great humanitarian and the most historically revered US President, possibly apart from George Washington. Harder heads have suggested this Republican Party leader was more concerned with eliminating the South's economic advantage over that of his own supporters, but his iconic status as the President who freed the slaves is never likely to diminish.

(In Marvin Gaye's 1968 Motown hit, 'Abraham, Martin and John', his name is invoked along with that of Luther King and Kennedy to epitomise how 'the good die young' via the assassin's bullet. Given its timing, the song also had the vocalist asking, 'Has anybody here seen my good friend Bobby?', marking the assassination of JFK's younger brother. Somebody should have broken it to Marvin that Bobby had been shot dead – a fate he would sadly share himself.)

Major Rathbone tried to apprehend the assassin, but received knife wounds for his pains. Booth would remain at liberty for another eleven days, before being besieged by federal troops at a farm in the neighbouring state of Virginia, the gateway to the Old South. Like the much disputed assassin of President Kennedy, Lee Harvey Oswald (as with Booth, dignified by history via use of his full name), Lincoln's assassin would not live to see trial.

Perhaps the only significant mystery surrounding the Lincoln assassination is why a stage actor like Booth should have taken it upon himself to be the Confederate avenger. True, he appeared as the archetypal Southern gentleman, resembling with his side-parted hair and fussy moustache none other than onetime resident of Richmond, Virginia, the tormented author Edgar Allan Poe.

But in acting as Confederate agent and assassin, Booth was taking on the greatest part of his career. '*Sic semper tyrannis*,' ('thus always with tyrants') he announced with a theatrical flourish after killing the man who freed the slaves.

It was a performance that eclipsed even those of his more successful brother, the actor Edwin Thomas Booth, and foreshadowed those 20th-century assassins who kill as an act of self-realisation rather than from devotion to a cause.

In this case, however, there can be little doubt that John Wilkes Booth acted as part of a conspiracy. Nine supposed co-conspirators were rounded up, four of them so hastily convicted and hanged that it suggests the Union was seeking its own revenge. (One of them, Mary Surratt, was the first woman to be executed in the newly created United States. Her only crime may have been that she was landlady to Booth and the other conspirators.)

Some have suggested a conspiracy from within Lincoln's own circle – why, they argue, was it so easy for Booth to attack the president in his private box at the theatre? But this seems to be answered by the circumstances of the time: Lincoln was attending against the wishes of his advisors, who knew how vulnerable it would make him to attack. It is only in our own, more security-conscious age that the man who espoused 'government of the people, by the people, for the people' might have been protected *from* the people.

As the USA, a fledgling superpower in the making, was still reeling from its own violent birth throes, in Europe political assassination became something of an epidemic. Nowhere was this more apparent than in the region where east met west, the seemingly monolithic state of Tsarist Russia. Long the subject of arrogant or autocratic rule from its emperors (tsars), the tension between rulers, ruled and disaffected intellectuals led to an upsurge in radical ideas: socialism, anarchism, even random acts of nihilism were increasingly common in this period of ferment, before the vast nation was eventually overtaken by the Bolshevism (state communism) that made it the USA's deadly ideological rival.

In 1881, Tsar Alexander II became the first of many European heads of state to be assassinated over the twenty-year period that extended into the twentieth century. Ironically, perhaps, Alexander had been enough of a liberal (by Tsarist standards) to emancipate Russian peasants from the slavery of serfdom, whereby their very existence was owned by the landed gentry.

By 1881, however, Alexander II was little other than a symbol of repression to the various radical groups that had formed in Russia. His assassins, *Narodnya Volya* ('the People's Will'), have been called the first modern terrorist group. In a genuine innovation, rather than good old-fashioned bullets, the Tsar's assassins made use of a newly invented explosive substance called nitroglycerine.

The terrorist who dropped the bomb through the Tsar's carriage, Ignatai Grinevitsky, may or may not have realised that he had no time to get away and that he, too, would be blown apart. Maybe by default, Grinevitsky became the first suicide bomber, motivated by secular ideology rather than religious faith.

In this bloodstained late 19th-century climate, there were deep fissures between the materialist ideals of Karl Marx and the utopian (if still ultimately violent) idealism of Mikhail Bakunin and his fellow anarchists. While the unworldly theorising of Bakunin – who believed (or perhaps hoped) that mankind would reach its social apex when unfettered by any form of government – was occasionally translated into grenades thrown by his followers, younger idealists were developing an appetite for violence for violence's sake.

One such was Sergey Nechayev, who would die in prison at the age of thirty-five. He was originally a disciple of Bakunin (also rumoured to be his gay lover), but the elder anarchist began to break with Nechayev over the broodingly violent worldview expressed in his 1869 essay, 'Catechism of a Revolutionary': 'A revolutionary has broken all connection with the intellectual order and the social world, with all of its laws, moralities and accepted conventions. He is an implacable enemy of this world and if he continues to live in it, it is only to destroy it more effectively.'

As Nechayev veered into a nihilism that sought joy in destruction rather than any form of social justice, he became the model for Fyodor Dostoyevsky's character Pyotr Verkhovensky in his 1872 novel *The Devils* (sometimes translated as *The Possessed*) – still one of the greatest literary musings upon terrorist or nihilist mentality. An agonised traditional moralist, Dostoyevsky detected and feared the various wild offshoots of radicalism in his troubled nation. He would die in February 1881, three weeks before Alexander II was assassinated in the novelist's native St Petersburg.

As a terrorist, Sergey Nechayev was a non-starter. His sole victim was a pitiful sap named Ivanov, shot and strangled to death by the little revolutionary cabal of which he was a dissident member.

But is not not via his solitary kill that Nechayev, who died in 1882, foreshadows the self-styled modern assassin. While many exert their imaginations by delineating the vast conspiracies that they imagine lay behind such men, in the USA – land of the solitary, alienated individual – the assassin often takes action as an army of one, whose internal agenda, hard to discern, shares little common ground with those prepared to kill for an imagined common good.

But in the ferment of pre-revolutionary Russia, individualism was seen as the province of the despised ruling classes and the bourgeoisie. Much blood would be shed, but it was in the ideological name of collective justice or, after the historic rout by the Bolsheviks, the so-called 'dictatorship of the proletariat'.

When a failed assassination attempt was made on the new Tsar, Alexander III, in 1887, one of those hanged for the crime was nineteen-year-old student Alexander Ulyanov. His younger brother, Vladimir, rather than being deterred, became increasingly active in revolutionary politics fuelled by the economic theories of Marx and Friedrich Engels. Promising a heaven on earth to the disenfranchised workers, Marxism made some astute observations on the nature of Europe's newly industrialised societies – to the extent that Marxian terms like 'means of production' and 'economic alienation' have even been parroted by conservative politicians in our post-ideological times.

But when Marxism moved from observation to prophecy, it took on the tones of a secular religion, or Christianity and Islam at their most apocalyptic. Promising that the collapse of exploitative capitalism would usher in the dictatorship of the proletariat (to be administered, of course, by the Bolsheviks themselves), it also predicted this would magically create an era of social justice for the workers and their defenders. Such an imagined worker's paradise was surely to die for – or at least to kill for.

So it was that a tumultuous Russia edged ever closer to revolution. The suppressed uprisings of 1905 did not stop the momentum, resulting in the revolution of March 1917 that deposed the Romanov dynasty – the last Tsar, Nicholas II, his wife Alexandra and their five children. At first, the Romanovs were housed in safety in Siberia. But revolutionaries have long memories and bear grudges.

After the Tsar's 1894 accession to the throne, it was believed that he would be a milder ruler than his father, Alexander III. When workers' councils made modest requests for Nicholas to approve a form of localised (rather than state) democracy, they were met with the shouted response, 'I intend to maintain the principle of autocracy, like my father.' During the failed 1905 revolution, he instructed his troops to open fire on a peaceful delegation of workers, women and children, killing and wounding dozens.

So it was that, when the revolutionary agitator Vladimir Ulyanov – having rechristened himself, in the manner of many Bolsheviks, 'Lenin' – returned to Russia from exile, there was unfinished business on his mind. Nicholas II had effectively written the death warrant not only of himself but of his wife and children.

After the October Revolution of 1917, the Bolsheviks exerted total control due to the defeat of their more liberal revolutionary contemporaries, the Mensheviks, in internecine warfare. Lenin became supreme leader of the newly formed Soviet Union (a conglomerate of Russia and her satellite states), and the Romanovs were doomed.

Nicholas, Alexandra, the thirteen-year-old Tsarevich Alexis and his four sisters Olga, Tatiana, Maria and Anastasia were moved to the city of Ekaterinburg. On 16 July of the following year, with civil war between the Bolsheviks and White Russian royalist forces breaking out, their captors telegrammed Lenin in Moscow for permission to 'execute' the Romanov family immediately. His silence gave consent.

It is said that there were eleven assassins to kill eleven victims – the family, their doctor and their servants. No witnesses were to be left alive. According to the commander of the guard who later gave his account, in the smoky aftermath of the crossfire the Tsarevich lay moaning in pain and had to be put out of his misery with a bullet. The youngest child, Anastasia, was finished off by bayoneting.

In order to perform the mass execution, the Romanovs' assassins could not have seen the children in the same way as they would have done those innocents the Tsar himself had killed back in 1905. To the terrorist or the ideological assassin there are no innocent victims, just symbols or by-products of a greater injustice they believe themselves to be overcoming – or, at best, in the 20th-century term coined by the US military to describe civilian victims of warfare, 'collateral damage'.

In the early years of enforced collectivisation and the Stalinist purges which followed, the deaths were on too grand a scale to be described as targeted assassinations. Lenin once remarked that, 'In order to bring about the dictatorship of the proletariat, it may be necessary to eliminate eighty per cent of the population.' Such was the cost of heaven on earth, it seems.

Lenin remains a hero to many on the vestiges of the old Left, largely because his early death in 1924 left the ruthlessness of such statements untested. (Through the cultural looking glass, JFK is regarded as the greatest US president by many liberals, principally because his own assassination left him precious little time in which to betray their values. See Chapter Twelve.)

The policy of mass murder in pursuit of an elusive social justice was left to Lenin's successor, Josef Stalin, one of history's greatest ogres. His much feared secret police, the NKVD (later the KGB), had little need of a domestic assassinations programme when the policy of mass arrests, show trials, executions and banishments maintained perpetual state terror.

In terms of foreign policy, there was more scope. Certainly, fellow veteran Bolshevik Leon Trotsky realised he would probably never escape Stalin's reach. One of the leaders of the Bolshevik revolution alongside Lenin, this Ukrainian-born Jewish intellectual had founded the Red Army and propagated a radical philosophy of 'permanent revolution', whereby all aspects of society were continually under a microscope of revolutionary scrutiny.

Understandably perhaps, Comrade Stalin had little sympathy for a political philosophy that might undermine his monolithic presence. After losing a power struggle with Stalin and being expelled from the Soviet Union, Trotsky began a decade of overseas exile in 1929, moving gradually from Turkey to post-revolutionary Mexico. Stalin's agents finally caught up with him in August 1940, when a supposedly friendly visitor to his fortified Mexican villa bludgeoned him in the head with the blunt end of an ice-pick. (Contrary to the old song, the ice-pick did not 'make his ears burn'.)

Trotsky died slowly in hospital from his injuries. His assassin was finally identified as a Spanish communist, Ramón Mercader, who the Mexicans imprisoned for the killing in 1943. Upon his release in 1960, Mercader went to the Soviet Union to receive the Order of Lenin from the supposedly post-Stalinist government of Nikita Khrushchev.

As the post-World War 2 Cold War played out between the two superpowers in small conflagrations around the world, the USA's overseas intelligence service, the CIA, was slightly more circumspect about engaging in dirty deeds. Indeed, with its military advisors backing Southeast Asian governments and Central American dictatorships hostile to communism, there was little need to engage in an assassination policy when the host countries had the matter in hand themselves. It was only when communism turned up, unannounced, seventy miles off the coast of Miami that things took a definite turn for the absurd.

Fidel Castro's revolution in Cuba had rid the Caribbean island of its Mob-friendly leader, General Batista, in 1959. Cautiously received at first by President Eisenhower's administration, it soon became clear that Castro's industrial nationalisation policies were not flying a flag for the American spirit of free enterprise. Increasingly ostracised by a US trade embargo, Castro turned more and more to his ideological allies in the Soviet Union for support.

Even before the apocalyptic near-miss of 1962, when Castro recklessly allowed the Russians to station nuclear missiles on Cuban soil, the CIA was already suggesting means by which their nearest red-under-the-bed could be eliminated. After such comic-book schemes as spiking him with LSD when he made a TV appearance or poisoning him to make his famous beard fall out, the assassination schemes got seriously underway during the presidency of John F. Kennedy, the USA's new young liberal leader.

The disastrous, CIA-funded Bay of Pigs invasion by Cuban exiles had been hatched during the later Eisenhower years, and fell flat in 1961; after that, much testimony exists to confirm that gangsters Sam Giancana and Santos Trafficante – heads of the Chicago and Florida branches of the Mafia respectively – were recruited to 'hit the beard', as the title character says in the 1983 version of *Scarface*.

Both failed to deliver despite receiving funding, and one of the numerous JFK conspiracy theories (see Chapter Twelve) suggests that Giancana – annoyed with Jack Kennedy for allowing his Attorney-General brother Bobby to pursue the Mob, in spite of this and various other favours performed for the Kennedy clan – may have engineered the killing of the president.

Certainly, it was only after the post-assassination swearing-in of

Vice-President Lyndon Johnson to the top job that the CIA were told to call off their assassination attempts against Castro. And this from the politician who escalated US involvement in Vietnam, something many are convinced that Kennedy never would have done, had he lived.

So, have the CIA always had a covert assassination policy to be applied around the world when it suits them? Former President Bill Clinton certainly seems to think so. Speaking after the 11 September 2001 attacks on the World Trade Centre, Clinton claimed he had authorised the CIA to assassinate Osama bin Laden in the wake of al-Qaeda's bombing attacks on the American embassies in Kenya and Tanzania, which caused substantial loss of life. Now that communism had collapsed under the weight of its own contradictions (just as Marx had claimed that capitalism would), the USA had a new nemesis in radical Islam. These were the theological descendants of the Assassins, and they were seeking to take their holy jihad worldwide.

Some disputed the strength of Clinton's response, while others pointed cynically (and perhaps realistically) to his directive for bombing raids on supposed al-Qaeda bases in Afghanistan and Sudan, as an attempt to deflect attention from calls for his impeachment for lying about his sexual liaison with White House intern Monica Lewinsky.

The only apparent certainty is that, for all Clinton's support of the newly incumbent President George W. Bush in seeking out the world's only truly iconic radical Islamist, bin Laden was neither apprehended nor assassinated.

If he is still alive, we are led to believe he may reside hidden in the rocky terrain of the Afghan Northwest Frontier, issuing distant directives like some latter-day Old Man of the Mountain – more myth than man.

***

In modern fiction and screen drama, the archetype of the Assassin became equated with 'cool' on account of its aloofness and detachment. Far removed from the political or theological commitment that swerved the course of history with one thrust of a dagger or click of a trigger, he/she was no longer the fanatic that would kill for a cause – but the professional profiteer who would perform the fanatics' dirty work for them. All at the standard market rate, of course.

Just as the fictional blueprint for the politically committed murderer can be found in Dostoyevsky's *The Devils* and Conrad's *The Secret Agent*, the modern template for the detached pro killer in pop fiction is

Frederick Forsyth's *The Day of the Jackal*. Forsyth, a teeth-clenching British conservative whose novels excel in alternately riveting/numbing procedural detail from the lives of his spy/mercenary/terrorist/assassin antagonists, bridges the gap between the Cold War morality of John Le Carré and the technophile espionage blockbusters of a Tom Clancy. The strength of his early novels – as exemplified in *Jackal* – is that he was able to stitch modern history quite seamlessly into the exploits of his pulp-fiction characters.

The Jackal's telescopic rifle sights are focused on the form of General Charles De Gaulle, hero of the Free French movement in World War 2 and long-serving French president. While basically a right-winger himself, De Gaulle was enough of a realist to accept, in his last long period of government, that France's days as an imperial power were over. Granting independence to Algeria in 1962, he curtailed a long and destructive guerrilla/terrorist war in the former North African colony, in a way the British were never quite able to do in their annexed neighbouring territory of Northern Ireland.

It may have meant that fewer hand grenades were thrown in the Kasbah, but it earned De Gaulle enemies at home. The *Organisation Armée Secrète* (OSA) was a terrorist organisation largely comprising former members of the French Army, who regarded the liberation of Algeria as a major betrayal of Mother France. In a direct inversion of our own times, the Gallic supremacists targeted Muslim groups and communities along with their perceived enemies in government. De Gaulle became the subject of no less than six assassination attempts. The last and most serious, in August 1962, left his chauffeured car riddled with bullets but the general almost unscathed. For this, one of those accused of leading the conspiracy, Colonel Bastien-Thiry, would face a firing squad the following year.

The fiction takes over one year after the OSA machine-gunned the President's car. Seeking vengeance for Bastien-Thiry and the completion of their failed mission, the OSA commission a foreign contract killer to the tune of a cool half-million in sterling. In a further meshing of fact and fiction, Forsyth credits him with the assassination of Franco-ist dictator General Rafael Trujillo in the Dominican Republic, during 1961. (In reality, those accused of the assassination conspiracy were tortured, shot by firing squad and fed to sharks.)

'The Jackal' is an archetype writ large; any hint as to his possible real identity is a red herring, as he routinely lifts false identities from sources such as a buried child and forges his papers. Aloofly professional and an expert in ballistics, he quickly becomes (anti)heroic in the eyes of the reader through his moral parity with the French security services, who are prepared to torture an OSA operative to death to gain information. So it is that we follow him noiselessly strangling the woman with whom he's having a sexual liaison to protect his identity, or ruthlessly killing an old lady, while admiring his self-reliance and ingenuity.

(He does, of course, eventually go down in a hail of bullets as his own attempt to shoot De Gaulle at a Liberation Day ceremony fails. Thus the 'factional' context is maintained by the anonymous Jackal dying in obscurity, the world unaware of his deeds.)

When Forsyth's immensely successful novel was filmed as an Anglo-French co-production, Hollywood veteran/*High Noon* director Fred Zinnemann acknowledged 'the peculiar fascination of a man who was anonymous, nobody knows him including the reader.' For his Jackal, Zinnemann chose Edward Fox, the epitome of the cravat-wearing, cold-blooded, upper-crust Englishman, 'against the type of what one would think a professional killer looks like.'

Fox's Jackal is part of a lineage of coolly-detached cinematic assassins, quite apart from the low-level hit-men of the Mob. The ethos of thug-kill-thug for money, advancement within the gang or simply prestige is an equally time-honoured tradition, but happens on a parochial level amongst the 'community' of organised crime. (The apologia 'They only killed their own kind' was often applied to the Kray twins, 1960s London's predatory pair of Mafia wannabes. 'Yuss,' retorted cockney comic Arthur Mullard, with a wit for which he was not renowned, 'human beings.')

Infamous Mob killers such as Louis 'Lepke' Buchalter, Albert Anastasia and Abe 'Kid Twist' Reles became known collectively as Murder Incorporated, middle-management troubleshooters who settled the US Crime Syndicate's personnel problems via the bullet, the blade, the garrotte or the ice-pick. They also became the template for decades of movie anti-heroes. In the fictionalised 1950 film *Murder Incorporated*, Mob-busting District Attorney Humphrey Bogart was the hero; by the time of the 1974 *Lepke*, audience sympathy belonged to Tony Curtis as the title character, the ruthless over-boss of Murder, Inc., depicted as a dapper, sword-fencing, self-made man.

The all-American capitalist hit-man has long been a laconic anti-hero of the movies, from Lee Marvin's sharp-suited, grizzled Mob assassin in 1964's Hemingway-inspired *The Killers* to his wise-fool descendants in Tarantino's 1994 *Pulp Fiction*. The archetype was so well established that it permitted such romantic subversions as 1994's *Leon*, where Jean Reno's pro killer is a childlike innocent whose homicidal skills help him protect a young girl orphaned by the Mob.

Leon was directed by Luc Besson, luminary of the modern French 'cinema du look' (i.e. visual style with only a cursory smattering of substance). He pre-empted it four years earlier with *Nikita*, which made a heroine of a prepossessing ex-junkie/French governmental assassin played by Anne Parillaud. Owing more as a character to Modesty Blaise than the Jackal, her seductively lethal exploits also filled a Hollywood remake (*The Assassin*, 1993) and a cult TV series (*La Femme Nikita*, beginning 1997) which softened both her lowlife origins and her homicidal aptitude.

As outlandish as these latter-day pulp scenarios are, they maintain the archetype of the fictional political assassin: any icy-cool passion will be channelled strictly into the assassination itself, or the assassin's subsequent flight from the consequences; the political impetus behind the hit is strictly the business of the controllers or paymasters.

***

The 'real Jackal' would never have been so dispassionate. Ilich Ramírez Sánchez was born to a far-left-wing Venezuelan family, who named him after Vladimir Ilich Lenin. Fully embracing revolutionary politics by his mid-teens, his privileged family background (his Marxist father was a wealthy lawyer) allowed him an expensive education and a globetrotting existence which began a process of self-reinvention. After expulsion from university in Moscow in 1970, Sanchez tied his revolutionary flag to the mast of the Palestinian cause, seeing its displaced and marginalised people as an oppressed group worthy of his liberator's zeal.

As a recruit to the People's Front for the Liberation of Palestine (PFLP), the Central American Sanchez was provided with the affectionate *nom de guerre* 'Carlos'. (As if a South American revolutionary group had recruited an Arab and renamed him 'Abdul', perhaps.) Directing assassination attempts at prominent Zionists in Paris and London, Carlos would later claim to be responsible for a grenade attack on a Parisian restaurant which killed two and injured many more. Wanted after two failed rocket attacks on El Al airliners, he went on the run after shooting two French detectives who tried to apprehend him in the summer of 1975. In London, a search of his flat unearthed a copy of the Forsyth novel and his soubriquet, 'Carlos the Jackal', was completed for him courtesy of the *Guardian* newspaper.

(Some assume the novelist took the title *The Day of the Jackal* from the Venezuelan terrorist rather than the other way around, a classic instance of where fact merges with pop culture to produce legend.)

Later that year, Carlos led an attack on the Vienna headquarters of OPEC (the Organisation of Petroleum-Exporting Countries) which took 60 hostages to exchange for the release of Arab activists. Fast becoming the world's most wanted terrorist himself, the Jackal was also an assassin for hire. Sheltered by various Middle Eastern states, he also enjoyed the patronage of Eastern European communist governments. Suggestions exist that, for a short time, Carlos targeted Romanian political dissidents on behalf of the dictator Ceausescu. According to his accusers, such political hits allowed the Jackal to line his own pockets.

Considering himself an honorary Palestinian, he formed a group called the Organisation of Arab Armed Struggle (OAAS) which largely conducted a parochial war against French interests, including the bombing of two trains which left four dead and many maimed. Between this late-1983 atrocity and Carlos's own kidnap and extradition to France in 1994, the Jackal became an increasingly shadowy figure, his surly, bespectacled photo-portrait appearing increasingly in the press as he became less of a presence in the world beyond the media. Like Osama bin Laden he became an absent figurehead for international terrorism, aligned with pan-Arab liberation movements rather than today's theological terrorists.

In his novel about a CIA assassin, *The Bourne Identity*, airport fiction writer Robert Ludlum took a leaf out of Forsyth's book and incorporated the Jackal as a fictionalised super-terrorist, supposedly even responsible for the assassination of JFK – when he would have been 14 years old. (By the time the novel became a hugely popular film in the third millennium, history had taken a different turn and Carlos was not even mentioned.)

By this point, the pro-Palestinian terrorist had been a long-term guest of the Syrian Government, who both granted him sanctuary and kept a lid on his activities. A move to Sudan would prove his downfall, as the African Islamic state's security services colluded to turn him over to their French counterparts.

Convicted of the murders of two policemen and a PFLP informant in 1997, Carlos the Jackal is now serving life in a French prison, where he faces further indictment for a series of Parisian bombings in the early 1990s that left eleven dead. Formerly the face of international terrorism, he is now a prolific letter writer and essayist. In his 2003 book,

Revolutionary Islam, he accepts the demise of the communist ideology that once sustained his activities and acknowledges the turning of the historical tide. 'From now on terrorism is going to be more or less a daily part of the landscape of your rotting democracies,' promised the honorary Arab and Muslim convert, now a vocal champion of Islamism.

Several years later, Carlos would criticise the supposed al-Qaeda activists who detonated themselves as human bombs on the London transport system in July 2005, claiming, in defiance of the outstanding charges against him, that their indiscriminate terrorism had nothing in common with his targeted assassinations. In fact these were homegrown young British Islamists, al-Qaeda – translating as 'the base', or 'the fundamentals' – being more of an ideology than an organisation.

Such a born-again Islamist would presumably have been aware of al-Qaeda's roots in the revolutionary Muslim Brothers movement that began in Egypt at the end of the 1920s. The Brotherhood's most influential figure, Sayyiid Qutb, was martyred by President Nasser's government in 1966, when he was hanged for revolutionary sedition. The Brotherhood's Arab liberationist creed ('liberation', in Islam, equating with freedom from despotic government but total submission to the will of Allah) had in fact influenced the younger Nasser, who was nonetheless not willing to submit to Qutb's vision of a total Islamic state ruled solely by Sharia law. So it was with Nasser's successor, Anwar Sadat.

Sadat, too, had been influenced by the liberation theology of the Muslim Brothers, but damned himself forever in the eyes of its fundamental adherents by making peace with Israel in the late 1970s. By kissing both Prime Minister Menachem Begin and President Jimmy Carter – respectively the Zionist and American infidel – on the cheek, he legitimised his targeted assassination in the eyes of the nascent Islamist movement.

Ironically perhaps, Sadat was gunned down at the eighth annual commemoration of the 1973 Yom Kippur War with Israel, in October 1981. As he watched an air force display from the podium, a cadre of military conspirators leapt from a truck and opened fire for a full two minutes, leaving the President and eleven others dead. At the 1982 trials of the 24 accused of plotting to assassinate Sadat, the main triggerman, Lieutenant Khalid al-Islambouli, clearly felt he had committed no crime but had secured himself a place in Heaven. He wrote a prose-poem address to the court which would not be read at his own trial but at that of a co-conspirator, eight months after al-Islambouli's execution:

'I have known my end and I am content with it. I will meet angels of the Most Merciful. Virgins [houris] of Paradise will conduct my procession, and all the creatures of the universe will sing the sweetest of songs for me.'

The unidentified assassin of former Pakistani president Benazir Bhutto will have regarded his self-obliteration as a similar one-way ticket to Paradise. As the female heir of an allegedly corrupt political dynasty, Bhutto was nonetheless popular, charismatic and – most damning, to the Islamists – relatively Westernised. While the cause of her 27 December 2007 death remains disputed, there can be little doubt that she was finished off by the self-detonation of the suicide bomber who approached her car, as she campaigned for the Pakistan People's Party in Rawalpindi – assuming the two gunshots that many claim they saw fired had not already inflicted the fatal injuries.

Ultimate responsibility still remains a controversial issue. If the killer was not a self-sanctioned army of one, then the responsibility may rest with al-Qaeda – certainly, the theocrat guerrillas themselves were quick to say so, claiming that bin Laden's deputy, Ayman al-Zawahiri, had issued a fatwa against Bhutto two months previously. But the invisible men of the Northwest Frontier cannot extend their pious tentacles everywhere, and the Pakistani Interior Ministry has pointed its finger at the ideologically linked group Lashkar-e-Jhangvi. The late Ms Bhutto, for her part, had expressed fears that senior figures in the government of President Musharraf were conspiring with Islamists against her.

Whatever the name or the label bestowed on the killer, we can be certain that whoever committed the deed did so in the name of fundamentalist Islamic tenets, but also that he shared the faith of the ancient heretical sect of Assassins, assured that the Garden of Paradise would welcome him at the moment of his martyrdom.

III

THE FIRST JIHAD?

The landscape that the victorious Crusaders surveyed from the walls of Jerusalem in 1100 was already fractured by deep divisions of race, creed and allegiance. It was this, perhaps, as much as any holy miracle or skill at arms that had paved their bloody way to the Holy City. The Christian invaders effectively established themselves on a political fault-line. To the north were the forces of the Seljuq Turks who they had fought to get to Jerusalem; to the south the Fatimid Caliphate, whose capital lay far to the south in opulent Cairo. Both empires were Muslim and both regarded the other as heretical, at least as invidious as the invading Christians. Among both Islamic factions, local leaders watched ally and enemy alike for weakness, eagle-eyed for any opportunity to strengthen their own positions at the expense of their neighbours.

If the Crusaders had known what to look for, they might have noticed that they were not the only new faction contesting for power in the region of Syria. By 1100 the first Ismaili agents had begun to infiltrate the district. They came from the castle at Alamut, the newly-established Assassin headquarters in Persia, the best part of 1,000 miles to the west, but along basically the same political fault-line that ran through Syria. Like the Seljuqs and Fatimids, the Assassins would also claim to be true Muslims, though this claim was treated with contempt by their supposed brothers of the faith. Islamic chronicles of the day routinely refer to the Ismailis simply as the *malahida* – heretics, a term heavy with murderous venom when apostasy means death. The phrase 'at daggers drawn' could not be more appropriate. Hugely outnumbered and metaphorically outgunned by their established Muslim opponents, anything that destabilised the Islamic status quo suited the Assassins, who otherwise stood to be crushed by one powerful neighbour or the other.

Regions of conflict and unrest drew in the Ismailis like vultures to a fresh battlefield. In Persia they could draw converts from the local population who chafed at the heavy-handed rule of the Seljuq Turkish overlords. In Syria, they could benefit from the fierce political, religious and military friction on the border between the Seljuq and Fatimid dominions, the region's inherent instability aggravated in no small way by the unexpected arrival of a highly trained Christian invasion force. Hasan Sabbah, the founder of the Assassins, correctly identified Syria and Persia as perfect territory for waging what we now call 'asymmetric war' – a term coined for a conflict between two opponents substantially mismatched in terms of numbers, military technology or other significant tactical factors.

In modern terms, fighters who have sought to overcome such odds have been labelled 'guerrillas' – or terrorists. The Vietnam War is a classic example of guerrilla warfare, and the Soviet invasion of Afghanistan is in many respects its Cold War mirror-image. In Vietnam, despite being a superpower which should have had no problem in defeating a small nation already torn by civil war, the USA was delivered a humiliating defeat in 1975 by its communist Viet Cong opponents. (The Soviets learnt a very similar painful lesson in Afghanistan in 1989.) Despite enjoying an overwhelming logistical superiority, the Americans were beaten by an effective use of other factors. Just as the Ismaili Assassins turned the terrain to their advantage, creating strongholds in mountainous regions that negated their enemy's numerical superiority, so the North Vietnamese used the jungles to compromise US military might. Like the Viet Cong guerrillas, Assassin agents hid among the local civilian population until the time was ripe to strike. Both North Vietnamese and Ismaili leaders made masterful use of psychological warfare; the Ismailis effectively paralysed effective political opposition using the fear of assassination, while the success of the North Vietnamese in sapping the enemy's will to fight – with relentless guerrilla campaigns, night operations, even subterranean tunnel complexes – helped ensure their ultimate victory.

Dr Farhad Daftary, leading expert on the history of the Ismaili sect, accepts the authors' comparison. 'I see an analogy,' he agrees. 'The Viet Cong were much more motivated for combat than the Americans. The Americans had gone to a foreign land, perhaps very often against their will, they had no choice. The Viet Cong were fighting for their own land; the Ismailis were fighting for their very survival in a specific fortress community. They were being attacked.' But of course, the Viet Cong were not seen as 'freedom fighters' by their enemies any more than the Assassins were, some 750 years earlier.

The Seljuq Vizier Nizam al-Mulk (improbably rumoured to be a school friend of Hasan Sabbah, more plausibly identified as the first official victim of an Assassin plot in 1092) stated, 'never has there been a more sinister, more perverted or more iniquitous crowd than these people, who behind walls are plotting harm to this country and seeking to destroy the religion . . . and as far as they can they will leave nothing undone in the pursuit of vice, mischief, murder and heresy.'

To the orthodox Muslims of the day, the Ismailis were a cancer, a revolutionary enemy within that weakened Islam, leaving it dangerously vulnerable to exterior attack. By way of contrast, in his 1938 book *The Assassins*, socialist author F. A. Ridley challenges the view of the Ismailis as a 'subversive menace'. Instead he depicts them as

> 'the last stand, the final oasis of the classical civilisation of the Mohammedan East, before it went down under the incoming flood of the destroying waves of barbarism represented successively by the Seljuq and Ottoman Turks and the Tartar armies of Jenghis Khan, Hulagu and Tamerlane. The strongholds of the Assassins represented oases amidst the flood.'

Much of medieval history suggests human tides swelling inexorably from the east, sweeping all before them. A succession of nomadic peoples emerged from the harsh vastness of the Asian plains to fall upon the fertile fields and opulent cities on their western borders – their inhabitants made indolent and complacent by too much comfort. The conquerors then inevitably yielded to the temptations of the civilised lifestyle of their predecessors, softened by luxury only to fall victim in turn to the next nomadic people to emerge from the windswept steppes, lean and hungry from a life in the saddle. The warlike Goths that thundered into Europe in 376AD, eventually bringing the mighty Roman Empire to its knees, were themselves fleeing westward from the formidable horsemen of the Hun tribes. The gradual collapse of Roman power under these tides would herald the dawn of the Dark Ages and, just as 'Assassin' would survive in many European tongues as testament to ancient fears of those who pursue a strategy of murder, so 'Gothic' came to describe anything dark, barbaric and desolate.

'Vandal' is another pejorative word that has passed down to us from this period, from another warlike tribe who ransacked the Roman Empire. In the early fifth century the Vandals devastated Europe, leaving a trail of destruction through the regions now known as Italy, France and Spain before turning their gaze southward, to the wealthy ports of North Africa, once the pride of haughty Carthage. In 455 they captured Rome itself, subjecting it to the rough treatment that would immortalise the name 'Vandal' as a synonym for senseless destruction. It would take the armies of Eastern Rome – now commonly known as the Byzantine Empire – to avenge the insult nearly a century later. In the mid-sixth century the fledgling Vandal empire was obliterated, its forces scattered by the military genius of the Byzantine general Flavius Belisarius. The elite of the defeated Vandal army were conscripted by the victorious Byzantines to serve on their eastern frontiers, where the Empire was locked in conflict with the mighty Sassanid dynasty, the last of the proud Persian emperors.

Byzantium had been adopted as his capital – a 'New Rome' – in 330 AD by the Roman Emperor Constantine I, who also left his domains with the ambivalent legacy of Christianity as its official state religion. After his death the city became commonly known as Constantinople until 1453, when it was captured by the Turks who would much later provide its current name, Istanbul. As the western Roman Empire slowly decayed and collapsed, Byzantium became the focus for surviving Greco-Roman culture and values, a shimmering beacon of wealth and sophistication amid the impending darkness. It was by far the biggest city in Christendom – some ten times the size of Rome, with perhaps 30 times the population of humble London. Byzantium survived by a combination of military expertise, economic might, complex diplomacy and the three rings of all-but-impenetrable defences that surrounded the thriving metropolis. Though the Sassanid armies reached these walls in 626, the Byzantine forces prevailed. Byzantium stood as the gilt gate between east and west, the richly bejewelled stopper that prevented the djinn of the Asiatic hordes from escaping the bottle to run rampant in Europe.

The next such manifestation resulted from the foundation of the Islamic faith under their inspirational warrior prophet Muhammad. He united the Arab tribes from a people of feuding desert raiders to forge a devastatingly disciplined fighting force. By Muhammad's death in 632, the entire Arabic peninsula was under Muslim control. Subsequent caliphs demonstrated the vigour and vitality of this young religious power with impressively rapid expansion. Between 633 and 651 the Rashidun caliphs thundered into the Sassanid territories, overrunning an empire already weakened by its wars with Byzantium, and bringing most of the Middle East under the crescent.

The Byzantines were also badly depleted by their long wars with the Sassanids and made easy prey for the advancing Muslims. By 640 the Byzantine territories of Syria, Palestine and Egypt were under the control of the Arabs. Under the Umayyad Caliphs, the Muslim tide swept ever westwards along the northern coast of Africa, taking one Byzantine city after another, until they reached the shores of the Atlantic. To the north lay Europe, across the Strait of Gibraltar which takes its name from the Umayyad general who led the Islamic invasion of Spain. By 718, after an eight-year campaign, the Iberian Peninsula was also under Muslim rule.

It looked at this point as if nothing could stop the Islamic advance. Far to the east the forces of the Caliphate massed around the walls of Byzantium, upon the very threshold of Eastern Europe. But its redoubtable defences held, and with the aid of their Bulgarian allies, an unusually bitter winter and Greek fire – Byzantium's secret weapon, an incendiary that adhered to its target like medieval napalm – the Byzantines repelled their Arabian foe.

Meanwhile, in Western Europe, the Umayyad armies began moving northwards over the Pyrenees into the region now known as France. Their success may have made them overconfident, and they began to experience setbacks at the hands of the local forces. Duke Odo of Aquitaine delivered a surprise defeat to the Arabs at Toulouse in 721. When the Umayyad invasion force reassembled in search of revenge, they were met by the Frankish ruler Charles between the cities of Tours and Poitiers in October of 732. Though outnumbered by two to one, he commanded the only force in western Europe capable of credibly confronting the Umayyad army, and must have been keenly aware that the fate of Christian Europe rested in his hands.

The tightly-packed phalanxes of battle-hardened Christian infantry held fast against repeated Arab cavalry charges. Then a rumour spread through the Muslim ranks that the booty and slaves they had taken were under threat from a flanking force. Some raced to the rear to protect their loot, which triggered a wholesale retreat. The Umayyad general was cut down in the ensuing chaos, and the Muslims fell back to the safety of their Iberian strongholds, effectively ending the Islamic threat to northern Europe. The Frankish leader was given the nickname of 'Martel' – meaning 'the Hammer' – for his role in smashing the Umayyad threat. Some fellow Europeans are fond of mocking Belgium as a small, inconsequential nation that has conspicuously failed to produce any men or women of great note. They might do well to remember the Belgian-born warlord Charles Martel, without whom we might all be speaking Arabic today.

The Christian fight-back in Spain became known as the 'Reconquista' ('Reconquest'), taking some 800 years of sporadic warfare, and is often seen as paving the way for the Crusades. It began a tradition of Christian warriors doing penance for their sins by battling unbelievers, coming from all over Europe in the hope of cleansing their souls and claiming some Islamic booty in the process. In a sense, almost all of the Crusades were reconquests of a sort, taking territory that the Muslims had themselves previously captured from the Christian Byzantines and Zoroastrian Persians. These Empires in turn had largely taken their lands by force, in an ongoing process that can be followed back as far as historical records allow. Or, indeed, as far as it suits national or religious sensibilities. Modern Muslim claims of indigenously Islamic territory cannot logically go back any further than the foundation of the faith in the seventh century any more than claims of England as a Christian nation, for example, can pre-date the country's conversion at around the same time.

What followed Umayyad defeats at the walls of Byzantium and on the hills outside Tours might be described as the tide turning. The Christian cause was aided by problems the Umayyad Empire was experiencing at home, as fractures in the Arabic unity Muhammad had achieved yawned wide. A rival Arabian dynasty also rose to power; the Abbasids accused the Umayyad Caliphs of corruption and questioned their right to rule. The Umayyads represented the traditional Arabian aristocracy, their love of luxury contrasting sharply with Muhammad's modest lifestyle and disdain for decadence. Their critics maintained that many of the dynasty had opposed the Prophet in his lifetime, and were now far more interested in the political power that came with adopting the mantle of his spiritual successors than any of his actual teachings. In practical terms, the Umayyad Caliphate's meteoric rise had left the empire overstretched. Their racist ideology that regarded their growing population of non-Arab subjects as second-class citizens was also a recipe for resentment.

In 750 the Abbasid clan led an army of the Umayyad's many enemies to victory at the Battle of Zab. Only one member of the Umayyad dynasty escaped the slaughter, fleeing to their Spanish territories in a doomed attempt to regroup. They would eventually fall victim to the Christian Reconquista.

Significantly, the Abbasid revolt against the Umayyad had begun with a campaign of preaching, underlining the links between religion and political power. He who held the caliphate held the key to one of medieval Europe's most efficient war machines, yet such power would take a heavy toll on its bearers. From the very start the question of succession had plagued Islam, with ancient rivalries and betrayals echoing down the centuries to create deep internal divisions. The Ismaili Assassins are the product of several such ruptures – in effect the consequence of a schism within a schism within a schism – a veritable Russian doll of religious discord. Peeling away the layers of this catalogue of dissent takes us back to the troubled birth of the caliphate.

The position of Muslim Caliph has much in common with that of Catholic Pope. The holder is regarded as God's direct representative on earth, but in practice the post also carries a great deal of political weight. Just as many medieval and Renaissance popes fielded armies, so the early caliphs were also the commanders-in-chief of Islamic empires. Popes and caliphs have waxed and waned throughout history, as secular princes, pragmatic politicians and ambitious warlords have challenged their authority over non-religious matters.

Rival dynasties attempted to manoeuvre their own candidates into the papacy or the caliphate, to lend divine sanction to their cause. While a growing Christian obsession with celibacy meant that heredity never entered into papal succession (even when relatives did inherit the post), it was important for caliphate candidates to be able to demonstrate a bloodline stretching back to Islam's founder.

After Muhammad's death, there had been two principal candidates to succeed him from among his retinue: Abu Bakr enjoyed the support of the majority of influential voices within the Muslim leadership. Ali, Muhammad's cousin and son-in-law, was supported by those who believed him to have been the Prophet's divinely appointed successor. Abu Bakr prevailed, pushing Ali into the background and establishing the first caliphate. It also established the schism between Abu's supporters who became known as the Sunnis – and the Shiites, who endorse only Ali's claim, which divides Islam to this day. The divisions that separate Sunni and Shiite soon became more profound than simple political loyalties. As with Catholics and Protestants, debate has frequently descended into violence.

Muslim theology remains a complex minefield even among experts, and there is a wide variation of opinion. But certain characteristics broadly define the two Islamic traditions: The Sunnis represent the Muslim majority and thus became the denomination traditionally favoured by the authorities. They tend towards a more practical interpretation of the Islamic holy book, the Koran, and emphasise the central importance of the sacred laws of Sharia. By way of contrast, Shiite

Muslims believe that the Koran contains deeper, hidden meanings only accessible to enlightened religious scholars. Sunnis believe that the true path can be found by consensus – as it was with the effective election of Abu Bakr as first caliph. The Shiites believe that only divine revelation can unveil the truth – as with their claim that Ali was the legitimate caliph by sacred sanction.

As the minority within Islam, the Shiite faith by default attracted the underdog and the rebel against the Sunni status quo. There is a greater mystical and messianic tendency in Shiite Islam and, while Sunni imams are often simply local spiritual community leaders, among many Shiites the position of imam has a far greater significance as a direct representative of God. For some believers, imams have taken on the character of divinely sanctioned saviours – like King Arthur who lies sleeping, awaiting the moment of Albion's greatest need, according to British myth – poised to smite the infidel and elevate the righteous when the allotted time arrives.

Abu Bakr's reign lasted less than three years. Both of his successors were assassinated by fellow Muslims – proof that political murder plagued Islam centuries before Hasan Sabbah was born – and Ali finally became caliph in 656. Ali too was murdered after a five-year reign, cut down with a sword while at prayer by Muslims who rejected his leadership. Civil war had blighted Ali's reign, and threatened to tear the caliphate in two when he died. To avoid further bloodshed, Ali's son relinquished his claim to his rival, Muawiyah, who established the Umayyad Caliphate.

Muawiyah is rumoured to have had his rival poisoned, earning the eternal enmity of subsequent generations of Shiites who reject the rule of his successors. The Umayyad Caliphs would preside over the expansion of Islam for nearly a century, until they were dethroned and butchered by the rival Abbasid clan in 750. While the Abbasids enjoyed the support of many dissident Shiites in their struggle with the Umayyad Caliphate, once they came to power the new Caliphs embraced Sunni Islam, snubbing their erstwhile Shiite allies.

Under the Abbasids Islam enjoyed a golden age, when science and the arts flourished as the caliphate became a cultural magnet, attracting scholars and philosophers, craftsmen and inventors, from across the known world. The city of Baghdad was made the capital of the caliphate in 762, taking advantage of the region's rich supply of trained clerks and scholars as a legacy of the Persian Empire.

The arts also thrived. *The Thousand and One Nights* is one of the most popular legacies of the flowering of literature and poetry. A compilation of tales all supposedly told by a vizier's beautiful daughter, Scheherazade, to forestall her execution by a cruel king, the book has done much to shape Western views of 'the mysterious East'. (The stories of Aladdin, Ali Baba and Sinbad were added to the original tales when first translated in Europe in the early 1700s.) Many of the clichés about arcane Arabia that we grew up with – of bustling bazaars, opulent palaces and scheming viziers – have their roots in the anthology that became known in Europe as *The Arabian Nights*. When we watch films like *The Thief of Baghdad* we are looking at a fantastical version of the Abbasid Caliphate, when *The Arabian Nights* was first put down on paper.

Yet not everybody was dazzled by such cultural achievements. *The Thousand and One Nights* was theoretically set in Ancient Persia, and featured many folk tales that pre-dated Islam, emphasising cultural elements that medieval Muslim purists regarded as decadent or even heretical. It was an unwelcome reminder of a magical world before Muhammad.

Some Muslims felt that, in opening wide its gates to Chinese inventions and North African literature, to Greek philosophy and Persian medicine, the Abbasid Caliphate was severing its religious roots. It seemed as if, in the familiar pattern, the invaders were becoming softened by the temptations of civilisation. Simmering Shiite resentment would boil over into open rebellion, culminating in an armed uprising in the holy city of Mecca in 786. The Abbasid war machine slid smoothly into action, however, now principally manned by Turkish mercenaries, quashing resistance and scattering many of the rebels southwards.

By this time the Shiite sect had divided. The Twelvers, now in the majority, took their name from belief in twelve divinely appointed imams, beginning with Ali. The Ismailis, while endorsing Ali as the first legitimate caliph, differed on details of the succession. During this period the Twelvers were largely content to quietly await the ordained imam, who they believed would institute a Shiite revolution. The Ismailis, however, took a more proactive approach, preaching active rebellion against what they regarded as a false caliphate.

In the wake of their military defeat by the armies of the Abbasids, the Ismaili cause would be principally fought by covert religious conversion and infiltration, forming a quiet coalition against the caliphate just as the Abbasids had against the Umayyad. It was a process that took generations of patient effort, eroding Abbasid authority from beneath by concentrating their efforts where it was weakest – far from the caliphate's capital in Baghdad.

It's difficult to overestimate the importance of Shiite missionaries to their denomination's survival. Analogies can be drawn with the rise of communism in the twentieth century. The Russian Revolution of 1917 was resolved with bullets, but the groundwork was laid by leftist political agitators, propagandists and union organisers. Parallels can be drawn between America's response to the rise of communism and the attitude of the Sunni establishment to Ismaili revolutionaries. Their dogma spread like a virus through susceptible populations, particularly those who enjoyed the least rewards under the status quo and had most to gain by radical change. American society was gripped by 'red scares' in the 1920s and 1950s, where concerns over the growing influence of communist ideology among idealists and the disaffected led to political purges. Just as 20th-century America feared 'reds under the bed', so the Abbasid authorities of the medieval Middle East dreaded the propaganda activities of the Ismaili missionaries, which threatened the very fabric of their caliphate.

By the beginning of the tenth century Ismaili efforts bore fruit. The first Shiite Caliphate was founded in North Africa by the Fatimid dynasty, claiming direct descent from Muhammad and attracting support from renegade tribes in the south. Just as medieval Europe had seen more than one pope claiming the title – each dismissing the other as an 'anti-Pope' – so the Islamic states now played host to three rival caliphs, each claiming exclusive right to the title.

The glory days of the Umayyad Caliphate, now struggling against the Christian Reconquista in Spain, were over, leaving the Sunni Abbasids and Shiite Fatimids to fight over the soul of Islam. Throughout the century the preparatory work of the Ismaili missionaries would pay dividends, as the Fatimid territories expanded steadily across northern Africa, seizing the coastal regions lapped by the Mediterranean via a combination of religious conversion and force of arms. In 969 AD, after several failed attempts, the Fatimids finally captured the ancient kingdom of Egypt where they founded their caliphate's new capital in Cairo.

The burgeoning new city was to be a showcase of growing Fatimid wealth and power, designed to rival and ultimately eclipse Abbasid Baghdad some 800 miles to the north. Cairo became a hothouse of religious scholarship, preparing new generations of highly trained and motivated missionaries to send east towards India and north into the enemy territories of the Abbasid Caliphate. As with the Abbasids, the Fatimid armies that followed in their wake were increasingly led by recently converted Turks from the vast Eurasian plains of Turkestan, on

Islam's easternmost borders – widely regarded as the fiercest Islamic warriors. It would ultimately prove a costly mistake for both caliphates.

Like Baghdad, Cairo cultivated a cosmopolitan character, employing Sunnis, Jews and Christians in positions of authority and trust, emphasising talent over birthright, encouraging a climate conducive to learning and scientific enquiry. As in Baghdad, however, such policies created bad feeling among religious reactionaries, who thought that those in power were growing fat on the bounty of empire and in danger of forgetting the fundamental truths and simplicity of Islam's Arabic ancestry.

Those that accused the Abbasids of similar sins could take grim satisfaction in the Sunni Caliphate's fortunes. There are limits to the maximum manageable size of any empire, imposed by practical considerations such as indigenous manpower, the sophistication of its bureaucratic backbone or the communication technology available. When these are stretched beyond endurance, without the great mind of an inspired leader or the infusion of new blood from fresh conquests, empires ultimately die.

The Fatimids had the good fortune to clash with the Abbasid Caliphate when it was in just such a condition. The Abbasids were losing control. The Persian administration and Turkish generals were becoming powers in their own right, their provinces acting independently, while rogue states – some of them Shiite – erupted on their very doorstep.

Most damagingly on a religious level, in the tenth century a radical sect with Shiite roots, known as the Qarmatians, became effectively a sacrilegious brigand army – murdering countless Muslim pilgrims on the road to Mecca, while vocally dismissing orthodox Islam as superstition. The Abbasids appeared powerless to react. In 930 AD the heretic horde raided Mecca itself, stealing the sacred Black Stone – the first altar on earth, which supposedly fell direct from heaven according to Islamic tradition – and compounding their crime by desecrating the holy Zamzam Well which contained the corpses of pilgrims. In 934 AD a faction known as the Buyids – nominally Twelver Shiites and mainly Persian Muslims – took advantage of the shattered reputation of the Abbasids to stage a takeover. The Abbasid Caliph retained his post, but he was reduced to the role of a puppet subject to the will of the Buyid Emirs (which roughly translates as 'princes'), who split the former territories of the Abbasids among themselves.

By the early eleventh century a new force emerged in the shape of the Seljuqs, Turkish warriors from the east newly converted to Sunni Islam, who saw themselves as saviours of the Abbasid Caliphate. Their leader, Tugrul, successfully dethroned one Buyid Emir after another, finally taking Baghdad itself in 1055 at the Abbasid Caliph's request.

The price was high. From being the pawn of his Persian politicians, the Abbasid Caliph now found himself a mere religious figurehead for the new Seljuq Empire. Neither had the Ismaili Caliphate in Cairo been idle during these turbulent and humiliating years. They had struck northward deep into Abbasid territory, their zealous missionaries preparing the way for the invading armies that took Syria, Palestine and the Lebanon. A confrontation with the Sunni Seljuqs was inevitable, though when it happened it was by proxy, pitting one Turkish warlord against another.

When the Seljuqs took over Basasiri, a former Buyid general of Turkish origin pledged allegiance to the Ismaili cause in return for support from the Fatimid Caliphate in Egypt. His rebellion was initially rewarded with success, and in 1058 Basasiri took Baghdad. This had been the goal of the Ismailis for centuries, and represented a spectacular accomplishment for the sect. The Sunni Caliph was humbled, his insignia of office sent south to the rival court in Cairo.

But Basasiri's achievement was as short-lived as it was impressive. Mindful perhaps of how the Abbasid Caliph's Turkish generals had slipped the leash, the Fatimid Caliphate cut off its support for its erstwhile champion while Tugrul gathered his forces. Basasiri was driven out of Baghdad after holding the city for just a year; after his army disintegrated he was chased down and killed by the pursuing Seljuq forces. It had been a high watermark for the Fatimid cause, after which their re-energised Sunni rivals, now led by the Seljuq Sultans, would slowly but surely begin driving the Shiites back.

This conflict provides the backdrop to the Crusades and the rise of the Ismaili Assassins. The advent of the First Crusade, hitting the Seljuq Sultanate's western borders in Anatolia, did not go unnoticed in Cairo. The Fatimid Caliphs sought to take advantage of the distraction, marching armies north to recapture the territory they had lost to the Turks. It paid off. In August 1096 they recaptured Jerusalem from the Seljuqs.

The Fatimids sent friendly messages to the Crusaders, assuring them they would ensure that Jerusalem was once more a Christian city that would welcome pilgrims and that there was no need for their campaign to continue. As far as most of the Crusaders were concerned, however, one heathen was much the same as the next and their quest was not complete until they had captured the Holy City.

Meanwhile, Hasan Sabbah – then merely an Ismaili missionary and in theory a minion of the Caliphs in Cairo – had established his first stronghold, deep in enemy Seljuq territory. He was sending his agents westwards into the turbulent frontline between Fatimid, Turk and Crusader. The stage was set for one of the most explosive conflicts in history.

IV

THE CASTLE OF DEATH

The Venetian ship that seemed so heavy and solid in harbour was beginning to look small and fragile against the backdrop of a vast, unfriendly ocean. The vessel had begun its long journey in distant Italy, but even the most seasoned of Arabic captains could not confidently predict the moods of the seas, and on this day the western Mediterranean was dropping her mask of sultry calm to reveal something far uglier.

The merchant vessel making her way along the Syrian coast, from Egypt to the Palestinian ports to the north, carried a mixture of human and commercial cargo — Arab passengers and precious goods destined for Christendom. Two mules bucked and brayed apprehensively in the hold, while their human masters stared upwards at the blackening sky with building apprehension. The captain whistled nervously through his teeth while the crew – Italian sailors now keenly feeling the distance from home – kept their own fears at bay by working well-worn routines. The sails were lowered in quick flaps of cloth and whips of rope, then secured along with everything else that could be tied down in the face of the building storm, leaving only the Venetian flag fluttering spasmodically from the mast.

The storm hit like a hammer of angry brine, wind and rain. The sky seemed to howl, angry and strange, as cold, wet hell descended in a squall of titanic waves and needle rain. The ship rolled violently, dropped, then rolled again. Once pilots of their vessel, the tiny human forms aboard now clung to anything at hand – some had even tied themselves to the ship's wooden skeleton to avoid being cast overboard as it rolled skyward and downward, heaving audibly with every rolling blow. Each second, cold-numbed knuckles clamped against pitching timber and sodden rope, and faces were stung raw with salt spray. The huddled, shivering figures shared wide-eyed glances, believing these horrible moments to be their last. Some cried out, some prayed loudly, some did neither as the motion made them retch bile and tears onto the deck. Among the chaos a lone figure sat, cross-legged upon the brine-washed deck. He also prayed, but as if he were a child seated in the garden of his mother's house.

When the storm abated, a few bolder souls, whose legs and tongues had steadied, approached him. He was, quite evidently, a holy man, and his dress was modest, but this was no travelling beggar. A man of learning, in happier hours he had engaged the merchants on board in lively religious debate, impressing listeners with his agile mind and powerful vision. This passenger had paid his passage with gold and carried letters from important personages in Cairo – documents one might expect to find in the hands of a pampered diplomat, not a lone traveller on a windswept deck.

'Why are you not afraid?' challenged one sailor in broken Arabic as the storm's fury built once more.

The passenger looked up with disconcerting calm. The ship still rocked and his interrogators struggled to keep their feet. 'My mission is God's will,' he said 'God protects me. What have I to fear?'

'The storm hasn't finished her work – I know that much.' The sailor looked nervously at the roiling clouds.

'Nor have I finished my work,' responded the holy man. A murmur crossed the deck – 'Seqina,' meaning the tranquillity granted the faithful in the face of deadly peril.

True to the sailor's warning, the wind picked up again and he returned silently to his post. This time, as the storm's howl heralded a renewed attack upon the battered craft, two of the crowd that had gathered around the holy man stayed, awkwardly sitting beside him as the ship found itself once more in the violent grip of the waves. They had already listened to the holy man's wisdom indulgently when the passage had been smooth, and in this turbulence somehow it made perfect sense. As the crew and their fellow passengers cowered beneath the storm, the two Arab merchants turned to their new comrade.

'I need only two good true men to start a holy war,' he said, fixing them with a stare that somehow eclipsed all of the sound and fury, 'and with them, two more. Wisdom is contagious.'

The ship reached port safely a day later. Miraculously, no one was lost. The holy man disembarked with his two new companions; the ship departed, while the shaken passengers shared stories of their close escape at dockside souqs, some now swearing that the holy man had actually calmed the angry storm with a wave of his hand . . .

***

The passenger was Hasan Sabbah, then still only an Ismaili missionary on his passage from Egypt to Syria in around 1080. The central character in our story, in a few short years this remarkable man was to carve a deep scar on the political map with the sharpness of his acute mind and the edges of his devotees' blades.

One of the attractions of the Shiite cause was its tendency toward meritocracy – the humblest man could achieve a lofty position according to his talent, rather than his birth. Hasan had been born in the Persian city of Qumm in around 1050. His family belonged to the Twelver Shiite faith, who favoured passive resistance to Sunni rule, and had a tenuous claim to blue blood via the Himyaritic kings who ruled Arabia before the advent of Islam. After moving to the ancient city of Rayy, a local centre for radical Shiite scholarship, the young Hasan proved a diligent student; one biographer, quoted by F. A. Ridley in *The Assassins*, later described him as 'able, courageous and learned in mathematics, arithmetic, astronomy (including astrology) and magic.'

However, theology was evidently the young Hasan's forte, and from an early age – seven, by many accounts – he was determined to dedicate his life to religion. Inevitably, in a religious hothouse like Rayy, the young Hasan was introduced to the divisions between the moderate Twelver beliefs of his family and the more radical Ismaili dogma. In particular, he came to the attention of an Ismaili missionary named Amira Zarrab, who identified the potential of this intense young man and began the process of conversion.

Giving an insight into this procedure, later records tell us that the young Hasan found all of his arguments steadily destroyed by the older man, who commanded his respect as 'a man of good character', according to autobiographical accounts preserved by later Arabic historians. Zarrab delivered the final blow with impressive subtlety, simply telling his young friend that, while he might vehemently disagree with him now, left to reconsider on a sleepless night Hasan would know that what he said was true. When the seed planted by Zarrab bore fruit, it would ultimately do so with fearsome fertility.

'There are no atheists in foxholes,' runs the old soldier's saying, and the fear of imminent death has certainly triggered countless conversions. So it was with young Hasan Sabbah, who contracted a disease that looked to be fatal. On his sickbed Hasan was haunted by his former mentor's arguments, and the fevered young man decided in his torment that, if he was to meet his maker, it was to be as an Ismaili devotee. But Hasan would survive and become a firm convert to the cause.

(Such near-deathbed religious epiphanies can be found on all sides of the religious divide. In 1248 the devout French King, Louis IX, launched the Seventh Crusade inspired by visions on his sickbed. The Crusade was a failure and the King was captured by his enemies. Louis, a pious bigot, would later be made a saint by the Catholic Church.)

Ismaili agents in Rayy, noting the dedication and ability of their new convert, flagged Hasan as a promising new agent. In 1072, he received the official endorsement of the Ismaili head of operations, taking sacred oaths of loyalty at the movement's Persian nerve centre of Isfahan, two years later. In around 1076, Hasan began the long journey to Ismaili Islam's international headquarters in Cairo to receive further instruction. The journey would take some two years – a long time even allowing for the difficulties of long-distance travel in the era.

The reason was that Hasan was travelling as a *da'i* – an Ismaili missionary – though a *da'i*'s role had as much to do with propaganda and espionage as preaching. (For reasons of clarity, just as Ismaili *fida'is* are referred to as 'Assassins' we shall henceforth call Ismaili *da'is* 'missionaries'.) We in the West may be inclined to see such missionary work in the light of freedom of conscience, but from another perspective the intrusion of potentially subversive alien agents is an act of cultural aggression.

This was certainly the way Hasan Sabbah's journey was regarded by the Sunni authorities, and he was ejected from at least one town he visited en route to Cairo. Hasan attempted to disseminate the Ismaili doctrine wherever he went. He also gathered information at every opportunity, collecting details of the local political, military and religious situations that might prove useful to his Ismaili superiors, and ultimately his own sect.

Hasan's route was impressively circuitous. He began by heading north – the wrong direction – to the region now known as Azerbaijan, then headed south into Syria. Once the young missionary reached Palestine, however, further progress proved impossible. It was then the frontline in the ongoing wars between the Seljuq and Fatimid forces, and so Hasan headed to the coast, from where he took a boat, reaching Egypt in August 1078. What he had seen on his travels cannot have been encouraging – the Seljuq presence appeared strong and well organised, the overstretched Fatmid forces unlikely to prevail in a prolonged conflict.

Hasan's experiences in Egypt might have given the keen young strategist strong indication as to why this was so. In Cairo, Mustansir enjoyed the longest rule of any caliph, holding the position for nearly sixty years. It was an impressive achievement in an era when so many of his peers had their careers cut short by violence. This may well have reflected Mustansir's hands-off approach to government, preferring to live in opulent, silk-lined seclusion while important decisions were taken by his Persian viziers and Turkish generals. But several years of famine had weakened the Fatimid Caliphate, deliberately exacerbated by rebels to the south who destroyed farms and wrecked irrigation. One account says that Mustansir's stable was reduced from ten thousand beasts to just three emaciated horses, while large parts of Egypt became depopulated ghost towns.

Meanwhile, factions within the Fatimid army vied for power, the Turks finally prevailing over the Sudanese regiments in open civil war. By the time Hasan reached Cairo, a warlord named Badr al-Jamali was in effective control. Just as the Abbasid Caliphs had been reduced to puppets by their Turkish generals so now the Fatimid Caliphs were little more than figureheads, dominated by their former servants in the armed forces.

This can scarcely have pleased a devout Ismaili like Hasan Sabbah, as the Fatimid Caliph was also the Ismaili Imam and hence still his divinely appointed superior at this point. Some accounts suggest Hasan became actively involved in a plot to reassert the authority of the caliph. This inevitably irritated Badr, who had Hasan imprisoned. But in truth, aside from the facts that he never managed to secure an audience with Mustansir himself and that he spent time in Alexandria after leaving Cairo, we know very little of what happened in the years Hasan spent in Egypt. At some point around 1080 he left – either under his own volition or else expelled by Badr – and took a ship north to retrace his steps. It is this journey that is recreated at the start of this chapter, the story of Hasan's miraculous survival after a near wreck being one of many legends surrounding this remarkable man. Another legend insisted he had only been released from prison in Egypt after one of its minarets collapsed, which nervous gaolers interpreted as a sign of divine disfavour.

Now in his thirties, Hasan Sabbah began his life's mission in earnest. His travels had convinced him that if the Middle East was to be freed of Sunni domination then it would not be courtesy of the Fatimid Caliphate in Cairo. They had abandoned Basasiri, conqueror of Baghdad, to the mercy of his Seljuq enemies, and would no doubt do the same again in a similar situation. The native Shiite presence was too weak and disunited to stand a chance against the professional armies of the Seljuq Sultanate, so a conventional armed insurrection was out of the question.

Instead, Ismaili missionaries were to be the principal secret weapon of Hasan's asymmetric war. The Fatimid Caliphate had been won not on the battlefield so much as in marketplace sermons and private religious debates, winning hearts and minds over a period of decades or even generations. Hasan believed that the same methods could prevail in the Middle East if brought to bear by a man of ability and patience.

We do not know whether Hasan's ambitious endeavour was endorsed by his superiors of the day. Certainly, his first destination was the Ismailis' Persian HQ in Isfahan, which Hasan reached in 1081, where he may have received authorisation for his audacious plans. He continued his missionary work for the best part of a decade, roaming throughout Persia, spreading the Ismaili doctrine deep in Sunni territory and probing the Seljuq position for weaknesses. When a new convert showed particular promise he would in turn be trained as a missionary, so the Ismaili cause would gain gradual momentum. The reaction of the Seljuq authorities paid testament to Hasan's success; he became a wanted man, actively sought by those serving the Sultan. For his part, the Ismaili missionary was developing a strategy that involved exploiting not just religious factors but social and even racial fault-lines running through the Seljuq Empire.

Three cultures then competed for dominance in Iran. The Persians, who had been established the longest, were heirs to a series of mighty empires that flourished in the mists of antiquity. They still dominated scholarship and the arts and provided most of the administrators essential for effective government. When the Arabs arrived in the seventh century, they toppled the last of the Persian dynasties but still could not run their own growing empire without the assistance of Persian bureaucrats and administrators. As direct descent from the Prophet is so important to Islam, Arabs continued to dominate religious life, though in military terms they were largely superseded by the Turks who were, by the 11th century, very much in the ascendant.

The Turks had originated on the steppes of central Asia, and at this point were only starting to colonise the region we now call Turkey, rolling back Byzantine power across Anatolia. As far as many of the Arabs and Persians of the day were concerned, the Turks were just the latest wave of aggressive barbarians to emerge from the eastern steppes – fellow Muslims, but only recently converted and regarded as vulgar parvenus. While it's true to say that the Seljuqs were doing their best to combine Persian sophistication with Turkish martial virtues – and would leave an impressive cultural and architectural legacy – many Turkish governors ruled with a heavy hand, imposing punishing tax burdens on the subjects they treated with scant respect.

Hasan Sabbah expressed a popular opinion when he dismissed the Seljuq Sultan Malikshah as an 'ignorant Turk', comparing him to a djinn. (Djinns – or genies, in the West – were powerful but subhuman entities composed of smokeless fire, the Koranic equivalent of Christian demons. Like pre-Christian demons, they had enjoyed a more benevolent reputation in pre-Islamic lore.) Arabs resented the way in which these upstarts had taken control of the caliph, treating the blood descendents of the Prophet as mere pawns to add a veneer of respectability to their sultanate. The Persians nursed their wounded pride at being sidelined, the offsprings of an ancient civilisation that stretched back to the eighth century BC. Its humbling stone legacy – vast ruined palaces and crumbling lofty mausoleums – were still evident throughout the Seljuq heartlands, bearing silent, melancholy testament to the fallen empire that was once the envy of the world.

In one of the first firm indications that Hasan's mission was both politically revolutionary and religiously radical, he abandoned Arabic as the sacred language for his growing band of followers in favour of Persian. This unexpected move suggests that, as some of his biographers have suggested, Hasan probably had Persian blood running through his veins, or perhaps he was merely being practical. If his mission could appeal to Persian cultural sentiment as well as the religious resentment of the Shiites, then Hasan could broaden the appeal of his quiet rebellion against the Turkish-Sunni Sultanate.

But did his adoption of Persian values go further than that? Was he raising the banner for a lost culture? Perhaps he was even adopting elements of the forbidden pre-Islamic fire-worship of the Persians (Zoroastrianism) into his developing secret doctrines? We simply do not know but, as we will see later, it is at least possible.

Certainly Hasan focused his efforts on the regions of the sultanate with the largest concentration of deviant religions, where the bones of the fallen Persian empires lay all around. Forgotten friezes survived of high priests and kings with their ornately curled beards, staring impassively at the desolation, as did a scattering of statues of the strange gods and animal-headed demons that once stood sentinel over a vibrant empire. Most such ancient edifices were weathered by the elements beyond recognition; some were defaced by the Persians' Roman, Greek and Arabian enemies, while others had tumbled when the earth shook with the seismic shocks that plagued the region. It seems somehow appropriate that a territory riven by so many religious, cultural and political fissures should also lie upon a natural fault-line.

Daylam, in north-west Iran, lay between the modern capital of Tehran and the shores of the Caspian Sea which suffers earthquakes to this day. (In May 1990, tremors killed some 45,000 people in the region). The Buyids, the Persian Shiite warlords who briefly dominated the Abbasid Caliphate before being crushed by the Turks in the mid-eleventh century, hailed from Daylam. While technically a Seljuq province, it remained stubbornly independent, its warlike people fiercely resistant to authority, its rugged landscape a mixture of precipitous mountains and secluded valleys. This made it perfect guerrilla country, poor territory for large armies to manoeuvre or hold territory, and a magnet for fugitives from Seljuq justice. Followers of failed rebellions, preachers of forbidden faiths and desperados of all shapes and sizes made their homes in Daylam – in effect Persia's 'Wild West'.

It was an obvious target for Hasan's missionaries and by 1087 he was concentrating his efforts in the region. The following year he identified the ideal location for his new centre of operations – a castle in the forbidding mountains of Alborz known as Alamut, derived from the Persian for 'eagle's teaching'. The name refers to the legend that the first king to build a castle on this inaccessible spot was inspired by seeing an eagle. Hasan preferred to think of the castle as the Eagle's Nest, suggesting an eagle still nested there almost as a totem.

Alamut was also sometimes known in Arabic as the 'Castle of Death'. It sits at the head of a valley, teetering ominously atop a mountain crest, the only practical approach being along a treacherous path where intruders were exposed to the missiles and arrows of the defenders above. At the time it was occupied by a governor called Mahdi, who ruled the district on behalf of the Seljuq Sultan. The story of Hasan Sabbah's bloodless capture of Alamut has become the stuff of legend, a curious tale that throws a strange light on the future tactics of his burgeoning secret empire.

In tried and tested fashion, Hasan prepared the ground by slowly flooding the locale with his missionaries, preaching his radical new doctrine of revolt. Each new convert was cautioned to show patience as their leader prepared his masterstroke. There were efforts to convert the governor himself which initially appeared promising. (One account says that Mahdi was a Shiite, already sympathetic to the revolutionary cause.) But then, after agreeing to see the representatives of the rebellion in the castle, he had them expelled.

It may have been evidence of a divided conscience. Mahdi had pledged loyalty to the Sultan who had appointed him; he commanded an isolated outpost and the local population were looking increasingly hostile. But when Mahdi invited Hasan's followers to further talks, then ordered them to leave, they simply ignored them. He had lost control of his own castle.

In the meantime, the author of all his woes had been smuggled into Alamut. Some accounts suggest Hasan Sabbah had been living for some time in the Eagle's Nest, unnoticed. Mahdi's men had no doubt been expecting such an esteemed leader to stand out among the numerous tradesmen and servants that ensured the everyday running of the castle. If so, they missed Dihkkhuda – the identity that Hasan had taken on in order to infiltrate the fortress, in classic Assassin style. When Hasan chose to unmask himself, Mahdi was presented with a *fait accompli*.

***

Almost as curious as the capture of Alamut was the fate of its erstwhile governor. Mahdi took a draft he had been given for 3,000 gold dinars to a prosperous merchant stipulated by Hasan. It was honoured in full. This poses some interesting questions: Who was 'Muzaffar Musataufi', who paid this considerable sum at Hasan's bequest? Was it an 'inside job' – a simple case of a sympathetic governor taking a hefty bribe to abandon his post? In any case, the cash exchange – voluntary or otherwise – gave a certain legitimacy to Hasan's acquisition. It also indicates that, at this early stage, his revolutionary mission included some wealthy converts, or at least opportunistic businessmen willing to back Hasan's rebellion with hard cash. While most begin recruiting among the dispossessed, no radical cult survives without sound financial backing. The lure of gold would prove as significant a tool as religious conversion or the threat of cold steel in the Assassin armoury.

One story that underscores this comes from an episode in the late 12th century. An eminent and influential Sunni theologian in the city of Rayy named Fakhud-Din ar-Razi was becoming increasingly vocal in his denunciation of the Ismailis. An Assassin was sent from Alamut to silence this prominent critic. In classic fashion, the Ismaili agent infiltrated his target's social circle, posing as one of Razi's students. Once he had won the theologian's confidence, the Assassin asked his tutor for a private conference after class. Once they were alone, the Assassin drew a knife; when asked what he wanted by the terrified scholar, he announced his allegiance to Alamut, and coolly expressed the desire to 'slit your honour's body from the chest to the navel, because you have cursed us from the pulpit.' After a struggle the young Assassin wrestled his foe to the floor, exacting a promise from Razi that his denunciations of the Ismailis would cease.

Satisfied, the Assassin handed him a bag containing 365 dinars and told him he would receive the same every year so long as he kept his promise. (The sum matched the number of days in the year. Numerology seems to have been significant to the Assassins.) Razi kept his promise, as did the Assassins. Quizzed later by another student as to why he had abandoned all criticism of the Ismaili heresy, Razi simply replied that it was not wise because their arguments were 'weighty and trenchant' – as heavy as the bags of gold he received and as sharp as the knife that had been held to his throat. Effective Assassin policy frequently employed a balance of these two elements – the carrot of bribery and the stick of threatened assassination – as the most effective method of silencing opposition.

While the capture of Alamut in the autumn of 1090 was a remarkable achievement, Hasan was well aware that he had no time to rest upon his laurels. If his missionary activities had made him a marked man, this audacious seizure of a stronghold deep in the Seljuq Sultanate's turbulent flank set off alarm bells. It also made him a focus of the Seljuq vizier, Nizam al-Mulk.

'Vizier' is a position roughly analogous to that of prime minister in Western politics. In theory, the vizier's job was to act as the chief advisor and assistant to the ruler – in practice, the adviser could eclipse the authority of his master if the monarch was weak, as has happened so often in European history. The powerful Seljuq Sultan, Malikshah, was certainly no pushover, but Nizam was a formidable politician, an erudite and energetic Persian who had risen through the ranks to become the Sultan's right-hand man. Some whispered that he was the true power behind the throne. While Malikshah's military muscle had helped establish the Seljuq Empire, it was Nizam's brilliant brain that had created the administrative sinews that bound it together as a Middle Eastern superpower.

A curious story links Nizam al-Mulk and Hasan Sabbah. It was said that three friends went to school together – Nizam, Hasan and the poet Omar Khayyam. The trio were inseparable, and agreed that, if one should enjoy great success in their future lives, they would share their good fortune with the other two. Nizam's career as a politician at the sultan's court flourished first, and he made good his promise by offering Omar and Hasan lucrative jobs in government. Omar declined, preferring to ask for the ways and means to continue his studies, which would ultimately make him medieval Islam's counterpart to the Renaissance man. Hasan accepted, but things did not go well. When he threatened to rival Nizam's influence at court by outshining him, Nizam had his former friend exiled.

Historians have dismissed this story. While there are gaps in Hasan's history which may allow for a period at the Seljuq court, differences in age and geography make the trio as schoolmates all but impossible. Most now think it a legend in which the three men – the most accomplished voice of authority, the consummate rebel and the era's foremost thinker – are imagined as symbols of the conflicting forces in society.

But, just as the tale of Hasan's conflict with Badr al-Jamali in Cairo justifies the future acts of the Assassins, this story of Hasan's betrayal by a former friend gives the unfolding events a compelling personal angle. When news of Hasan's triumph in Alamut reached the Seljuq capital, now located in Isfahan, preparations began at once for a powerful force to recapture the castle. The Ismailis saw Nizam as the architect of this armed Seljuq response, and may well have been right. But it does not take any personal animosity to explain the military response. Nizam, or indeed Malikshah, was reacting in the way you might expect a superpower to respond to the sudden threat of a rogue state on its doorstep. The Shiite rebels were to be terminated with extreme prejudice.

Back in Alamut, Hasan was taking steps to try to fortify his position against the imminent whirlwind. His followers were put to work not just in strengthening the neglected defences of the castle, but improving the infrastructure of the valley beneath. Cisterns and channels were laboriously dug from the solid rock face to collect and supply water for the castle from the region's frequent rainfall, and to irrigate the fields beneath. (Even if the castle of Alamut was effectively impregnable to conventional military attack, any garrison without water would fall even more quickly than one without ammunition.) This vigorous improvement of any fortified position they captured became standard Assassin practice, and reflects more than the obvious practical advantages of improving its military strength. In the years to come, Alamut would become an oasis of verdant fertility among the forbidding Alborz mountains – not just a self-sufficient community in hostile territory, but a vista of natural beauty, a 'Garden of Paradise' which would play a profound part in Assassin mythology.

***

It is possible to draw some parallels here between Hasan – then fast becoming the most effective guerrilla leader in the medieval Middle East – and his most controversial modern counterpart. Robert Fisk was the first Western journalist to be granted an interview with Osama bin Laden in 1993, then best known as one of the Islamic *mujahideen* instrumental in driving Soviet troops from Afghan soil. Fisk found bin Laden and his men busy building a road in Sudan, using the same machinery and construction equipment he had employed in Afghanistan to build the infrastructure necessary to wage guerrilla war on the Russians. (The underground complexes he built would later shelter bin Laden from US attempts to assassinate him in the wake of the 9/11 atrocities.) The self-styled Saudi sheik described himself to Fisk as simply 'a construction engineer and an agriculturalist'.

Was not this hard labour a bit of an anticlimax for men used to fighting jihad on the battlefield, wondered the British journalist. 'They like the work and so do I,' said bin Laden. 'This is a great plan which we are achieving for the people here, it helps Muslims and improves their lives.'

It is easy to imagine that, if Fisk had been able to interview Hasan Sabbah as he supervised the work at Alamut, he would have received similar answers. By quite literally getting his hands dirty, Osama bin Laden demonstrated his credentials as both a practically-minded leader and a man of the people, in contrast to the Saudi Government, which he denounced as pampered traitors to the Islamic cause, wholly divorced from the true struggle by privilege.

In the same way, with the policy of personally overseeing structural and agricultural improvements to the places he captured, Hasan and his agents contrasted strongly with the caliphs and sultans who claimed to rule according to the austere example of Muhammad, from gilded palaces and perfumed harems.

Hasan's preparations demonstrated a keen understanding of the principles of fighting an asymmetric war. His missionaries had not let up the campaign of conversion and subversion, and preparations were in place to extend his power base from Alamut to other appropriate strongholds. (Indeed, some accounts from the era suggest that Alamut was not the first to fall to Assassin subversion.) But the cold steel of Seljuq retaliation was drawing ever closer, and Hasan had less than 100 men to garrison Alamut against a besieging force of thousands.

However, he had a plan, one that would carve his sect's name into the history books. The sultan's force, heavy with armour and weapons, was trailed by the baggage trains necessary to wage a campaign and making slow progress west, into the unwelcoming embrace of the Alborz mountains. Meanwhile, a lone agent named Bu-Tahir travelled eastwards from Alamut, carrying nothing but a knife.

V

ARRIVAL OF THE ASSASSINS

The progress of Nizam al-Mulk resembles an episode from The Thousand and One Nights – *an almost fairytale spectacle of pomp and grandeur. The vizier himself may be finally showing the marks of age and responsibility in his grey beard and lined face, but his air of authority and dazzling attire all but eclipse any such impression. Nizam is bedecked in expensively dyed silks, gold and precious stones, the best his vast territories have to offer, shimmering and sparkling in the heavy afternoon sun. Such magnificence demands a toll; constant travel and endless political duties in the far-flung cities of his master Malikshah are the price the ageing potentate pays for power and privilege.*

But such duties need not be too onerous. Nizam is borne upon a litter, four broad-backed slaves carrying his cushioned throne upon their shoulders, their stride expertly synchronised. After a day addressing a thousand questions of administration and governance, he is borne to his harem, a tent where deft fingers soaked in perfumed oil and the music of feminine laughter will wash away the dust and burdens of the day. A curious crowd follow at a respectful distance, cowed by his aura and the presence of the grim, narrow-eyed guards that form the vanguard and rear of this little procession, their mail marking out a rhythmic percussion. A figure stumbles to the fore of the throng, his hands held out in entreaty to the mighty vizier. His dusty robes and humble demeanour mark him out as a Sufi holy man.

Some say that the Sufi creed is strange, even suspect. But they are devout, and their blessing is said to bring peace to a world that has seen too little of it. Nizam gestures for his guards to let the man through. His bearers carefully lower the litter to the ground, and Nizam holds out his hand to receive a blessing.

There is a sudden, brief flash of silver as the holy man leaps forward, drawing a knife from the sleeve of his robes. It arcs in the sun three, four, five times as the blade drives through Nizam's silk robes into his soft flesh, barely giving him time to cry out.

Within seconds the guards are upon the Assassin, their swords making short work of him. He falls beneath their blows without a murmur. Nizam's lifeblood pumps into the thirsty sand, the greatest statesman of his age now a twitching carcass.

***

So, cliché has it, everyone alive in 1963 can remember where they were when they heard President Kennedy had been shot. The same may well have applied nearly a thousand years before in the Middle East, when Nizam al-Mulk was assassinated in 1092. The shocking news of his murder hit the region like a thunderbolt. The foremost statesman of his day, Nizam had served as Seljuq vizier for some 30 years, bringing stability and peace while establishing institutions which some regard as the prototype for modern Western universities. His death created a dangerous power vacuum. As with the assassination of JFK, conspiracy theories soon followed his violent demise, flourishing in the labyrinthine politics of the era. Some said that his master, Sultan Malikshah, had ordered Nizam's murder, wary of the growing influence of his most able and powerful servant. Others speculated that the Sunni vizier had secretly been converted to the Shiite faith, and had to be silenced by religious conservatives before his new beliefs became public.

But Nizam al-Mulk was almost certainly the first victim of Hasan Sabbah's Assassins. There were celebrations in Alamut when news arrived of his death. The chaos that ensued throughout the Seljuq Sultanate must have allowed even their serene leader a satisfied smile. 'The killing of this devil is the beginning of bliss,' Hasan is reputed to have said. It set the template for the policy of political murder which would ensure the place of the word 'assassin' in the popular imagination.

If Sultan Malikshah had actually orchestrated the murder it would have been a massive miscalculation. Nizam's personal skills as an administrator and diplomat made him irreplaceable and, in his absence, the network of government holding the vast sultanate together began to unravel. Even if Hasan had not been directly responsible for ordering the murder, the impact it had upon his foes must have proven inspirational.

According to the account by Arab historian Rashid al-Din, the assassination had been triggered in Alamut when Hasan exclaimed, 'Who will rid this state of the evil of Nizam al-Mulk Tusi?' An Ismaili named Bu Tahir Arrani took the Grand Master at his word, and took the road eastward, dressed as a harmless Sufi mystic. Carrying only a knife, he subsequently entered the history books as the first of the Order of Assassins.

A number of historians have noted a striking echo between Hasan's words and a famous outburst that led to another of medieval history's most infamous assassinations. Nearly 80 years later, in a distant north-western corner of Europe, the English monarch Henry II concluded an angry address to his court with the words, 'Will no one rid me of this troublesome priest?'

Henry was a force to be reckoned with – vigorous in government, decisive on the battlefield, a Plantagenet powerhouse who helped put England on the map. His son and successor, Richard the Lionheart, would undo much of Henry's good work by neglecting England in favour of the Crusades – in which capacity he would encounter the Assassins.

The troublesome priest who inspired Henry's fateful words was Thomas Becket, then Archbishop of Canterbury. Becket had originally been Henry's closest friend and ally – his equal in determination and ability – and in 1155 the King appointed him as Lord Chancellor (a role roughly analogous to that of vizier in the Middle East). Having brought his independently minded aristocracy to heel, Henry then focused his attention on the ongoing struggle between sacred and secular power that characterised the era. He was determined to assert his authority over the English clergy, who believed themselves answerable only to the Pope. In 1162, when Henry managed to elevate his friend to the most influential religious post in England, he anticipated a valuable new ally in his battle with the Church. He was to be bitterly disappointed.

When he took his new post, Thomas Becket experienced a sudden religious epiphany. In modern parlance, he was 'born again'. The new archbishop turned his back on the pomp and splendour of his past, donned a hair shirt and became a devout champion of the Church. Henry's old friend was now his implacable foe, opposing all of the King's attempts to reform the legal system which then held many clergymen effectively above the law. In exasperation, Henry charged Becket with contempt, and his former friend threatened to retaliate by excommunicating the King.

After it briefly looked like a compromise might be found in 1170, Becket excommunicated three bishops sympathetic to the crown. When word reached Henry of this latest display of disloyalty, the monarch was wintering in his Normandy territories. It was this that inspired his immortal rant about the 'troublesome priest', echoing Hasan Sabbah's invective against Nizam al-Mulk and setting in motion another momentous murder.

A quartet of Henry's knights decided to take the matter in hand and headed north, across the Channel, to Canterbury, where Becket was ensconced in the city's imposing cathedral. In the ensuing struggle, tempers frayed, then snapped, and Becket fell beneath a flurry of sword blows, one so powerful that the blade shattered on a flagstone, another nearly severing the arm of a monk who attempted to intervene. When the dust settled, Becket's blood and brains made a horrific slick across the cold cathedral floor. Most chronicles of the day were written by clergymen, so it is no surprise that accounts depict the episode as the brutal slaughter of a saintly innocent at the hands of four heavily armed thugs. England's senior churchman was butchered on sacred ground.

The ensuing scandal spelled disaster for the King. Henry almost certainly had not intended or anticipated the murder, and his exasperation with the archbishop was justified. Popular accounts of the day compared Becket with the martyred Christ, and described him meekly offering himself up as a holy sacrifice with the words, 'For the Name of Jesus and the protection of the Church I am ready to embrace death.'

Just three years later the Vatican declared the murdered Archbishop of Canterbury a saint and Henry was obliged to undertake a humble barefoot pilgrimage to the site of the crime, where monks flogged his naked back. It was a terrible humiliation for a proud man – no doubt already wracked with guilt over the death of a former friend – and a resounding propaganda victory for the Church, which successfully resisted Henry's proposed reforms. This was a pivotal point in the political history of medieval England, but does it tell us anything about assassination in any broader sense?

Richard Helms thought so, describing it in 1975 as an episode that 'spans the generations and the centuries'. As the director of the CIA, who presided over notorious covert operations such as the MKULTRA programme (of which more later), Helms was uniquely qualified to comment. He was addressing the Church Committee, convened to investigate the undercover activities of the US intelligence agencies in the wake of the Watergate scandal, which had shaken America's faith in its elected officials.

It seems odd that a murder that took place over eight centuries before, some 4,000 miles away, should become a burning issue on a US Government committee. According to author Richard Belfield in *Assassination*, it related to the extent to which post-war presidents such as Nixon, Johnson and (ironically perhaps) Kennedy had been aware of, or even ordered, missions of dubious legality by the FBI and CIA. Attempting to explain what qualified as an implicit order to assassinate, Senator Charles Mathias employed historical analogy: 'when Thomas

Becket was proving to be an annoyance, as Castro, the king said who will rid me of this man? He did not say to someone go out and murder him. He said who will rid me of this man and let it go at that.' Was this the kind of vague authorisation given to CIA assassination operations by the American presidents?

The committee resulted in President Ford issuing Executive Order 11905, effectively outlawing the use of assassination by US Government agencies. (This may or may not have remained effective, as we will see later.) It also underlined certain key issues regarding the art of assassination. The martyrdom of Thomas Becket remained a striking example of how badly a political murder could backfire. Even though he could plausibly deny any real involvement, it did immense damage to Henry II. Taking this lesson on board, the CIA had gone to great lengths to avoid leaving any evidence linking them with assassination plots, and to ensure that no US President appeared directly responsible for ordering such an operation. Instead, a wide range of euphemisms and inferences were employed in the Oval Office. The Kennedy administration were typically coy, debating evasively with the CIA on how to 'get rid' of Castro – though both Hasan Sabbah and Henry II had used very similar language with differing intent centuries before.

If the intent had differed, there was an even more radical difference in the reaction. While Henry became mired in a backlash of grim recrimination, Hasan began a macabre roll call that was kept by subsequent Assassin Grand Masters, recording successful assassinations in the same way victorious regiments record military triumphs. For those waging asymmetric war, an assassination is a propaganda coup worth advertising, while for an established ruler the reverse is true. This can be clearly seen in a modern conflict where one side used assassination as a propaganda tool while the other made every effort to deny involvement.

***

Modern terrorist strategy in the West was often exemplified by the Irish Republican Army. Born out of centuries of bloody British oppression, from Cromwell's Roundheads and King William of Orange to the murderous 'Black and Tan' mercenaries of the early 20th century, the IRA evolved an assassin's ethos that aspired to be almost as ruthless. 'To paralyse the British machine it was necessary to strike at individuals,' admitted their overall commander, Michael Collins, towards the end of his short life.

Collins, who remains a heroic icon to many Irish Catholics, had taken part in the abortive Easter Rising in Dublin during 1916 but was only briefly imprisoned by the occupying Brits. In November 1920, his was the guiding hand behind the first 'Bloody Sunday', a synchronised assassination of fourteen men accused of being military intelligence agents at large in the Irish capital. The response was unequivocal, the British Army firing into an Irish football crowd in an act of random retaliation worthy of the Waffen-SS.

Almost two years later, by which time Collins was military commander-in-chief of the newly formed Irish Free State, he was accused of masterminding the assassination of Field Marshal Sir Henry Wilson in London, in June 1922. Wilson, a highly decorated Irish-born career soldier, was fiercely defensive of the culture of Protestant 'Orangemen', and suggested during the Irish War of Independence that, for every British serviceman killed, five Fenian (i.e republican) activists should be shot. The chickens came home to roost for Wilson after he presided over the unveiling of the Great Eastern Railway War Memorial at Liverpool Street, commemorating the dead of World War 1. Trailed home, he was shot dead by two IRA gunmen.

Collins was not the only Fenian leader in the frame for the assassination, and historians have suggested it was more likely one of his republican allies who sent the triggermen. Whatever the truth, it might have spelled the end for them all but for the strength of will shown by Collins. For the IRA had already forced the British to the negotiating table for the first time, demonstrating the great unspoken historical truth of the last hundred years: terrorism works.

By December 1921, Collins and the Brits had negotiated the first Anglo-Irish Treaty. It was a *realpolitik* compromise, with the counties of Southern Ireland granted the right to self-government but not the status of a republic (which would come later), and the six counties of Northern Ireland remaining under British rule. The legacy of a divided Ireland would reap bloodshed for decades to come, and the pragmatic Collins remarked that, in signing the agreement, he knew he was signing his own death warrant.

So it was that, on 22 August 1922, Collins' small convoy of military vehicles was ambushed by a group of dissenting republican 'Irregulars'. In the gunfight that ensued, the back of his head was blown off; Collins was the only fatality and had clearly been the target. His state funeral procession in Dublin was on a scale little seen again until the assassination of JFK; hundreds of thousands of public mourners thronged the streets in a nation comprising just a couple of million citizens.

The IRA's battle against the British political and military establishment continued after Collins was killed. Now, however, they were fighting in the cause of a united Ireland and the joining of Ulster (as Brits and Protestants called Northern Ireland) with the southern counties. In the years ending World War 2 the IRA made few inroads into the public consciousness, although counter-terrorist activities were launched against their British mainland campaign in the late 1940s. While explosive devices were among their tactical armoury, they had not yet reached the low benchmark of modern terrorism whereby any passer-by would be regarded as fair game.

After the late 1960s, all that was to change. Stoked by the oratory of hellfire-and-brimstone Protestant preachers, the Fenians' counterparts in the loyalist paramilitaries launched a paranoiac campaign against the Catholic minority they believed would destroy their dominance of Ulster society, ushering in foreign rule from Dublin and Rome. The shots that precipitated what became known as the Irish Troubles were fired by the Ulster Volunteer Force on the streets of Belfast in 1966, killing three unarmed Catholics.

When the province's occupiers, the British Army, returned as peacekeepers to safeguard the besieged Catholics in 1969, their initial presence was seen as a relief. But the decision of Government and Army to fight a counterterrorist war only on one front – against the republican Catholics, rather than alienating the ultra-violent loyalist paramilitaries – opened up the fissures in Ulster society. Street battles in 1970 with IRA gunmen led later to the massacre of civilians by the Army in the second Bloody Sunday, and internment without trial of known IRA members and Sinn Fein political activists in the early 1970s.

Ironically, the fact that military intelligence were acting on old information proved an unforeseen boon to the latest paramilitary group on the block, the Provisional IRA. For many of the younger 'Provos' had not made the security forces' list of the usual suspects, while their older, less hot-headed counterparts – the official IRA, who had veered increasingly into the Marxist politics of the 1960s and were seen by Catholics as having failed to defend their communities – were taken off the streets.

Post-Bloody Sunday, the relevance of the old guard continued to diminish, producing a violent power change. While high-level political and military assassinations were beyond the Provos' reach at the time, they would match (and some say exceed) the violence of their enemies with a mainland terror campaign. Army bases, courts of law and even public places like railway stations and pubs were seen as legitimate targets for bombs, symbolic of the British way of life and the new IRA's ability to strike at it.

Civilian casualties were regarded by the Provos in a similar light to how the US military saw such 'collateral damage' in Vietnam, and the Provos' statements of responsibility and their recurring phrase, 'The IRA regrets . . .', became a running black joke of the 1970s and 80s – along with the conventional wisdom that ran, 'Never stay drinking in the pub once the Irishman has left.'

But not all the violence was untargeted. The Provos scored the occasional direct hit, such as Ross McWhirter, shot dead on the doorstep of his suburban London home in November 1975. An unlikely assassination target, McWhirter created the bestselling *Guinness Book of Records* with his twin brother Norris, both of whom were regulars on a BBC kids' TV show based on the book. He was also a member of the Conservative and Unionist Party (the Tory Party's full name, emphasising its former commitment to keeping Ulster British) and had personally offered cash rewards for information leading to the arrest of IRA members, while calling for capital punishment for terrorists.

More directly political assassinations struck deep into the heart of the British establishment. In March 1979, Airey Neave, the Conservative Party's spokesman on Northern Ireland, was killed on leaving the underground car park at the Houses of Parliament. As a young man he had been one of the British POWs to escape from the prison at Castle Colditz, but no such heroic resolution was on hand when the lower half of his body was blown away by a car bomb. Neave's murder was in retaliation for his stance on Ireland (echoing the Orangeman mantra of 'no surrender'), and most likely the work of the Irish National Liberation Army, a hardline republican splinter group.

The INLA was formed from the ashes of the official IRA by younger members who wanted to see action, not content with staying on the margins of left-wing politics. With fewer members and less paramilitary discipline, they briefly made their mark by the extremity of their actions. The better-organised Provisional IRA, however, were not far behind.

Five months after the Neave assassination, on 27 August 1979 there was a huge explosion aboard a yacht in the bay of Mullaghmore, County Sligo, in the Irish Republic. Two of its fishing party were dead in the water, another (the target) died minutes later, and a fourth died in hospital. The three survivors were seriously injured. What made the atrocity exceptionally newsworthy is that the boat belonged to Earl Louis Mountbatten of Burma, the Queen's second cousin and ageing favourite uncle of Prince Charles.

The former Viceroy of India had been appointed back in the late 1940s to oversee that British colony's transition toward political independence. In more recent times, he habitually holidayed every year in Sligo, ten miles from the Northern Irish border, dismissing the security staff who warned him he was a target for republican assassins.

Lord Mountbatten, as he was commonly known, believed his neutrality on the issue made him an irrelevance. The IRA did not see it that way, regarding him as a symbol of the colonialism he had played a role in dismantling. Mountbatten briefly remained alive when taken from the water but, like Neave, was severely mutilated and had lost the lower part of his body. Among the other fatalities were his fifteen-year-old grandson, Nicholas Knatchbull, and a sixteen-year-old Irish boy, Paul Maxwell, who was onboard to help with the fishing. Both were floating facedown in the water when their bodies were retrieved. The Provos were embarrassed that young Paul would never live to see a united Ireland ('The IRA regrets . . .'), but Mountbatten was still regarded in republican circles as a big catch. In *Assassination*, Richard Belfield suggests not only that Mountbatten was regarded as being suspiciously cosy with the Soviets, but also that well-informed rumour connected him with an unsavoury homosexual clique.

According to some accounts, Mountbatten's murder also threatened a secret accord reached between the IRA and the British security services. The Troubles in Northern Ireland claimed many innocent lives but never became a full-fledged civil war – the type of bitter conflict in which generations of brutality suddenly erupt on a massive scale. Both sides, to their credit, appreciated that there was too much to lose. Even in this state of asymmetric war there were rules.

'One aspect of containment was an early agreement with the leaders of the IRA,' writes Belfield. 'In a round-table meeting, British Army commanders warned their IRA counterparts that the royal family was off limits. The British admitted that ultimately it would not be possible for them to totally protect the royals against attack so they told the men sitting across the table that if anything should happen to any member of the royal family and the IRA was responsible then they would kill them all before midnight. It is a tactic straight out of the Hashshasin handbook and it worked. Hasan ibn el-Sabah would have been proud of them.'

According to Belfield, Mountbatten did not benefit from this arrangement for a number of reasons – not least because he was highly unpopular among the secret servicemen charged with his security. As Saladin might have confirmed, if you cannot rely upon those you entrust with your protection you are in a precarious position.

When Israeli Prime Minister Yitzhak Rabin was assassinated in 1995 by a lone Jewish fanatic, conspiracy theorists challenged the official version of events. While the theory that Rabin was actually killed by his own security services remains highly controversial, there is a powerful case suggesting that Shin Bet, the agency entrusted with his protection, were at least complicit in the crime. Shin Bet's chief, Carmi Gillon, resigned after the assassination, describing it as 'an operational failure'. Some critics suggested that such negligence was deliberate, because high-ranking officials shared the killer's conviction that Rabin's peace initiatives endangered the Israeli state. The Rabin affair swiftly blossomed into Israel's answer to the JFK assassination, with theories of secret-service complicity ranging from suggestions that Shin Bet deliberately left their charge vulnerable to attack to those that insist ballistics evidence proves that Rabin was not killed by the original gunman, who shot him after a rally in Tel Aviv, but murdered afterwards – most likely on the suspiciously lengthy limousine journey to nearby Ichilov hospital.

The assassin convicted of the crime, a student named Yigal Amir, who, it was alleged, had previously been employed by Shin Bet, fed the conspiracy theories at the court hearings: 'If I were to tell the whole truth, the entire system would collapse. I know enough to destroy this country.'

Assassination can be contagious – blood follows blood, with paranoia an occupational hazard. After Hasan Sabbah had dispatched his first Assassin from the Eagle's Nest he never left Alamut, only emerging from his quarters twice and then only onto the roof terrace. Henry II may have only avoided the prospect of civil war by undertaking his humiliating penance at the site of Becket's murder. Some of the more colourful conspiracy theories concerning the murder of President Kennedy suggest it was his tacit approval of CIA assassination programmes that triggered his own assassination, becoming a target in turn for retaliatory plots.

In Britain the security services calculated that the Mountbatten assassination (and the corresponding loss of young boys' lives) might actually damage the reputation of the IRA. 'They do not want Irish unity,' a 'Dublin workman' was quoted as saying in *Time* magazine in November of 1979. 'All they want is power, like the Ayatollah or Fidel Castro.' The consequences of assassination can be dangerously unpredictable.

Despite the homicidal attentions of the Irish republicans, a new Conservative Government had been elected less than two months after the assassination of Airey Neave. In tune with her black-and-white thinking on the Irish problem, Prime Minister Margaret Thatcher was determined to give no quarter. She refused to recognise the 1980 demands of the IRA's hunger strikers in the Maze Prison for political prisoner status, leaving Bobby Sands and nine others to starve themselves to death. Her much-parodied 'hard man' deputy in the Tory Party, Norman Tebbit, was equally resolute in insisting the Irish Troubles were a criminal, rather than political, problem, and should be met by the full force of law enforcement. (Unusually, however, much of that enforcement was being administered by the British Army.)

By the autumn of 1984, both Thatcher and Tebbit had earned the undying enmity of the republicans. It was in the early morning of 12 October that an IRA bombmaker attempted the biggest mass assassination in British history, engineering a massive explosion at the Grand Hotel in Brighton where the Tory Party were holding their annual conference. The grand prize walked away unscathed; Margaret Thatcher had left her hotel suite just minutes before it was totally obliterated. Others were not so fortunate, with five Tory activists or their partners killed outright. Many others were seriously hurt – including Tebbit, who fell through several storeys but whose injuries were mostly short-term, while his wife (not a politician but a nurse) was left confined to a wheelchair and condemned to years of pain. To the terrorist mindset, of course, this is irrelevant – human casualties exist only as symbols of their struggle, rather than as suffering flesh and blood.

On the smaller stage of Northern Ireland itself, paramilitary assassination policy was pragmatic and Machiavellian. It has long been believed – and very few would dispute it – that the British security services and Special Forces fed republican targets to gunmen in the UVF and the Ulster Defence Association, sometimes even allegedly supplying the weapons. The UDA, unlike most paramilitary groups, would remain a legal organisation throughout most of the Troubles.

Most remarkable was the internecine warfare that bloodied the ranks of both the loyalist groups and the INLA. Jimmy 'Pratt' Craig, head of the UDA's armed wing, the Ulster Freedom Fighters, developed a risky policy of eliminating rivals or liabilities among his own people by conspiring with his supposed mortal enemies, the IRA. According to Belfast investigative journalist Martin Dillon, author of the *tour de force* *The Shankill Butchers*, this included the butchers' charismatic psychopath leader, Lenny Murphy.

Murphy, as described by Dillon, was a mass-murdering sadist more akin to serial killer Ted Bundy than to most paramilitaries. His sadism also seemed infectious, the cronies within his little UVF subgroup sharing his glee in abducting, torturing and killing hapless Catholics at random. To the Provos, Murphy's death was a non-negotiable necessity. They cornered him in November 1982, at the end of his ten-year reign of terror, putting twenty-six bullets in him from a submachine gun and a .38 special.

Murphy was one of several such hits set up by Jimmy Craig. So it can have been little surprise even to him – though we can assume it was still a shock – when two gunmen from his own loyalist group perforated Craig with lead as he stood at a bar, in October 1988.

The INLA's last major coup would be the December 1997 shooting assassination of Loyalist Volunteer Force leader Billy Wright, which took place within the walls of the Maze prison. Before long, however, both internal warfare and peace negotiations between the Provos and politicians seeking an end to bloodshed on the British mainland would make the INLA redundant.

In 1998, Tommy McMahon, the Mountbatten assassin, and Patrick Magee, the Brighton bomber, were released from their multiple life sentences along with many other convicted terrorists under the terms of the Good Friday Agreement. While sectarian killings would continue in Northern Ireland, many of them territorial disputes over the supply of drugs and other criminal commodities, British politicians had lifted the threat of terror campaigns on the mainland – or so they hoped.

The outcome of the peace agreement was a power-sharing government that was surreal to behold. Reverend Ian Paisley, the ageing Protestant firebrand whose rhetoric inspired the UVF onto the streets in the mid-1960s, was photographed sharing a joke with Sinn Fein political leaders Gerry Adams and Martin McGuinness, both reputedly active IRA men in their youth. (American political humourist P. J. O'Rourke once imagined Bill Clinton asking Adams, 'Do you ever actually kill people? Or do you just do the spin?')

It may have brought the Provisional IRA not one jot nearer their goal of a united Ireland, and inspired the scorn of former fighters for the cause like Dolours Price, bomber of the Old Bailey courtrooms. The British Government, however, were canny in recognising that, as the original generation of Provos were reaching late middle age, and Paisley was still roaring in his dotage, it was the right moment for offering them the mainstream political power they would otherwise never achieve. For all the pious talk about the futility of violence, for Adams and McGuinness at least (both of whom risked making themselves republican targets for selling out to the Brits) terrorism had been seen to work.

***

In the years between the IRA's last British mainland attack, on the Docklands financial centre in 1996, and the transatlantic watershed of 9/11, New Scotland Yard's anti-terrorist squad identified the Animal Liberation Front and its splinter groups as the most active terror grouping in the UK. As absurd as it sounds, the militant bunny huggers had developed a crude strategy of attacks on medical research labs and destroying the cars of research scientists with incendiary devices.

For all their enraged rhetoric, however, they never took the lives of any of their 'species-ist' foes. Intelligence in the late 1990s suggested a doorstep assassination *was* planned at one point – possibly of neurologist Professor Colin Blakemore, whose sin had been to offer words of support for colleagues engaged in animal experimentation and to invite veggie fundamentalists to engage in debate. Whichever side one may stand on the lab-rats-are-the-same-as-human-babies argument, it is fair to say that these were the years of calm before an altogether more compelling cultural storm.

When the clouds of dust from the collapsed Twin Towers seeped like misty portents across the Western world, radical Islam was already entrenched in the UK. With its burgeoning Muslim minority population (many of whom were shocked to see desperate human dots jump from windows hundreds of storeys high), it was inevitable that 'Islamism' – a political ideology rooted in the otherworldiness of religion, unlike the predominant Marxism of the previous century – would take hold among some of the young faithful.

Radical Islam in Britain (and Europe) had first felt its collective strength with the Iranian *fatwa* against Salman Rushdie, in retaliation for his 1989 novel *The Satanic Verses*. A dense piece of 'magic realism' which included such wilfully provocative details as a cadre of whores named after the prophet Muhammad's wives, its more fantastical elements parodied the style of the classic *Thousand and One Nights* (whose Iraqi translator also produced the first recognised English version of the Koran).

Rushdie clearly felt he was the bad boy of the intelligentsia, a real Kensington Sex Pistol. What he never banked on was that the resultant outcry would take the matter way outside the parameters of literary debate and onto the streets, putting him under police protection for nine years and entailing an apologetic conversion to Islam along the way. It was also a turning point for the formerly silent ranks of European Islamism.

One of the co-authors of this book recalls listening to a conversation on a London tube train between three young Asian students. Two were at a loss as to how to take the theocratic death sentence passed on the anglicised Indian author; the third held no such reservations: 'Kill him,' he asserted with quiet moral certainty. Both the idea of Islam as a religious culture internationally besieged by the *kuffar* (unbeliever) and the concept of becoming a martyr (or at least an assassin) in defence of Allah's holy word were gaining legitimacy in the West.

In the England of the 1990s, apocalyptic preachers such as the hook-handed, self-styled imam, Abu Hamza al-Masri, evoked visions that made the Reverend Paisley seem the very spirit of liberal moderation. The concept of *jihad* – invoked in the Koran as a personal battle against the baser side of one's own nature – was now depicted in more literal, blood-and-thunder terms as a holy war against the enemies of the faith. ('Jihad' had first been evoked as a military term by Nureddin, commander of the young Saladin, in his campaign to drive the Crusaders from the Holy Land.)

Oft parodied for the way they let their capital city become 'Londonistan', the UK's intelligence services seemed at first to hold the pragmatically civilised view that, as long as we are not the targets, what does it matter to us what these chaps believe? History, however, would ultimately scorn any such equivocation.

In the wake of 9/11, the Muslim religion *per se* would come to seem like a blanket threat to many bewildered onlookers. However, a closer look reveals how facile it is to perceive any universal danger within the Islamic community – or, indeed, to even think of a cohesive community, when the religion is divided between the mainstream creed of Sunni, the rival tradition of Shia and their various sub-sects.

Islam contains a set of authoritarian edicts for conducting one's social behaviour; it also stresses compassion for society's unfortunates and prescribes a fixed rate of alms from the adherent's income, almost as a form of theological socialism. The debates are still raging, however, as to how the more medieval passages of the Koran should now be interpreted: 'slay the idolaters wherever you find them', insists one of the *suras* under the subheading 'Repentance'. 'Arrest them, besiege them, and lie in ambush everywhere for them.'

Even here there are ambiguities: 'idolaters' may be interpreted as

Pagans, rather than as the more often-cited Jews and Christians, and mercy is even suggested for the Pagans if they repent and pay the alms levy. (Any Pagan readers may be wondering why they are singled out as the enemy. Islam, however, as with the other great monotheist religions, is intolerant of the idea that worship is not solely given to one almighty god.)

The Koran, as a book, is less of a linear narrative than either the Torah or the Bible, but makes frequent reference to the mythologies of both. It does not explicitly attack either religion but, rather, adopts a tone of admonishment to Jews and Christians for not following the word of the Lord their God. In its statement of the Word, the Koran seeks to rectify such wandering from godliness.

But the new wave of radicalism had given rise to the almost fascistic theologies of the Salafi or Wahhabi sects, products of late 19th-century Saudi Arabia which allowed little leeway for interpretation and brooked no opposition. They also set the stage for a new form of identity politics.

In the late 1960s and 70s, some university-bred radicals had formed tiny Marxist-Leninist terror units such as the Red Brigades or the Baader-Meinhof gang, relatively privileged young people who believed they could transcend their bourgeois origins with supposedly revolutionary acts of violence. It was the mindset of an era which now seems much longer ago than it actually was.

Around the turn of the third millennium, with all dreams of the Marxist utopia long since dead, radical Islam became a new form of self-reinvention for disaffected youth. Raised in a materialist society which they did not believe had fully accepted them, the young *jihadis* cleaved to an unforgiving Muslim identity which condemned their own families as westernised *kuffar*.

Martin Dillon, in his many writings on the Irish Troubles, has characterised those years as an authentically religious war, insisting that the traditions of Catholicism and Protestantism gave a dimension beyond the violent clash of two socially opposed groups, which is how many other commentators have interpreted it. However, it is hard to see any of the bloodshed in Northern Ireland as perpetrated out of a belief in supernatural doctrine.

In this sense 'Jihadism' may be seen as unique at this point in history, its greatest excesses made possible by belief in a world beyond our own. As the Koran says, 'Never think that those slain in the name of God are dead. They are alive and well provided for by their Lord; pleased with His gifts . . . rejoicing in God's grace and bounty.'

For all the condemnations of 'cowardly' terrorists over the years, anyone not blinded by moral indignation can see the risks in planning a public outrage. The Provisional IRA, however, would always factor escape into their game-plan. Whether religiously or socially motivated, political or criminal, their bloody actions were at least *rational*.

The Provos must have realised decades ago that it would be relatively easy (at least under the security regime of the day) to leave tightly-packed explosives on a London tube train, reaping maximum carnage. The reason that they did *not*, and that the civilian casualties of their bombings could continue to be rationalised away ('The IRA regrets . . .'), was because they were seeking to triumph in a seemingly intractable political situation, and recognised that abandoning all restraint might make even their most fervent apologist regard them as nothing but butchers.

Not so the jihadists. As the pioneering stand-up/social commentator/ freebase cocaine addict Richard Pryor noted of what he called 'double Muslims', during his time in prison, 'them's the ones you do not want to fuck with . . . 'Cause them motherfuckers cannot wait to get to Allah. And want to take eight or nine motherfuckers with 'em.'

Mohammed Siddique Khan was a post-9/11 *jihadi* who wanted to take the maximum number of bystanders with him. Effectively the ringleader of the so-called '7/7 bombers', he and his brethren brought carnage to London's public transport system on the morning of 7 July 2005, a grim retort to the previous evening's orchestrated euphoria when the capital city was designated host of the 2012 Olympics. After the detonation of suicide bombs on three underground trains and a bus, 52 people were dead (excluding the four bombers) and hundreds injured, some maimed for life.

The rationale was that the British people were responsible for their government waging war in Iraq, despite the massive public protests against UK involvement, and were therefore aggressors against the 7/7 cell's Islamic brethren. (How many Muslims reigning despot Saddam Hussein had killed never seemed to enter the equation.) To the terrorists, every butchered body was just a symbol in microcosm of a greater enemy they believed themselves to be striking against.

Unlike the Provos, dodging the Anti-Terrorist Squad would not be a consideration for the *jihadis*. They were apparently sincere in the belief that, as soon as they blew everyone else to hell, they would be passing through the gates of Heaven. (Although, according to descriptions provided by survivors, agitated bus bomber Hasib Hussein seemed painfully aware that his immediate prospects were of being reduced to a bag of offal.)

In an accusatory rant he left on the 'martyrdom video' that acts as his last will and testament, Mohammad Siddique Khan identified some of the contradictions in present-day Islamic belief: modern religious scholars, he complained, 'tell us ludicrous things, like you must obey the law of the land. Praise be God! How did we ever conquer lands in the past if we were to obey this law?'

To Khan, Islam was still the religion of his namesake prophet (Muhammad, or its variously spelled derivations, now being one of the most common forenames in the UK), who made many early converts at the point of a sword when his army invaded neighbouring Middle Eastern territories. Khan saw no reason not to martyr himself for Islam – though it is a very thin line between martyrdom, which is revered, and suicide, which is forbidden. As a warrior of the faith, he would enter the Garden of Paradise justified.

Subsequent to the 7/7 outrages (and the abortive 21/7 attacks two weeks later, perpetuating a state of terror in which an innocent Brazilian was shot dead by the anti-terrorist squad), some well-intentioned commentators (and even one outgoing security chief) began to ask why the British Government did not sit down at a negotiating table and talk to the terrorists. After all, they reasoned, we did so with the IRA, so why not with the Islamists?

Indeed, such a dialogue would be fascinating. The Islamist has a very distinct viewpoint, an entirely theocratic worldview unlike that of the ostensibly Catholic IRA (many of whom were atheists anyway). While the republicans were willing to accede to a power-sharing compromise (which had been placed on the table several times in the thirty-year history of the Troubles, before its acceptance by both sides), the *jihadi*'s demands may be rather more far-reaching.

The most moderate demand of the Islamists is that the West withdraws its armed forces and business interests from all Muslim countries, particularly the oil producers of the Middle East. Should such an arrangement prove unconscionable to the economic forces that rule the Western world, perhaps we could take the religious option: acceding to the dominion of a worldwide Muslim caliphate, with every nation ruled by the diktat of Sharia law?

In the strange times that we live in, we may respect the purity of the *jihadis'* vision while recognising that it goes far beyond the parameters of reason – indeed, beyond the realms of earthly life and death itself.

As Umar Islam, one of the British Islamists tried for an alleged 2006 conspiracy to take down airliners over US airspace, said in his pre-emptive martyrdom video, 'We love to die in the path of Allah. We love to die like you love life . . .' In this sense, radical Islam is a form of extreme death-worship that eclipses even Christianity, for all its pie-in-the-sky promises of the next world and symbols of the messiah's crucifixion.

It is insulting to the legend of Hasan Sabbah and the Assassins to equate them too directly with the modern-day *jihadi*. The acolytes and disciples of Hasan are said to have gone to great and dangerous lengths to target those who presented a threat to their religion, or the creed of their heretical sect. In the eyes of the modern Islamist – who would violently decry the Assassins' heretical subversions of the faith – such heroic ends are not attainable. To him, the wider population must substitute for the powerful political figures against whom he cannot directly strike.

But the key, the trigger, the mnemonic to killing for Allah remains. Whether conscious of the Assassin legend or not, the *jihadi* acts in the belief that Jinna, the Garden of Paradise, and the love of the 72 houris of Heaven will be his at the moment of his death. In this, at least, he aspires to be one of God's Assassins.

VI

A VOICE IN THE WILDERNESS

If the salvation of Alamut from the invading forces of Malikshah in 1092 was regarded as a miracle by the castle's defenders, subsequent events must have confirmed to them that Hasan Sabbah enjoyed divine favour. The death of Malikshah's hated vizier, Nizam al-Mulk, at the hands of one of Hasan's followers delivered a powerful blow to the Seljuq state, one that Malikshah was obliged to avenge. But events also gave extra impetus to Hasan's growing rebellion. Wherever Seljuq authority was weak, their rule unpopular or the population restive, the missionaries took full advantage. Pockets of Assassin territory began to emerge across the Persian landscape and beyond – beacons of revolutionary fire to the Ismaili faithful, the foundations of Hasan's rogue state-within-a-state; cankers of heresy to Sunni devotees.

Most of the Assassins' conquests fitted the successful blueprint established at Alamut. Dedicated missionaries converted susceptible targets in pivotal positions, infiltrating strategic strongholds by stealth, only then declaring themselves disciples of Hasan once they had quietly outmanoeuvred and outnumbered the Seljuq incumbents. The fortress of Girdkuh was taken when a local governor named Muzaffar secretly converted to the cause. He convinced the Seljuqs that the defences of the region's most significant strongpoint needed fortifying, and they put him in charge. Only once Girdkuh had been fully reinforced and supplied did Muzaffar reveal his new allegiance, expelling any dumbfounded Seljuq loyalists among the garrison.

In the following years the castle's new Ismaili commander followed his master's example, matching the fortified defences with logistical and agricultural improvements that made Girdkuh both a verdant showcase for Assassin governorship and capable of withstanding prolonged attack. (Muzaffar did his job so well that Girdkuh was the last Persian Assassin stronghold to fall to the Mongol onslaught, some 200 years later.)

'Hasan exerted every effort to capture the places adjacent to Alamut or that vicinity,' according to the hostile chronicler Ata-Malik Juwayni. 'Where possible he won them over by the tricks of his propaganda while such places as were unaffected by his blandishments he seized with slaughter, ravishment and war. He took such castles as he could and wherever he found a suitable rock he built a castle upon it.' At this stage in his asymmetric war, Hasan was playing a defensive game, using a keen strategic eye to ring his headquarters with outlying defence posts. At the top of his hit list was Lamasar, the resilient fortress that sat atop a rounded rock guarding the western approach to Alamut.

As Juwayani suggests, religious conversion and subterfuge were not always enough. The castle's commander, a man named Rasamuj, had shown sympathy towards the entreaties of Hasan's missionaries, but at the last minute had appealed for support from his Seljuq masters. Like many of the local lords and governors in the increasingly volatile region, Rasamuj was doubtless hedging his bets, attempting to placate the rebels at the gates without burning his bridges with the powerful sultanate.

Unusually, Hasan responded with a conventional military assault upon the castle, sending his trusted lieutenant Kiya Buzurgummid to take Lamasar by force. The attack proved successful, illustrating both the expanding power and confidence of the Ismaili rebel forces and the vulnerability of the Seljuq chain of command, whose representatives ceded a defensive position through incompetence and indecision. Lamasar was probably the largest castle the Ismailis possessed, and would play a leading role in Hasan's power base – as indeed would its conqueror, Buzurgummid.

The Ismailis enjoyed successes in several other locations, such as Quhistan – located on the current border between modern Iran and Afghanistan – an arid desert region where settlements clustered around the region's life-giving oases. When their Seljuq overlord inflamed local sensibilities by demanding the daughter of a local lord in marriage, Hasan's missionaries turned outrage into open rebellion and the region became another Ismaili outpost. Another Ismaili commander – under cover as a shoemaker – successfully took two castles near Arrajan in southern Persia. A native of the area who, like Hasan, had made the pilgrimage to the Fatimid Caliphate in Cairo, his name was Abu Hamza – which may be familiar to any reader well-versed in the recent history of Islamic extremism.

Hamza's modern namesake is an Egyptian-born, British-educated Muslim preacher whose hook-hand and missing eye combined with his incendiary anti-Western rhetoric to make him into a crude cartoon villain for the popular press. 'Killing of the kafir [unbeliever] for any reason you can say it is okay, even if there is no reason for it . . .' he has declared. 'You must have a stand with your heart, with your tongue, with your money, with your hand, with your sword, with your Kalashnikov. Do not ask shall I do this, just do it.'

The modern Abu Hamza is a fanatical Sunni Muslim, who would see his historical Ismaili namesake as just as much a deserving target for his demented invective as the Western *kuffar*; similarly, the medieval Assassins may have considered such an outspoken Sunni a legitimate target for their knives. Yet the coincidence is difficult to pass over, if only because it throws into sharp relief the strategy of indiscriminate mayhem conducted by al-Qaeda's fellow travellers and that of the agents of Hasan Sabbah, who targeted their foes with dogged precision. (There are several other prominent Abu Hamzas involved in contemporary terrorism, such as Abu Hamza al-Muhajir, the Iraqi al-Qaeda leader, and Pakistani al-Qaeda leader Abu Hamza Rabia, killed by an unmanned US Predator drone aircraft in 2005.)

The mission of the medieval Abu Hamza, Muzaffar and Buzurgummid was made possible by the final stroke of fate that blessed Hasan Sabbah's cause in 1092. Within months of the death of the Seljuq vizier, Nizam al-Mulk, at the hands of the first Ismaili Assassin, his master Malikshah died. The Sultan most likely perished of natural causes, but even though his death was not at the hand of an Assassin it seemed like a propitious sweep of the hand of destiny for the embattled Ismailis. Military efforts to avenge the Seljuq humiliation at Alamut and the murder of Nizam al-Mulk were abandoned, the besieging force around the Ismaili stronghold in Quhistan withdrawing from their posts. If Nizam's demise had shaken the Seljuq Sultanate then Malikshah's death shattered the empire, creating a struggle for power among claimants to the throne. It also gave Hasan's fledgling rebellion vital breathing space and intriguing possibilities for advancement.

An empire held together by personal loyalties – like the Seljuq Sultanate – is a highly vulnerable, brittle structure. The Seljuqs certainly appreciated this, which is why they continued to maintain the Abbasid Caliphs as religious figureheads even though they had scant respect for the institution themselves. The Sunni Caliphate provided the cement on which to build a powerbase. Yet the sultanate could not endure the twin blows of the death of its greatest statesman and its presiding overlord. Malikshah's oldest son, Barkiyaruq, was the obvious claimant to the throne, and managed to secure the support of the caliph. But rival claimants from among his family made their plays for power, and the mighty Seljuq war machine began to turn on itself as a family feud span into open civil war. The resultant chaos not only assisted the Assassin cause in Persia, but also ultimately helped pave the way for the Western Crusaders, as rival Islamic warlords vied for power within the Seljuq Sultanate.

Hasan Sabbah also had dynastic struggles to consider. In 1094, the Fatimid Caliph Mustansir – still, theoretically, Hasan's ultimate spiritual superior – died, after a reign of opulent impotence in Cairo. His eldest son, Nizar, was widely seen as his successor as spiritual leader of the Shiite Ismailis, their Imam. However, Mustansir's powerful vizier, the warlord Badr al-Jamali, had other ideas.

With sinister echoes of the way in which the Seljuqs sidelined the Sunni Caliph, Badr had arranged the marriage between his daughter and Nizar's younger half-brother, Ahmad. It established the vital bloodline between Badr's family and the Fatimid dynasty's descent from Muhammad, and should have set alarm bells ringing among Cairo's elite – though Badr's grip on the levers of power may have been too firm to allow much effective resistance.

Badr had died months before his master Caliph Mustansir. But Badr's son, Afdal, was a true chip off the old block, smoothly taking up the reins of power and putting forward Nizar's inexperienced and pliable younger brother Mustali as the new caliph, claiming it had been Mustansir's deathbed wish. Nizar and his supporters fled Cairo to seek support for his claim in Alexandria. After some initial successes, their forces proved no match for Afdal's professional army and, in 1095, Nizar surrendered. He was taken back to Cairo and executed.

His death sent shockwaves throughout the Ismaili world, dividing the faith yet again. There were a number of precedents for the murder of blood descendents of the Prophet in the Islamic world, but the spilling of sacred blood would lead to bitter schisms that echoed violently for generations. So it was with the execution of Nizar and the elevation of his brother Mustali to the position of caliph. Those that accepted Mustali as Mustansir's ordained successor became known as the Mustalis. Those Ismaili devotees for whom the murder of Nizar was a shocking blasphemy became known as the 'Nizaris'.

Hasan quickly joined the Nizari camp in dismissing the new Fatimid Caliph as an impostor and hailing his murdered rival as a martyr. It led to an immediate unbridgeable rift between the Fatimid Caliphate in Egypt and Hasan's guerrilla kingdom in Persia.

Perhaps such a rift was inevitable. It is unclear to what extent, if any, Hasan had been taking orders from Cairo in his campaigns, while there was scant support from the Fatimids for Assassin operations against the Seljuqs. There had always been a certain incongruity to the Assassins acting as both revolutionaries and agents of a distant imperial power. In order to gain more potential converts, Hasan had to offer something more than exchanging the tyranny of one overbearing overlord for another, to be able to preach in favour of a true new order. With his divorce from the Fatimid Caliphate he was free to do just that. But it also left Hasan Sabbah effectively alone in his struggle – with enemies now to both north and south, he was truly a lone voice in the wilderness.

The growing Assassin rolls of honour now began to include a number of Ismaili Mustali victims, alongside the Sunnis and Christians that fell beneath the knives of Hasan's agents. In 1121, when the Fatimid vizier Afdal was murdered, many believed the Assassins were responsible. The finger of blame also pointed towards Alamut in 1130 when Amir, Mustansir's successor as Fatimid Caliph, was killed in Cairo. Such outrages provoked responses from both the Seljuq and Fatimid regimes, and the Assassins soon found themselves the target of hostile armies and propaganda from almost every corner of the Islamic world, a creed under siege.

One of Hasan's most audacious conquests had been the castle of Shah Diz, taken by one of his former mentors in 1092, when the turmoil following the death of Malikshah was at its height. Shah Diz stands less than ten kilometres from Isfahan, the city which had been the nerve centre of the Persian Ismaili underground for generations, and where Hasan had received instruction while serving his apprenticeship as a young missionary. It was also the city which Malikshah had chosen as the Seljuq capital, making it both the sultanate's centre of government and a ferment of religious dissent.

Shah Diz controlled many of the most important roads into Isfahan, and the Assassins began exacting tariffs from passing merchants. This hit Malikshah's successor, Barkiyaruq, hard, both by depriving his exchequer of vital funds and damaging his prestige at a time when both were in short supply for the embattled Seljuq leader. While he lacked the military strength to dislodge the impudent Assassins from his doorstep, there was nothing to stop Barkiyaruq revoking the policy of religious tolerance that his predecessors had observed in the name of peace.

***

Isfahan sits upon a fertile Persian plain, cradled in a horseshoe of mountains. Its proud minarets and heaving marketplaces have witnessed fierce religious debate and spirited dissent among its cosmopolitan population. So the saying goes, the troublemakers and the misguided can sing their songs of heresy and rebellion in the very shadow of the palace, for what are they but caged songbirds who the Sultan can release or else wring their necks upon a whim? But such things change. With the coming of the arch heretic Hasan Sabbah a darker shadow begins to wreathe through the twilit streets of Isfahan. Some whisper that he preaches freedom, an end to bearing Turkish overlords on honest Persian backs. Others spit that he is the worst sort of dog, a heretic who hypnotises the unwary and knows no god but himself. But all speak of Hasan Sabbah.

When news reaches Isfahan that the vizier, Nizam-al Mulk, has been stabbed by an Assassin, such talk becomes increasingly febrile. Some rejoice at the death of the oppressor who imposes the Sultan's taxes to make himself rich. Others say that, when the Vizier perished, so too did peace and prosperity for the people of Persia. Perhaps they are all right in their fashion. After the Sultan followed his vizier to the grave, everywhere was seized by great fear and dismay. All of the news that reaches the capital is of war and strife, of brother falling upon brother, while it seems Hasan circles like a vulture, plucking at the ailing body of a wounded empire. His men know no shame, taking the mighty fortress of Shah Diz and taxing all who fall under its shadow as if Sabbah were the Caliph himself.

In 1101, Barkiyaruq, who occupies Malikshah's great palace, can brook the impudence of the heretics no longer. The mullahs whose tongues had been fettered by Malikshah are let off the leash. Some say that to spill the blood of the heretics is to cleanse yourself of all sin. Even those who do not preach extinction for the followers of Hasan Sabbah do not preach against it. A great fire begins to build in the blood of the good people of Isfahan. Then, one fateful night, that fire becomes a living reality as a mighty blaze is built in the main square of Isfahan, its flames licking high into the evening sky. The common people build it seemingly of one purpose, while Barkiyaruq's soldiers stand by in silent acquiescence. Across the city the cry goes up, an animal howl of vengeful mob fury – 'Assassin!' Those known to preach the word of Hasan Sabbah are seized first. Some are slain where they are found, beaten to the floor with sticks and rocks. Others are dragged, shrieking with defiance, to the square where dozens of hands propel their bound, still-living bodies into the hungry flames.

That hunger is not easily sated. A holy madness washes over the streets of Isfahan as those who have been heard to speak well of the Assassins or ill of the Sultan are hunted down in their homes. Neither their sex nor their age will spare them, as Isfahan struggles to cauterise itself in blood and flame. The city becomes a living window into Hell, echoing with anger and agony, its streets slick with blood, the terrible stench of burning hair and human flesh hanging heavy in the air. Some take full advantage of the madness for themselves. The spurned suitor searches out the woman whose father rejected him and slays her with a hatchet, telling all around that she had confessed to following Hasan. The merchant who believes he has been cheated leads the mob to the house of the man he accuses, pointing it out as a den of heresy.

When dawn rises on Isfahan, none know how many have died – is it hundreds, thousands? – or how many of them had truly been followers of Hasan Sabbah. Some feel cleansed by the butchery, confident that a message has been sent to those who would taint the soul of their city. Others wonder silently if such a night of shame can ever go unanswered.

***

The massacre at Isfahan was the first of many such violent pogroms aimed at rooting out Nizari sympathisers in major towns and cities, almost literally fanning the flames of religious sectarianism. Similar scenes of bloody mob justice meted out to alleged Nizaris were played out in several other important Persian communities, most notably Baghdad. There, the Assassin leader is reported to have taunted his tormentors with the question, 'You have killed me – but can you kill those that are in the castles?'

Whether such barbaric episodes achieved anything is open to debate, as is the efficacy of the Nizari policy of assassination. Some historians have suggested that assassinations only ultimately hardened the resolve of their opponents, just as the indiscriminate mayhem that resulted from anti-Assassin hysteria in Isfahan may well have increased revolutionary fervour among the Nizari faithful and potential converts. Similar questions continue to haunt modern debates about terrorism, where every response by either side just seems to escalate into further conflict. So it was in the medieval Middle East, where Sunni pogroms begat retaliatory Nizari assassinations, which in turn inspired further massacres.

Meanwhile, the heritage of the dead Imam Nizar remained a live issue. Some Nizari scholars and historians claim that he was survived by several sons and relatives of the dead candidate, for the Fatimid Caliphate continued to conspire against Mustali and his successors. But Nizar does not appear to have officially ordained anybody to succeed him, leaving the fledgling Nizari faith without an imam.

The success Hasan Sabbah was enjoying against the Seljuq State and Sunni Caliphate – and his growing reputation as a holy man who appeared to enjoy divine favour – would seem to make him an obvious candidate. But the Assassin Grand Master was always careful to stifle any such suggestion, styling himself merely the voice or representative of the True Imam, who would imminently make himself known.

Or perhaps he was simply being practical. It would have been difficult to argue any plausible bloodline between Hasan and the Prophet, and any attempt to fabricate one played into the hands of those who dismissed the Assassins as fraudulent heretics. The position of imam had also proven hazardous to the holder, religious office being no barrier to violent death. The aftermath of the death of the Seljuq Sultan had proven how vulnerable an organisation could be if all of its power was concentrated in the hands of one hereditary ruler, and Hasan probably calculated he could serve the cause better as a rebel leader than a divinely-appointed imam. When he died, the revolution was more likely to outlive him if he was a revered leader than if he encouraged rumours that he was more than a mere mortal.

The acts that best underline Hasan's merciless dedication to his cause may also reflect a similarly cold strategic thinking. He infamously had both of his sons executed at Alamut: one for drinking wine, another for alleged involvement in the murder of another Assassin. (Most sources agree that the latter son was probably innocent of the charge.) Such a policy obviously sent out a powerful message. It broadcast Hasan's own fervent piety, willing to condemn his own flesh and blood if they strayed from the path, while stressing total impartiality and a blind dedication to Islamic justice, whatever the consequences.

It was a particularly important message to Shiite Muslims, for whom Sharia law is the cornerstone of their belief system. It also curtailed any likelihood of the position of Grand Master of the Assassins becoming a hereditary position, immune to the nepotism and corruption endemic among Hasan's opponents. It was an attractive recruiting tool among the dispossessed who saw no route to advancement within the Fatimid and Seljuq establishments. Organisations with leaders appointed according to ability are naturally stronger than those whose leadership falls by accident of birth, and also less vulnerable to the consequences of a disputed succession.

The executions of Hasan's two potential heirs may also suggest a darker psychological motive. The dynastic struggle for the legacy of Malikshah is but one example of vicious family struggles that characterise not only medieval Islamic politics but those of the European Middle Ages. The cautious ruler did well to keep a careful eye on their nearest and dearest if they had any ambition to rule for long.

Hasan Sabbah presided over his unorthodox kingdom for some 35 years – a span most caliphs and sultans of the age conspicuously failed to match. He had eliminated the only two men with any plausible claim to succeed him. Was this evidence of Machiavellian paranoia running riot in his sparse private chambers? For assassination is a risky policy that breeds suspicion – once you begin the cycle it can prove difficult, even impossible, to stop.

From this point, Hasan's decision to become an effective hermit, self-confined to his quarters for over three decades, makes perfect sense as a precautionary measure. But what effect might this level of seclusion have on a person's mind – even one as resilient and acute as Hasan Sabbah's?

***

The modern world offers an intriguing selection of similarly exceptional, driven or – in the view of their enemies – deranged individuals who epitomise the psyche of the secluded messiah, the dynamic cult leader able to direct the actions of their devotees from a safe distance.

At the very beginning of the 1950s, science fiction author L. Ron Hubbard (a former associate of Jack Parsons, US rocket scientist and Luciferian occultist) founded a new religion on what seemed like an almost faddish basis. Its seminal holy book, *Dianetics: The Modern Science of Mental Health*, became a surprise bestseller for a publisher of academic psychiatry textbooks and had its origins in an unlikely place.

'We are back in a sense into a fictional universe, because Hubbard started as a writer of pulp tales,' observes writer and lecturer Ken Hollings, comparing the origins of Hubbard's religion, Scientology, with the legends of Hasan. Hollings' extraordinary study *Welcome to Mars* deals essentially with the media-saturated, technocratic consumerist utopia of the post-war USA, as evinced in its subtitle, *Fantasies of Science in the American Century 1947-1959*.

'It occurred to me that the whole issue of "mind control" – the proposition that the mind is somehow programmable and controllable through new technologies – certainly becomes a significant theme in 1950, where you get two rather interesting eruptions that happen within a few weeks of each other. You have on the one hand the first part of "Dianetics: The New Science of the Mind" appearing in *Astounding Tales*, when Hubbard unveils this terrific science of Dianetics to the public, thanks to John Campbell Jr.'

Campbell was better known as a scientific pedant who insisted on authentic detail in the pulp SF stories he published – and, later, as author of the tale which became the classic monster movie *The Thing* – than for any connection with radical theology. Thanks to his patronage, however, Hubbard would soon sell out the 6,500-capacity site of the Al Malaikah Temple in Los Angeles. (Not an Islamic place of worship but a Masonic glee club – rather like Laurel and Hardy's Sons of the Desert.) His new creed was, in effect, an alternative school of psychiatry to whom the mainstream practitioners in the field were anathema. As Hollings describes,

'And you also have a Florida newspaper running a story about what are described as "brainwashing" experiments going on during the Korean War. The story was written by a guy called George Hunter, who was actually a sort of low-level CIA operative/press figure, and he actually coined the phrase "brainwashing", coming from some Chinese term which meant "to cleanse the mind". What he was asserting was that the Chinese, and through them the North Koreans, had developed a method of programming the minds of captive GIs who had come out of the conflict. These were the individuals who appeared in newsreels denouncing their actions as imperialistic transgressions against the legitimate People's Revolution, who claimed they were carrying out biochemical attacks against North Korean soldiers. Hunter really laid it out, saying this is brainwashing, they've actually figured out a technique – through some chemical, mechanical or electronic means – to alter the minds of these captives.

'So you also have Hubbard proposing that the mind is a programmable, controllable thing, and his model is really the tape recorder – this notion that somehow our thoughts, our consciousness, are part of a linear "tape" which we can then wind back through, find the bits we do not like, erase them, record something else over them. This notion that somehow the mind itself is just this playback device fundamentally lies at the heart of what he's saying, his treatment of the mind, how it can be rendered mechanically perfect.'

As the theory of Dianetics was codified into the tenets of the Scientology cult (or religion, to its converts), the ever-controversial Hubbard made claims that his research into a 'technology of psychological warfare', which he intended to present to the US government, had been sabotaged by Russian spies. (The CIA's own forays into psychological warfare, inspired by the methodology of brainwashing, were neither as theoretical nor as innocuous – as we shall see later.)

With the Church of Scientology a growing fringe presence in both the US and UK, Hubbard relocated for a while to the Sussex countryside in England. In 1967, he would forsake leadership of his church to man one of several cruise ships on a semi-permanent eight-year voyage. In his absence, his professedly science-based theology would become both more elaborate and more widespread, eventually converting a cadre of Hollywood movie stars. Like the Old Man of the Mountain, his word was carried from afar.

Much has been made of the more extreme tenets of Scientology: its reductive analogy of the human mind as a recording device, as described by Hollings; or its myth of how human beings as a species were infected with negative memories by an alien race known as the Thetans. Supposedly a cure-all for depression, alcoholism, drug addiction and the distinctly American sin of not fulfilling one's career potential, the disputed process of 'auditing' has worked for a number of people seeking to 'go clear' of the negative life experiences they felt were holding them back. Hubbard's biography suggests he was far from clear of the habits from which he promised to save others, but the sci-fi doctrines of Scientology seem no more outlandish than some of the supernatural myths of Judaism, Christianity and Islam.

As Ken Hollings observes, however, as ambivalent a character as Hubbard may have been, some of the figures influenced by Scientology have been altogether less benign. It was in the 1960s, as Hubbard's church gained popularity amidst a whole explosion of alternative belief systems, that its tenets of reprogramming the mind were studied by an unsuccessful little petty criminal incarcerated in McNeil Island Federal Penitentiary, Washington. His teacher was an armed robber who claimed to be a 'Doctor of Scientology' (a rank since abolished by the church itself).

'Manson used a few Scientology expressions – "come to Now", and what have you,' says Hollings, cautious not to attribute the psychedelic cult leader's mind games to one source. For Charlie Manson was equally adept at juggling biblical imagery, the Luciferian creed of the Process Church of the Final Judgement and the type of psychological self-help dogma that today finds its corporate apogee in neuro-linguistic programming (NLP). Add to this a white supremacist dogma, the free love of the hippie era and the psychedelic drug explosion and you have one extremely potent mixture. For like the Hasan of myth, little Charlie, a former car thief and would-be pimp, realised that the power of hallucinogenic sexual experiences would bind his devotees to his word. Unlike the Assassin leader, however, he was erotically active, participating fully in acid-tinged orgies with young people more than a decade his junior.

'I think that what makes Manson interesting in relation to the way that drugs and technology develop,' describes Hollings, 'is that he's very much a kind of Faustian version of the kind of environmentally immersive worlds that were being designed in the mid-to-late 60s. I'm thinking of Tim Leary's stage show, where they were using slides and films and tape-recorded sounds and setting it to the music to conjure up an LSD experience onstage. Or you've got Warhol with his Exploding Plastic Inevitable – admittedly this is more amphetamine-based, but again it's the idea of playing back films, tapes, feedback sound, that the whole thing has to come together to create this environment that you give yourself up to, a little like Hasan-i-Sabbah's Garden of Jinna. And then you've got Manson playing around with tape recorders, slide shows, TV cameras, etc., trying to do a similar sort of show with a floorshow undertone to it. It is very hard not to think of [Church of Satan founder] Anton LaVey's vampire girls coming out of their coffins.'

LaVey's vampires put on an altogether more kitschy, striptease-style revue, but, as Hollings notes, 'Manson was a slightly older guy as well, in terms of saying, "I was never a hippie, I was a beatnik." Feeding his 'Family' on a daily diet of acid (which he habitually partook of in lower doses), Charlie took his growing retinue of early twenty-something hippies and misfits through a variety of living environments, from a travelling bus to a spooky mansion to a movie-set ranch near Death Valley in the Californian desert. As those who were nervy or sceptical of Charlie's assumed leadership fell away, the remaining hardcore included sexual disciples like Susan 'Sadie Mae' Atkins, once a vampire girl in the Church of Satan's burlesque revue.

Manson's ultimate term of imprisonment has now lasted four decades, with no end in sight until he ceases to exist. In the 1980s and 90s, the US 'Apocalypse Culture' and disaffected young people all over the West looked to him as a kind of folk hero, based largely on his innate charisma and a free-riffing verbal style that ties together commonsense parables, environmental dogma and borderline schizo gibberish. It did not hurt that Charlie was the dark icon that forever tainted the psychedelic naivety of the hippies either, and that he is forever linked to an infamous 48-hour orgy of murder.

Those who got off on Manson's image the most tended to have it both ways by claiming he was never proven guilty of the act of murder (as if their admiration for him would have been as great without the homicidal edge). Leaving aside the shooting of a ranch hand – never effectively denied but of which he was not convicted – in August 1969, Manson intruded into the home of supermarket owner Leno La Bianca and his wife, tied the couple up at gunpoint, told them they were safe and then sent in his young, addled 'acidassins' (to quote Manson biographer Ed Sanders) to do their worst. It is hard to see how this would not fit the definition of murder under any legal system.

But it is on the first night of their 48-hour Hollywood Hills killing spree, 7 August, that the Manson Family's infamy rests. It is also true that Charlie was not present when a small group of his acidassins, led by Tex Watson and Sadie Mae, went on 'creepy-crawl'. The victims were Sharon Tate, starlet wife of filmmaker Roman Polanski (director of *Repulsion* and *Rosemary's Baby*), then eight-and-a-half months pregnant; playboy Vojtek Frykowski; coffee heiress Abigail Folger; society hairdresser and drug dealer Jay Sebring, and young caretaker Steven Parent.

All were mercilessly butchered with knives; the pregnant Sharon was strung up by her wrists to a ceiling beam before she was slaughtered. Like the Family members themselves, most of the group were tripping on drugs, their terror unbearably heightened by the hallucinogen MDA. The Family had tempered their own acid trip with hits of speed, in itself forbidden by Charlie (who had a policy of not ingesting any drug that might kill him). According to Ed Sanders, the murders were committed 'by some new form of zombie-spore'. As a counterculture figure himself, Sanders was no abstainer, but he saw Manson's continual process of indoctrination under the influences of sex and drugs as somehow usurping the group's collective will.

As for the motive for the killings, it remains much mythologised and obscured to this day. The media's favourite, as repeated in court, is that Charlie, the Old Man of Death Valley, had sent his young assassins to start a race war between blacks and whites by writing opaque slogans like 'Political Piggie' in the victims' blood. Following the acid-addled chain of logic, the legends were derived from titles on the Beatles' newly released White Album and their actions were indirectly supposed to free Family member Bobby Beausoleil, already down on another murder charge.

Manson later contradicted the burbling rationale of his flock, stressing the generation gap by claiming, 'I'm not a Beatle fan, I'm a Bing Crosby fan!' But his major talent lies, as he has said, in reflecting back what people want to see, and if it served his purposes for the Family to hear the chords of apocalypse in the White Album, he'd surely play along.

He also indulged in a little magical thinking himself – claiming, for example, that the Tate-LaBianca murders had stopped the Vietnam War. But the real spur for the killings may be as banal as the fact that Terry Melcher was the Tate house's former tenant – a record producer who failed to win a contract for Charlie's own discordantly compelling folk-rock – and the Family did not know he had moved. Much is lost down the refracted corridors of acid-crazed memory.

None of the convicted Family members have yet been paroled. Patricia Krenwinkel, for one, attributes her dominance by Charlie and her crimes solely to her use of drugs – overlooking how other hippie kids, just as spaced out as she was, had exercised free will and moved away from the Family when they decided they did not like the dark trail they were following.

Few commentators seem to agree exactly on whether the Manson Family constituted a cult, a commune, or even just a gang. In Japan in the 1990s, there was no such hair-splitting over the collective body responsible for the nation's worst terrorist attack thus far.

Aum Shinrikyo was a Buddhist-based religious cult formed in 1984 by a bearded charismatic, Shoko Asahara, achieving short-lived but widespread respectability in Japan. ('Aum' is the phonetic pronunciation of 'Om', the monosyllabic Buddhist mantra said to recreate the breath of the universe.) Translating into English as 'Supreme Truth', Aum Shinrikyo espoused a hybrid religion combining elements of Japan's native Shinto, Yoga, Hinduism and Christianity. More ominously, it also namechecked the 16th-century French mystical writer Michel de Nostra-Dame, or Nostradamus, whose cryptic prophecies have often had grand claims made on their behalf by writers of very loose translations. (Nostradamus's famed warning about the coming of Hitler, for instance, can be attributed to his writings about 'Hister rising' – more likely referring to the River Ister in Germany.)

Asahara's own writings on the paths to transcendence and enlightenment gained a wide following across Japan, but it was in the 1990s that their tone became paranoid and apocalyptic. The Third World War and Armageddon were predicted, the result of an international conspiracy ranging from the Jews to the Freemasons to the British royal family. As the new harbinger of the Apocalypse, Asahara, who had previously preached humility, now announced that he was Jesus (as had Manson – as well as being Christ's apparent antithesis, Hitler). The grandiosity of these proclamations may well have been influenced by the use of LSD as a ritual sacrament.

It is perhaps a measure of Aum Shinrikyo's former influence that the cult began a policy of assassination a number of years before the crimes actually came to light. In October 1989, a lawyer actively campaigning against cults named Tsutsumi Sakamoto, his wife and their child went missing; their bodies have never been recovered and Aum Shinrikyo's responsibility was only suggested in the light of further atrocious events. It would take less time for the February 1995 disappearance of the 69-year-old brother of a renegade member to be attributed to the cult.

That previous June, the world's first biochemical terrorist attack on a civilian population had taken place in the city of Matsumoto. The release of the poison sarin into the air killed seven and injured 200 more, but the wider world paid little attention. This was to change on 20 March 1995, when a sarin attack on the Tokyo subway system killed twelve and seriously injured 54 others. Police raids on the cult indicated they had the means and the inclination to carry out both attacks; while hiding out in the wilderness, Asahara, his health now failing, promised to make the recent 'Kobe earthquake seem as minor as a fly landing on one's cheek'. His words would come back to haunt him when he was apprehended.

By the time that the apocalyptic cult members stood trial, there was some confusion as to whether their terror attacks had been intended to bring about or to avert the end of the world. To their various religious motivations was added speculation about the influence of *The Foundation Trilogy* by science fiction novelist Isaac Asimov, in which the hero seeks to prevent the onset of interplanetary decadence and cultural decay. (Manson had also been influenced by a work of one of Asimov's contemporaries, *Stranger in a Strange Land* by Robert A. Heinlein, the story of a messianic Martian outsider. But it would take a convoluted chain of logic to apply responsibility for his actions to a book.)

Asahara, by now blind, was sentenced to death for conspiring to implement the attacks. Despite his frail health and the activities of the heads of the cult's various 'departments', it was believed that it was the incendiary words of their prophet which brought death to the two cities.

In 2000, Japan's freedom of religion laws allowed the Aum Shinrikyo cult to continue, under their new name of Aleph – the first letter of the Hebrew alphabet; ever eclectic, the cult continues to borrow from belief systems such as the Jewish mysticism of Kaballah. That same year, Russian police arrested a former KGB agent and cult member for stockpiling weaponry such as machine guns, allegedly intended to break his guru Asahara out of prison. Now closely monitored by law enforcement agencies, Aleph has sworn against any contact with such extremists – just as it has placed distance between itself and the cult's former leader.

Meanwhile, at the time of writing, Asahara awaits his death sentence, with the dates yet to be confirmed for him and ten other cult members. Their sightless mystic sits silently in the condemned cell, confounding the mystery by refusing to talk about events. According to the authorities, the hirsute little blind man gave the orders for murder from afar, sending out his devoted assassins while preparing to flee into the wilderness. If accurate, it is a model of behaviour which transcends the ages.

Some – not least Ismaili Muslims – may find comparisons between Hasan Sabbah and controversial modern figures like Asahara offensive. But the polemics of the day leave little doubt that he provoked similar levels of suspicion, controversy, outrage and fascination to the cult leaders and self-styled messiahs of our age.

But, to many of his Nizari contemporaries, Hasan Sabbah was more of a Robin Hood figure. He did not take from the rich to give to the poor, or even preside over a band of merry men (in addition to the prohibition on alcohol, anybody caught playing a musical instrument in Alamut was exiled). But the Assassins were a frugal fraternity who appeared to share their wealth equally. Hasan was also an outlaw who challenged a ruling class that many regarded as exploitative and tyrannical. Just as the mythical Robin inflicted humiliations on Prince John's trained troops before retreating to the refuge of Sherwood Forest, so Hasan's men used the mountains to evade the superior forces of the Seljuq sultans. As in the legend of Robin Hood, racial elements also underpin the story: the crude, arrogant Normans, imposing an oppressive foreign rule over the native Anglo-Saxons, provide a parallel to how many Persians felt about their Turkish overlords. Just as Robin disdained any political position in favour of awaiting the overthrow of Prince John, so Hasan accepted only the role of the representative of the coming Imam.

The fact that, in Robin Hood's case, the impending rightful ruler of England was the brutal Crusader warlord Richard I brings us crashing down to earth again. But such comparisons may serve to illuminate the polarised views of the Assassins, both today and a thousand years ago. A pernicious threat to the state – or the last hope of an oppressed people?

VII

THE HASHISHIM

The aspect of the Assassin legend that most fascinated and alarmed early European chroniclers was their death-defying fanaticism. It parallels current attitudes to suicide bombers: sacrificing the lives of others in the name of your cause – politically motivated murder – is a tragic historical commonplace; sacrificing yourself changes the rules entirely. Assassins or terrorists who maintain the desire to complete the job and then escape alive are much easier to stop than those with no concern for their own survival. The rise of Islamist suicide bombing over recent decades has forced security forces worldwide to rethink every aspect of their tactics in light of a new enemy who requires no exit strategy. The advent of the Nizari rogue state in 11th-century Persia had a very similar effect in that era.

Hasan Sabbah's Assassins have aptly been dubbed 'suicide commandos'. Their weapon of choice was the knife, not the explosive belt, but it implied a similar ethos of self-destruction. While firing an arrow from a distance might give an Assassin some chance of escape, and employing a sword at least a fighting chance after the deed, the killer who got close enough to deliver a knife thrust to a well-guarded opponent in a public place was effectively signing his own death warrant.

The knife had obvious advantages. It was easily concealed and the killer who got close enough to use it had to be committed to do-or-die. For the death of the Assassin was as much a part of the message as the murder itself. The numerous accounts of the relatives of modern suicide bombers greeting the deaths of their nearest and dearest with pride has parallels in the era of the Crusades.

One account of the aftermath of the assassination of the Governor of Mosul and Aleppo, in 1126, relates how, 'when the mother of one of the youths who attempted Aksunkur's life heard that he had been slain, she painted her face and donned the gayest raiment and ornaments, rejoicing that her son had been found worthy to die the glorious death of a martyr in the cause of the Imam. But when she saw him return alive and unscathed, she cut off her hair and blackened her countenance, and would not be comforted.'

The quote is drawn from *Secret Societies*, one of the more colourfully speculative and less scholarly texts on the Assassins, penned by Arkon Daraul (very likely a pseudonym for the occult historian and Sufi, Idries Shah). The book was first published in 1961, and was instrumental in popularising the story of the Assassins among occultists, conspiracy theorists and left-field thinkers. Intriguingly, it emerged decades before suicide bombing became a standard tactic for Islamist terrorists (and two years before the assassination of President Kennedy launched the modern conspiracy-theory industry). Yet the scene Daraul describes is chillingly resonant of the attitudes of relatives of many modern Muslim 'martyrs', elated when one of their own gains entry to Heaven, courtesy of the slaughter of infidels by explosives strapped to the martyr's body.

Just as we have seen an ever-increasing catalogue of measures and laws to purportedly address terrorism, the authorities in medieval Cairo and Baghdad took action to counter the Assassin threat, whether real or imagined. They may not have had access to metal detectors or satellite-tracking devices, but local leaders enforced new policies forbidding anyone from carrying weapons in their presence while central government endeavoured to monitor the movements of its subjects. An account of the extensive precautions undertaken by the Fatimid Vizier al-Mamun in the 1120s sounds hauntingly familiar in the light of recent Western government initiatives. Officials without impeccable backgrounds were sacked. Merchants and camel-drivers endured routine in-depth interrogations and surveillance at every gate and border. The inhabitants of Cairo were subjected to an exhaustive and intrusive government census, and forbidden from relocating without official permission. Government spies were also despatched into local neighbourhoods to identify those with suspect opinions, who were then rounded up. Officials claimed that no Assassin could put a foot outside of Alamut without them knowing.

But how much good did it do? The assassinations did not cease, while the Nizaris could claim a victory of sorts via the strangulation of so many basic freedoms under a pall of paranoia. The same conundrum that faced the security forces of the twelfth century haunts the FBI and MI5 today. How do you engage a foe you cannot find, who strikes without any fear of the consequences?

The answer, at least in part, must surely lie in pinpointing just what might motivate someone to make a suicide attack. As with suicide bombers today, in the Middle Ages it was the suicidal fanaticism of the Nizaris that perplexed, appalled and fascinated Western commentators. One of the most infamous examples of such behaviour was witnessed by Henry of Champagne, the Crusader King of Jerusalem, who visited one of the sect's Syrian strongholds on a diplomatic mission in the late twelfth century.

***

Even as evening approaches, there is precious little wind to alleviate the pulsing summer heat that sucks the very air from the lungs of the Castle of al Kahf. Looming in bleak magnificence like a fist thrust in defiance over the Syrian landscape, al Kahf holds a secret in the dark recesses deep beneath the knuckles of its towers. It is whispered that in a cold cave, hidden from profane eyes, lies the tomb of Rashid al Din Sinan. Only recently interred, the Grand Master of the Syrian Assassins is widely reputed to have been not merely a cult leader or military commander, but the master of occult powers of sorcery. Some whisper that even now Sinan is not truly dead but sleeping in shadowed seclusion, ready to rise when his devotees need him most.

Henry of Champagne feels uncomfortably aware of the grim power that seems to echo from the very stone beneath his feet. Every inch the embodiment of the knight born to the sword, the tall Christian soldier looks somehow ungainly when his broad shoulders are not burdened with chainmail. But Henry maintains his haughty façade. In this year of his lord 1192, he has only recently been crowned King of Jerusalem – king of the city at the very centre of the world, clad in silk and steel, treated as a brother by King Richard of England. But Henry is also queasily aware of the true source of his new-found power. The same man who put him on the throne lies entombed in some lightless shrine below. Try as he might, Henry cannot dispel that thought.

The Crusader king has other matters to consider, concerning the living – in particular his genial host, Sinan's Persian successor, Nasr. Since his arrival at the Assassin stronghold, Henry and his party have been afforded all of the honeyed hospitality a spartan military outpost like al Kahf can furnish – delicate sweetmeats, saffron and rosewater; chambers bedecked in cushions where servants stirr the heavy air with giant fans. The conversation has been the essence of etiquette, deferential compliments and silver-tongued good will shown towards 'al-kond Herri' in reverential tones. Somehow it makes Henry feel worse. Here he is at the tender mercy of the men who had made him king, by coolly butchering his predecessor Conrad in the street.

As he tries to focus on the steady babble of mannered conversations around him, Henry cannot help wondering why he has come, why he did not remain seated in his own halls, playing chess and drinking wine. When the Assassin envoys presented themselves to him, their sincere apologies for the unfortunate demise of Conrad Montferrat, King of Jerusalem, seemed like some kind of crazy jest. Everybody knew who was responsible, but there they stood, offering profuse condolences. Conrad's murder may have been fortuitous, but how did these cold-blooded killers expect him to respond to their bizarre diplomatic mission?

The Assassins expected Henry to accompany them back to al Kahf, of course, to enjoy the hospitality of their master. He had not known whether to laugh or explode in anger. He looked over his shoulder to the advisors King Richard had left to guide him in his first difficult months on an unsteady throne. What he saw written on their faces told him everything he needed to know and did not want to hear. There are some offers you just cannot refuse.

It then became horribly clear to Henry that he was involved in a game where he was not privy to all of the rules. His advisors had tried to reassure him that the Assassins never kill their guests; that he is more at risk in his own bedchamber than in a Nizari castle; that the Kingdom of Jerusalem needs every friend it can find in such troubled times. For all of this, Henry feels the cold foreboding of a man thrusting his ungloved hand into a scorpion's nest . . .

'You seem distracted, my lord,' Nasr smiles pleasantly, gesturing for one of his men to proffer Henry a silver platter of dried dates. 'Are you unwell? Perhaps the air in here is too dry and makes you sleepy. Come,' the Persian lays his hand gently on Henry's shoulder, 'the evening air is most pleasant at this time of day. Let us walk the battlements where we may talk as men, with the benefit of privacy and the breeze to clear our minds.'

Henry gets to his feet and follows his host through an arched door, up a short set of stone steps that leads to the walls. 'We are not so different, your people and our own,' says Nasr as their eyes adjust to the fading sunlight. 'We follow our God even when all around us would put us to the sword, with words like "infidel" on their lips. And sometimes, even the most even-tempered of us must strike back . . .'

The words hang heavy in the evening air, as Henry feels the Persian's unflinching gaze upon him. Leaning on the stone ramparts, the Christian can think of no suitable reply.

'Your people are great warriors,' Nasr breaks the silence. 'But my men are brave too.' The Assassin gestures towards the sentinels that stand on al Kahf's towers, impassive in the diminishing heat, narrowed eyes focused on the horizon. 'Let me show you,' he continues with a strange smile, then shouts something in Persian. Nasr points towards one of the Nizari guards and makes three or four quick hand signals. The guard he has so curtly commanded carefully lays down his spear, clambers over the rampart as easily as a man might climb into his own bed, then steps over the edge. He plummets through the air for a few seemingly endless seconds, before the sharp rocks hundreds of feet below halt his descent. There is a sound like an overripe melon dropped on a stone market floor. But no scream . . .

Henry has seen dozens of men die – in the heat of battle, in the sweaty grip of the plague – but nothing like this. Nothing so casual, so cold.

'Men of faith need fear nothing. Is that not so, al-kond Herri?' Nasr gestures once more, this time to his right, and another sentinel repeats the ghastly exercise. He pitches himself over the walls with what seems to a horrified Henry like a beatific smile.

'Are your men so dedicated, al-kond, that they will follow you not only to the very lip of the grave but beyond, if that is their duty?'

When Nasr makes to gesture again, Henry seizes his arm. 'Enough!' is all he can say. 'Enough,' the Crusader repeats, his throat dry, 'this is mere butchery, it is profane.'

'All war is butchery, and we are warriors. No road that leads to Paradise can be profane,' the Persian insists quietly. 'Now, we have business to discuss.'

King Henry is not sorry to leave al Kahf, his business successfully concluded. Nasr has assured him that the Kingdom of Jerusalem no longer had anything to fear from the Nizaris or their Assassins, while Henry has solemnly sworn that the Nizaris' castles will not come under attack from any Crusader force, and that their people are free from all persecution in the kingdoms under his domain.

'Your enemies are my enemies,' concluded the Persian. 'Is there any man who stands in al-kond Herri's path that he would have removed?'

Henry had declined the implied offer, wondering silently if just such an exchange had sealed the fate of his predecessor, Conrad . . .

***

Henry of Champagne, the new King of Jerusalem, died just one year later. He fell from a high window at his palace in Acre, the fatal descent appearing to be an accident. While few deny that his diplomatic mission is a matter of historical record, most historians are adamant that stories of Assassins casting themselves from the castle walls to demonstrate their unswerving loyalty are mere myth, examples of what Nizari historian Dr Farhad Daftary describes as 'the black legend' – negative propaganda generated by the Assassins' Muslim foes and accepted as fact by credulous Christian chroniclers.

Records suggest, however, that this chilling display was witnessed not only by Henry but also by the Sicilian king, Frederick II, and by an ambassador of the Sultan Malikshah. The modern tendency is to dismiss it as a grisly rumour. It is too horrible – historians cannot quite believe that anybody in their right mind might take their own life in such a fashion, just to prove a point.

But is this any more implausible than monks dousing themselves with petrol and serenely setting themselves ablaze in the streets of South Vietnam, to protest against the oppression of Buddhists in 1963? Or more horrific than the numerous Islamist terrorists who turn themselves into human bombs, indiscriminately taking as many lives as possible? Even sceptics and Nizari historians concede that the sect's assassination missions practically guaranteed the deaths of the agents involved. How much real difference lies between dying at the blades of vengeful enemy guards or at the foot of a castle tower, if the aim in both cases is to spread fear among your enemies? If anything, the suicidal sentry is closer to the self-immolating monks of Vietnam than the Assassin, whose deadly intent toward an unsuspecting enemy brings him closer to the modern suicide bomber.

For those tasked with preventing suicide attacks, establishing what creates the terrorist's mentality is an enduring question. Arnold of Lübeck was a German monk who visited the Middle East in 1172. He was among the first to bring accounts of the Assassins back to Europe, including references to what Dr Daftary describes as 'the death-leap legend'.

Referring to the Nizari leader, Arnold wrote,

> 'this Old Man [of the Mountain] has by his witchcraft so bemused the men of his country, that they neither worship nor believe in any God but himself. Likewise he entices them in a strange manner with such hopes and with promises of such pleasures with eternal enjoyment, that they prefer rather to die than to live. Many of them even, when standing on a high wall, will jump off at his nod or command, and, shattering their skulls, die a miserable death. The most blessed, so he affirms, are those who shed the blood of men and in revenge for such

deeds themselves suffer death. When therefore any of them have chosen to die in this way, murdering someone by craft and then themselves dying so blessedly in revenge for him, he himself hands them the knives which are, so to speak, consecrated to this affair, and then intoxicates them with such a potion that they are plunged into ecstasy and oblivion, displays to them by his magic certain fantastic dreams, full of pleasures and delights, or rather of trumpery, and promises them eternal possession of these things in return for such deeds.'

Arnold of Lübeck suggested that three factors instilled the Assassins with suicidal loyalty – witchcraft, religious indoctrination and drugs. While most rational modern minds would discount witchcraft (perhaps too rashly) as a legitimate motivation for anything, few can plausibly contradict the role devout religion plays in extreme, irrational behaviour. But it is the issue of drugs which is the can of worms at the heart of the Assassin legend. Modern Nizari historians such as Dr Daftary are inclined to condemn Arnold's account as ignorant nonsense. His suggestion that the Assassins took mind-altering substances is rejected as quickly as the idea that they would cast themselves to their deaths at the whim of their Grand Master.

While Arnold first introduced Europe to the idea of the Assassins as a cult seduced into suicidal behaviour, it was Marco Polo who popularised the story. According to tales brought back to Europe by the Venetian merchant in 1295, Hasan fed followers with hashish (hence the 'hashishim') before taking them to a secluded garden to be indulged with forbidden pleasures, including the sexual favours of young women. On return to normal consciousness, the Assassin was told he had experienced the heavenly garden of Paradise and would spend eternity there provided he followed his master's every command, thus overcoming fear of capture and death.

Polo's travel memoirs remain controversial, some suggesting they were concocted from second-hand accounts and hearsay rather than personal experience. The accuracy of his account of the Assassins has also been challenged, not least because Polo's supposed visit to the Nizari stronghold took place well over a decade after the sect had been successfully suppressed. For all that, his account contains too many accurate details to be dismissed out of hand quite so easily.

Suggestion of drug use among the medieval Nizaris is a particularly contentious issue, when abstention is such an important virtue in every interpretation of Islam. Muhammad's strict prohibition on alcohol was arguably among the more radical aspects of his creed, and modern Nizaris tend to regard stories that the sect used intoxicants like hashish, and later alcohol, as simply further examples of the black legend.

The condemnation of alcohol in the Arab world strongly contrasted with Europe at the time, where the copious consumption of beer and wine was the norm practically from cradle to grave. It is not much of an exaggeration to suggest that Christendom spent most of the Middle Ages engulfed in an alcoholic fug.

Alcohol played a particularly important role on the battlefield and continued to do so long after the medieval era. It is easy to see why alcoholic intoxication might have suited the Western style of warfare in the Middle Ages, while being a positive liability for an army employing the Turkish tactics favoured by Saracen forces. A clear mind and a steady hand were essential for the mounted archers of the Islamic armies, who loosed arrows at their foe from the saddle before wheeling away to frustrate enemy counterattack. By contrast, the Crusader stratagem of soaking up the damage before delivering a devastating cavalry charge demanded raw courage and aggression, not incompatible with the belligerence found in drink.

Of course, strategies and tactics varied according to circumstances. Just as there were teetotallers among the ranks of the Crusaders, abstention among the Saracens was not as universal as some Muslim accounts might suggest. A number of the early Saracen heroes of the Crusades were notably heavy drinkers, including the formidable general Zengi, who successfully led the fightback against the European invaders until he was murdered in his bed in 1146 by his Christian slaves, whilst sleeping off an excess of wine.

But as long as courage remained the most important military virtue, alcohol would be a vital resource for many campaigning armies. Persuading your troops to stand firm against volleys of flintlock fire, or to charge headlong into a forest of spears, required overriding the natural instinct for self-preservation. The point where battlefields turned into slaughterhouses came when one side's will broke, and the ethos of 'every man for himself' took hold. Anything that could bolster the resolve of a soldier in the face of imminent death was of great value to any warlord.

Of course, military discipline – often severe to the point of sadism – had a large role to play. According to the celebrated 11th-century Prussian warrior king, Frederick the Great, 'the common soldier must fear his officer more than the enemy.' But the carrot of 'Dutch courage' was at least as important as the stick of court martial to Western armies.

'Armies have often deliberately employed drink and drugs to promote fighting spirit,' observe John Keegan and Richard Holmes in *Soldiers*. 'The Vikings sometimes used a dried fungus whose hallucinogenic effects blurred the images of battle, and pre-combat drinking has been common for centuries . . . The medical officer of a Black Watch Battalion told the 1922 Shell Shock Committee that "had it not been for the rum ration I do not think we would have won the war."'

While alcohol continues to play a central role in British regimental rituals – officially and otherwise – its place on the battlefield has radically diminished as military technology has advanced over the past century. As weapons have become more accurate and complex, the importance of quick reflexes and a clear head have wholly eclipsed the virtues of blind belligerence. Yet intoxicants have still played a part on the battlefield. Amphetamines were used extensively during World War 2 by both sides as performance enhancers – particularly by the German army – but the policy was rolled back when it became clear that the after-effects of the 'comedown' proved too debilitating. At the other end of the spectrum, the North Vietnamese actively facilitated heroin abuse among the demoralised US forces during the Vietnam War, to devastating effect, and many GIs returned home with crippling addictions.

But to return to our central story, how *does* hashish figure in the secret world of the Nizari Assassins?

***

The correlation between the term 'assassin' and the drug 'hashish' is now often believed to be a classic case of colourful myth engulfing authentic history. In *The Assassin Legends: Myths of the Isma'ilis*, Dr Farhad Daftary dismisses any association between the Nizari sect and psychoactive drugs, and regards the few references to the medieval Nizari as 'hashishim' as throwaway slurs. However, Daftary does record an account of a Persian Ismaili who provided a concoction made from hashish, honey and spices for the local aristocracy in Cairo in the 1390s – suggesting that, even if the Nizaris did not really indulge, there were those willing to trade upon the mythical association between the sect and the drug in the ensuing centuries.

As in modern Pakistan – where uncultivated strains of the cannabis plant grow all over the country, but are most potent in the mountainous border regions – 'hashishim' was simply a term applied to members of the lower classes, the scum whose use of a widely available but derided hallucinogen was proof of their lowly social standing. (According to those in the know, modern Pakistani sophisticates are more likely to pay over the odds for American whisky or Colombian cocaine than to make use of their region's natural bounty.)

It has been very plausibly argued that the use of dope would be anathema to anyone planning a high-risk guerrilla campaign, such as Hasan and his followers. Certainly, Uzi Mahanaimi, Israeli correspondent of London's *Sunday Times*, would agree. In the 1990s, Mahanaimi filed a report which revealed the Israeli army's role in supplying high-grade hash to their Egyptian adversaries, from the time of the Six Day War with their Arab neighbour in 1967. Despite the hippie stereotyping of cannabis as a catalyst for peace, one Israeli military leader spoke of his amazement as stoned Egyptian soldiers formed a front line of attack, running fearlessly but seemingly in slow motion toward the soldiers who mowed them down.

But in other Islamic cultures, the euphoric lift which made the Egyptians so unafraid of their Zionist enemy is ingrained as a part of the fighting spirit. The Mujahideen resistance to the Soviet invasion of Afghanistan, in the 1980s, seemed motivated in part by the illusion of invulnerability that protracted heavy cannabis use can instil. Interviewed by a British war correspondent, one young fighter explained, 'I do not smoke hashish very much – just about four times a day.' In present-day Afghanistan, a British soldier in a BBC documentary film was impressed by how their Afghan allies against the Taliban relied on a daily regime of hash smoking. Seemingly familiar with the disorientation of the novitiate, he observed, 'I thought it would make you more cautious or something.' But to the Afghans, natives of the region where the much disputed weed is first believed to have grown, the buzz only seems to bolster their will to fight.

Another apparent reason to disbelieve the role of dope in the Assassin legend is Marco Polo's description of Hasan administering it to his disciples in the form of a drink, rather than encouraging them to smoke or eat the brown resin. However, hashish is the condensed preparation of the psychoactive ingredients from the same plant which gives us marijuana, or herbal cannabis. In recent years, before specially-grown hydroponic strains of the weed became internationally popular, it was the most potent way of ingesting this relatively mild natural hallucinogen. In the raw distilled form of the oil that is used to make hash, it is much closer to the more extreme hallucination or dream states of LSD or opium. As licking one thumbnail covered in a Victorian-style cannabis tincture preparation can provide a full-blown and relatively benign trip, it is not hard to imagine how the Assassins might be lured into three days of intoxicated sleep, followed by a dreamily hungover awakening period when they believed the young women administering to their sexual needs were the houris of Heaven.

In this scenario, any reasonable scepticism about how the Assassins might fight under the influence of hash seems less relevant. According to the legend, they were not getting stoned before going out on a mission to kill – instead, they underwent a prior psychedelic/psychosexual experience that granted what they believed to be a glimpse of Paradise. It was the memory of Paradise, not hashish itself, which was the mnemonic to murder. Coloured by their faith, these warriors of the Nizari sect were prepared to lay their lives on the line, believing that Heaven – with all its sensory and erotic delights – would be theirs again once they had died as martyrs.

It is particularly hard to extricate history from myth in this case but, to anyone familiar with the drug, it does at least strike a chord. For in the closing days of the 13th century, when Polo first told his tales, the properties of hashish were little known in the West. Whether fictional or only part-fabrication, his stories of the Assassins' hallucinogenic indoctrination must have come from someone who was (as Jimi Hendrix would put it much later) 'experienced'.

Eating or drinking the drug has always produced far more powerful effects than the transient high of smoking. However, in the early days of tobacco consumption, during the Renaissance, it was also conventional to describe someone as 'drinking' the drug, before 'smoking' became an established verb – possibly explaining tales of the Assassins 'drinking' an intoxicating potion.

It would be several hundred years before the recreational use of hash began to slowly permeate the Western world, but even then it was in this more potent form. In 19th-century Paris it was the vice of the *demimonde*. The Club des Hashichins included among its membership the legendarily dissolute poet Charles Baudelaire. Baudelaire said of hashish that it was a substance with the power 'to bestow imagination without the power to make use of it,' paralleling Shakespeare's comments in *Othello* about the effects of alcohol on sexual desire.

When eaten, hashish is also a difficult demon to control or predict. Wild flights of fancy or paranoia can seem real, while hypersensitivity may exaggerate the feeling of a rapidly beating heart, driving the escalating pulse rate ever upward. Little wonder perhaps that Baudelaire

– widely regarded as the first of the 'decadent poets' – should temper hashish eating with much wine drinking to suppress its wilder elements, and considered it the equivalent of the physically addictive opium that he also dabbled in.

It is one of the great ironies of the modern world that, once a less obliterating method had been found for social cannabis use, so it became a social demon. Extracts and tinctures were used for decades to counter everything from the DT's among alcoholics to Queen Victoria's menstrual cramps. All contained high levels of THC, the main psychoactive ingredient, which suggest that many people were quietly undergoing psychedelic trips in the Victorian era.

It was only in the early 20th century, as the less potent dried leaves of the plant (marijuana, as the Mexicans called it) were added to the familiar hand-rolled cigarette, that moral alarmists invoked the legend of the Assassins. As the post-World War 1 Volstead Act was repealed in 1933, and Americans were legally able to take a drink again, upright descendants of the nation's puritan founders found themselves a new public menace to rail against.

Cannabis had already been criminalised throughout the British Empire and much of Europe in 1928, as an addendum to the international opium-trafficking treaty. The white colonialists regarded the marginalised weed as of little consequence, but the Egyptian Government insisted on the prohibition of hashish – by now enormously popular among the lower classes, seen increasingly by their rulers as a caste of indolent addicts.

In the USA, the media campaign equating the short-term mild psychosis of marijuana with full-blown madness began by the mid-1930s. Previous government-backed research into the small-scale use of the weed – among everyone from sailors to midwives – had not perceived a problem. But the director of the newly formed Federal Bureau of Narcotics, Henry J. Anslinger, would set the tone of drugs policy for many decades to come.

A careerist reactionary, Anslinger made criminalising marijuana into a crusade. He announced to Congress in 1937:

> 'This drug is as old as civilisation itself. Homer wrote about it, as a drug that made men forget their homes, and that turned them into swine. In Persia, a thousand years before Christ, there was a religious and military order founded which was called the Assassins and they derived their name from the drug called hashish which is now known in this country as marihuana.

>They were noted for their acts of cruelty, and the word "assassin" very aptly describes the drug.'

Anslinger's testimonial may have been a curious cocktail of half-truths, pure bullshit and wild historical inaccuracy. (Note how he traces the origins of the Assassins, an Islamic sect, to 1,600 years before the birth of Muhammad.) But it helped coin a catchy slogan for the earliest crusaders in the war on drugs: 'Marihuana – Assassin of Youth'.

In the 1936 church-tent 'educational' (i.e. exploitation) film *Reefer Madness*, the narrator warns us of 'the loss of all power to resist physical emotions leading to acts of shocking violence, ending often in incurable insanity.' To belabour the point he tells us of a reefer-puffing boy who axed his parents to death, before the movie gets on with the 'real' story. Other reports of psychotic violence conflated the cannabis plant with Jimson weed, a much more dangerous psychotropic plant that grows wild, containing the psychoactive toxin scopolamine, and which remains strangely legal.

Not so marijuana and hashish, which were criminalised in the US in 1937 thanks to Mr Anslinger. Presumably he believed his own alarmist propaganda; he may even (according to pothead conspiracy theorists) have been conspiring to deter cheap hemp paper production. But we can safely assume that, along with fellow ultraconservative FBI director J. Edgar Hoover, he was fighting back against the 'deadly narcotic' that led to white women dancing with 'coloureds' in jazz clubs. It was the beginning of a versatile history of subcultural associations. Reefers, or joints, became not only *de rigueur* but essential for beatniks to dig bebop in the 50s, hippies to groove to psychedelia in the 60s and Rastas to interpret the Old Testament edicts of Jah in 70s reggae.

Hippie minstrel Donovan may have sung of a 'violent hash smoker' in 'Sunny Goodge Street', but he'd just been busted and was trying to curry favour with the authorities by urging youth to forsake dope. (As you may have observed, he had limited success.) For the rest of the glassy-eyed counterculture it was not the harbinger of reefer madness but a hippie soporific. Even the authorities toned down the rhetoric about violence, shifting the emphasis to the dangers of dope as a gateway drug leading to heroin or coke – true for some users, but not the case for many others.

The controversy between moral interventionists and social libertarians (of all political stripes) would never die, but for a couple of decades weed and hash were no longer the devil incarnate. During this period, enthusiastic smokers were on a quest for the most potent high; Panama

Red (in the American hippie era) or Thai stick (in the 1980s) had a much higher than usual THC content and, especially if smoked pure, could take the user on the kind of sensory trip more readily associated with LSD. In short, they produced cannabis psychosis – not a psychiatric disorder for most, but a pleasantly desirable effect; for others it was an open door to fear, paranoia and disorientation, most often diminishing as intoxication passed but sometimes leaving that door open forever.

The huge international upsurge in hydroponically-grown cannabis in the 1990s was a boon to potheads at first. In the UK, now one of the most enthusiastic dope-smoking nations in Europe, the widely available 'soapbar' hash gave way in popularity to skunk weed, a pungent form of the plant that made the intense highs formerly associated with pure Thai weed increasingly common. It also produced a sea change in liberal attitudes that was amusing to behold.

Skunk's high levels of THC are in proportion to a smaller presence of the chemicals that produce the calming effect of cannabis. While no one can really call skunk a 'stimulant' drug (THC mimics some of the neuro-chemicals which flood our brain during sleep, and users can still fall asleep for hours as the high diminishes), its more intense high affects a large number of users in increasingly different ways. This mostly applies to the young, as middle-aged (and even elderly) users have tended to retreat quietly into their own private universes.

By the middle of the 'noughties' (first decade of the third millennium), liberal UK newspaper *The Independent* made a front-page *mea culpa* about its campaign to legalise cannabis just a few years previously, which may have influenced the British Government's temporary (and largely meaningless) lowering of the drug's 'classification of risk'. For now, contrary to the belief that a little civilised dope-smoking would keep British boozing in check, skunk weed had become the latest element of the modern culture of excess.

Concerned middle-class parents noted how it made their children rebellious, moody and idle – more like teenagers than ever, in fact. Hilariously, *The Independent* quoted a thirtysomething mother who revealed her own predilections by stating she would rather her children did coke or took pills – heart attacks or strokes in their late twenties notwithstanding, at least little Sophie or Nick would be energetic enough to pursue a career.

Another mother, a clinical psychologist, revealed the prejudices of her profession when she asserted she would rather her children got addicted to heroin than skunk – at least, from her viewpoint, smack addicts had a greater chance of recovery than skunk smokers. (She did not state whether she considered a heroin overdose more benign than 'throwing a whitey' on skunk. Perhaps the kids could have assisted Mum in her research by shooting some skag.)

Modern strains of cannabis have elicited a wholesale resurgence of the reefer madness scare, in a manner that would have been unfeasible just a few years ago. In part, this is due to the rise of the 'hoodie' – working-class (or unemployed underclass) kids who emulate the dress, speech and perceived attitudes of urban black hip-hop culture. Uneducated, hedonistic and culturally hostile to anything outside their milieu, these kids are as opposed to middle-class ideals as they could possibly be. They also tend to fill their ignorant little heads with a sweet-smelling smoke that makes them feel like God Almighty.

Cannabis psychosis has become a regular state of mind for a significant minority of British youth. But it is not the psychosis *per se* that's the problem – that can vary from person to person, and manifests itself in ways ranging from intense religiosity to hysterical laughter at dull TV shows. More problematic is how the hallucinogenic buzz feeds the wellbeing of young people whose primary instincts are violent.

One of your authors remembers a conversation between a group of young guys he worked with in his youth. The more assured of them were told by a smaller kid, eager to make an impression, 'I'll fight anyone when I'm buzzin'!' – all he needed was a smoke and the fighting demons would be released, so he claimed. This was in the days before skunk, when young people smoked hash resin and many believed cannabis to provide a totally peaceful experience.

Truth be told, a small minority of regular users have always experienced profound forms of cannabis psychosis. It may be that such incidences have increased since the advent of skunk, or have simply become more visible via the hoodie subculture. In one case of a hoodie jailed for causing death through dangerous driving, the court heard how his skunk habit made him feel invulnerable and believe he was skilful enough to steer the wheel with his feet. He might have been a harmless buffoon until he took his state of psychedelic ecstasy out onto the road. Other, more directly violent kids seem inspired by the buzz to take on the world, with a shank in their hands and casual murder in their hearts.

Reefer madness is a much bigger media story the second time around, but it is as well to remember that some aspects are still mythologised. When William Jaggs, an old pupil of the famed Harrow public school, was arrested for the hideous multiple stabbing murder of Lucy Braham, daughter of the arts master, much was made of his skunk habit. The fact that the entire panoply of recreational drugs – including crack cocaine – seemed to have aggravated his schizophrenia was only mentioned in the more analytical reports. It has always been obvious how a violent stimulant like crack can fuel acts of violence, but stories about it are *just so 1980s*. It is skunk that's on the agenda now.

***

Away from the privileged environs of the British public school, it is the spectre of the skunk-smoking hoodie that terrorises Middle England today. Unknowable behind the dark hood of his sports top, with his stoned gaze and mocking thin-lipped leer, he is their juvenile equivalent of the hash-crazed Assassin.

As evinced by the history of its colonial army, however, Britain is traditionally a nation that has run on booze, and never more so than in the present day. Indeed, the nature of some modern imbibers may come as a surprise to the abstemious.

Muslim youth in the UK seem to share the same attitudes towards hashish and related narcotics as the rest of their contemporaries, ranging from absolute tolerance to disdain. But, just as there are those who insist that Allah has only forbidden the imbibing of alcohol, and therefore the same restrictions do not apply to all other intoxicants, so there are those who take a detour to piety via the path of excess. Indeed, it used to be a regular experience for one of the co-authors to watch young Muslim men flocking to Friday prayers and then to stand at the bar of a local pub with their younger brothers, just up the road, as they got extremely shit-faced on beer and tequila chasers.

Such excess among the young is often a rite of passage, in the case of young Muslims most likely leading to conventional moderation and religious observance. But more profound states of intoxication have also been known to lead to more intense religiosity and, ultimately, to strict sobriety. More than one young jihadist in the UK has led a former hell-raiser's lifestyle on booze, weed, mushrooms and ecstasy – often followed by conversion to radical Islam in a young offenders' institute or prison. It may be the case that, perversely, the glimpses of Paradise afforded by psychedelic drugs are the precursors to an abstemious fanaticism.

VIII

THE KNIFE TESTED

The word that recurs in most accounts of the latter years of Hasan Sabbah is 'stalemate'. Holed up in the all-but-impregnable Castle of Alamut, beyond the reach of his many enemies, he was an equally distant and shadowy figure to his followers in the Nizari strongholds and underground congregations. We can only guess at what was going through his mind; we know Hasan was spending much of his time in religious study, vigorously committing his doctrines to paper during his decades of self-imposed seclusion. His writings joined numerous religious tracts, scientific texts and scholarly historical works in Alamut's extensive library, then one of the most impressive in the Islamic world. In subsequent years, some of the region's most celebrated scholars would overlook any reservations about the heretical beliefs of the Nizaris and become guests of the Assassins, in order to access Alamut's library.

The infamy of the Assassins has overshadowed the fact that, rather than a slavering psychopath, Hasan Sabbah was above all a man of learning, in many respects the typical product of an educated, middle-class Persian background. One of the only descriptions of Hasan we have with any claim to objectivity – it comes from a Byzantine envoy – paints a picture very much in keeping with his soft-spoken but highly charismatic persona:

> 'His natural dignity, his distinguished manners, his smile, which is always courteous and pleasant but never familiar or casual, the grace of his attitudes, the striking firmness of his movements, all combine to produce an undeniable superiority. This is fundamentally the result of his great personality, which is magnetic in its domination. There is no pride or arrogance; he emanates calm and good will.'

The description rings true because it makes sense. Hasan Sabbah's rise to power had been courtesy of his powers of persuasion, his missionaries more significant in the establishment of the Nizari state-within-a-state than the infamous Assassins. Conversion, not murder, was the key. Parallel to the vicious cycle of Nizari assassination and anti-Nizari pogroms, a war of words raged as the Sunni theologians, preachers of the Seljuq Sultanate and their Mustali equivalents in Cairo attempted to stem the flow of converts with sermons and tracts condemning their heresy.

It was at this point that terms like *hashishiyya* began to be employed in hostile screeds attacking the Nizaris. 'The damage caused by the Batiniyya [Nizari heretics] to the Muslim sects is greater than the damage caused them by the Jews, Christians and Magians,' according to one typical anti-Assassin document of the time; 'nay, graver than the injury inflicted on them by the Materialists and other non-believing sects; nay, graver than the injury resulting to them from the Antichrist who will appear at the end of time.'

This raises interesting questions about the presence of atheists in the medieval Middle East. History, so the saying goes, is written by the victors, but it is even more true to say that it is written by the literate. In medieval Europe, the Church maintained a monopoly on education that effectively stifled dissenting voices throughout the era, and the same may very well have been true in the Arabic world. Atheism was a charge levelled at the Assassins on more than one occasion, and would gain resonance centuries later. The reference to 'Magians' also echoes back through the ages. The Magi were the priests of the fallen Persian Empire, their creed suppressed by the burgeoning Islamic faith (and best known today as the 'Wise Men' who paid tribute at the birth of Christ). So did the doctrines Hasan Sabbah transcribed during his long, lonely hours contain elements of taboo Persian law, or even of naked unbelief?

By no means all of Hasan's time can have been taken up with theological study. He must also have been kept busy reading and responding to reports from the numerous outposts of his scattered realm. The library at Alamut doubtless contained maps by which he could chart the progress of his agents, applying his keen strategic mind to the constantly shifting jigsaw puzzle of Middle Eastern power politics. Barkiyaruq, Malikshah's nominal successor as Sultan in 1092, was too preoccupied fighting to protect his throne from rival claimants among his own family to launch effective action against the heretics within his realm. But Hasan's shadow still hung heavy over his court.

'No commander or officer dared to leave his house unprotected,' wrote one Arabic chronicler of the atmosphere of dread; 'they wore armour under clothes, and even the vizier Abu'l-Hasan wore a mail shirt under his clothes, Sultan Barkiyaruq's high officers asked him for permission to appear before him armed, for fear of attack, and he granted them permission.'

After a significant victory over his principal rival, Muhammad Tapar, Barkiyaruq sanctioned the brutal massacre of Nizari sympathisers in Isfahan in 1101. But the castle of Shah Diz remained under Assassin control, just eight kilometres south of the Seljuq capital, a humiliating challenge to his prestige. Barkiyaruq's brother and ally Sanjar took a more proactive approach, though with curiously inconclusive results.

Like Hasan Sabbah, Sanjar was a survivor, enjoying an unusually long and successful life for a leader in this turbulent age, though for different reasons. While Hasan prevailed with single-minded dedication, Sanjar was a wily opportunist. His brother convinced him to launch a well-equipped military expedition against the Assassin strongholds in Quhistan, which enjoyed some success until they were bribed to go home. One suspects that Sanjar was paid both to launch the campaign and abort it, taking money from both sides. A similar enterprise was undertaken three years later, the only difference this time being that Sanjar's general returned from the expedition with a solemn promise from the Assassins to curtail their activities.

Unsurprisingly, Sanjar had his critics at home who accused him of treating the Assassins with undue leniency. But the Machiavellian Sanjar always had his reasons.

When Sultan Barkiyaruq died, in 1105, his rival Muhammad Tapar took the throne. 'When the Sultanate was firmly in the hands of Muhammad and no rival remained to dispute it with him, he had no more urgent task than to seek out and fight the Ismailis and to avenge the Muslims for their oppression and misdeeds,' wrote the chronicler Ibn al-Athir. 'He decided to begin with the castle of Isfahan which was in their hands, for this was the most troublesome and dominated his capital city. So he led his army against them in person, and laid siege to them on the second of April 1107.' The new Sultan appeared far more determined than Sanjar, but the unfolding drama would prove every bit as bizarre a footnote in military history as Sanjar's abortive expeditions against the Assassins in Quhistan.

Just as many of the assaults on Hasan's isolated kingdom had been accompanied by a war of words, so Sultan Muhammad's siege of Shah Diz began with religious debate. The Nizari occupants issued theological objections to the siege, insisting that they were good Muslims and deserved to be dealt with as fellow believers rather than heretics. Their detailed arguments were passed on to the priests on Muhammad's staff, who considered them carefully. Supplies were even sent up to the besieged Assassins while the debate continued.

If the Sultan demanded the surrender of Shah Diz, the Nizari negotiators suggested that its inhabitants be permitted another fortress to occupy in exchange. This conciliatory avenue hit a brick wall when an Assassin was caught attempting to murder one of the more outspoken anti-Nizari members of the Sultan's entourage. Yet, even then, negotiations continued. A deal was struck, whereby the Assassins would vacate the fortress in three groups, the final defenders surrendering Shah Diz once they had confirmation that the previous contingents had reached friendly territory safely.

It was a manoeuvre that puts the best modern psy-ops units to shame. Faced with overwhelming odds in hostile territory with no obvious escape route, Assassin commander Ibn Attash successfully evacuated most of his force and dependents to safety, before reneging on the deal and resolving to inflict as much damage as possible to the enemy force, fighting to the last man. While Sultan Muhammad's men were preparing to take peaceful possession of the castle, Attash was fortifying the defences for a last stand, with less than a hundred men remaining to man the walls.

Once the Sultan understood the extent of the deception, a vicious struggle ensued. The Assassins contested the castle room by room, tower by tower. So the story goes, the Sultan despaired of taking the fortress until a traitor from the Nizari camp revealed that the defenders were so short of men that they had propped weapons and armour against one of the walls to create the illusion that it was manned. The Seljuq forces surged over the undefended wall, and Shah Diz fell. Legend also has it that Ibn Attash's wife refused to flee when she had the chance, preferring to stay with her husband and share his fate. As the enemy approached, she donned her finest attire then cast herself from the battlements to avoid capture. Her husband would not be so fortunate.

***

A lonely figure in white, heavily stained with blood and dirt, staggers in a daze through a sea of angry faces on the streets of Isfahan. To either side of him are his captors, soldiers in the characteristic black and green of the Abbasid Caliphate. Though they are victorious warriors parading their prize, the captured Assassin leader, they find themselves supporting Ibn Attash while attempting to shield him from the volleys of fists and stones hailing down from the bellowing crowd that hems them in. Their commander finally orders his men to lower their spears and take march briskly, virtually screaming to make himself heard over the cacophony. The roiling mass of shouting, spitting humanity reluctantly parts and their human burden is dragged forward to their destination, the main square.

The same place that witnessed the human pyre that devoured so many Nizari souls in 1101 now prepares to accept another sacrifice. A platform has been erected in the square. Atop it is a stout wooden frame positioned to face the podium upon which Sultan Muhammad sits. He is flanked on either side by his advisers, staring implacably, awaiting the bloody drama that is about to unfold. A milling crowd surrounds the stand, fists waving, eyes bulging, voices raised in deafening outrage. As the condemned man is helped onto the platform, then stripped naked, a strange silence descends. Nobody really hears the charges barked by the official on the platform as Ibn Attash is strapped to the frame, spreadeagled before the podium. The Sultan feels the need to meet the Assassin's gaze, to fix his stare with his own, but the man's face is but an empty, malformed mask of bloodied bruising, and he cannot help looking away.

As the ritual formalities cease, all make way for a surgeon who unrolls a leather pouch upon a table. The sun glitters mercilessly off a row of cruelly sharp blades. The surgeon runs his fingers through his beard for an impossibly long moment, then draws out a long, curved knife. With deft fingers, he slices neatly from Ibn Attash's sternum to his groin. A line of oozing blood follows his blade and the Assassin, previously inert, suddenly erupts in screams.

The surgeon stands back until the spasms of his subject subside, then begins anew, drawing his blade around the man's flank to his back. He pauses, carefully selecting a new knife, then turns his attentions to the skin around Attash's shoulders and neck with quick, careful cuts. Nobody witnessing this unholy operation can tell how long it takes before the surgeon carefully replaces his tools and grasps the skin on Attash's chest. The Assassin screams again, but this time the surgeon does not pause. Some wish Attash would continue screaming – anything to drown out the awful sound as his skin is peeled back from his raw, crimson flesh.

Once the Assassin has been flayed, the city executioner mounts the platform and, in one easy stroke, takes the head from his body. It is the only part of him still wearing any skin. This has been a redundant exercise, for the corpse stopped twitching about the time the surgeon pulled the skin on its stomach loose. But the Sultan demands the head be sent for display in Baghdad as evidence of his triumph, along with that of Attash's son. To complete the tableau, Attash's skin is assiduously being stitched back together by tailors, squatting in the slicks of fly-flecked blood beneath the frame, thence to be stuffed with straw. The crowd disperses, variously sated and disgusted. Or perhaps inspired. For the day's awful drama has had a different meaning to some citizens of Isfahan – soldiers, bakers, blacksmiths – who quietly share a secret, awaiting the order from Alamut to pick up the knife and join Ibn Attash in Paradise . . .

***

Once Shah Diz was finally in his hands, Sultan Muhammad made a rather perverse decision. Rather than garrisoning this powerful, well-appointed castle with his own men, he had it pulled down. It was almost as if he was afraid that, the minute he turned his back, it would be infiltrated by Assassins once more. This, and his willingness to engage in lengthy and fruitless negotiations with Ibn Attash, suggest the respect and fear that the Nizaris commanded in the Arab world of their day.

Having removed the immediate threat on his doorstep, the Sultan set about destroying the heresy at its root in the district of Rudbar, raising an army to march on Alamut and the surrounding Assassin strongholds in 1108-9. Wanting no repeat of the farcical campaigns waged by Sanjar, he put his vizier, Ahmad ibn Nizam al-Mulk, in command. Not only had Ahmad's father and namesake been the first victim of an Assassin's dagger, but his brother had suffered the same fate a year earlier. There was little prospect of him being so easily dissuaded or bribed to abandon his mission.

Hasan clearly took the threat seriously, sending his wife and daughters away from Alamut to the fortress of Girdkuh, and a number of his men followed suit. (Whether this reflects a rare example of sentimentality on the Assassin Grand Master's part, or simply his disinterest in anything besides his cause, is open to debate.) As Ahmad's force advanced upon the Nizari lands, they followed a scorched-earth policy, burning crops and slaughtering civilians, motivated by the vizier's personal grudge against the Assassins. It is said that the wave of destruction caused such famine in the region that many Nizaris were reduced to eating grass. Yet, once more, Alamut itself proved impregnable. After several futile months of siege, Ahmad was obliged to admit defeat and head home, leaving a skeleton force to try and suppress the Nizaris.

Inevitably perhaps, once Ahmad reached Baghdad he was the target of a Nizari assassination attempt – though, unlike his father and brother, the vizier survived.

Muhammad Tapar decided to follow up the campaign by mounting regular sorties into Rudbar, doing everything he could to prolong the famine in the region while his army engaged in the field with any Assassin forces they encountered.

After eight years of this relentless war of attrition, the Sultan decided his foe might have been softened up sufficiently, and prepared to deliver the knockout blow. This time command was entrusted to a professional soldier named Shirgir, who was provided with a large number of siege engines and the expert engineers required to operate them effectively. Shirgir's forces surrounded the Assassin fortress of Lamasar and then Alamut itself, the siege engineers set up their devastating machinery, and salvos of rocks and incendiaries began to rain on the Nizari defences. They did so with soul-sapping regularity for the best part of a year.

The defenders were starving, and could see little prospect of relief. It looked like they were faced with the same stark choices presented to Ibn Attash at Shah Diz – surrender, or go down fighting. But now there would be nobody to celebrate any noble last stand; if Alamut fell, Hasan Sabbah's rebellion would be over.

Then, as had happened enough times to suggest Hasan enjoyed some divine favour, events intervened. In 1117 Sultan Muhammad Tapar died suddenly, apparently of natural causes. As before, once the news reached Shirgir of his master's death he abandoned the siege. The period of regime change was the time to be at home, where you could promote your interests with whoever was taking the throne – not out in the field, fighting on behalf of yesterday's man. To the elation of the Assassins, Shirgir's forces left with such indecent haste that they abandoned most of their weapons and supplies, which the Nizaris fell upon, dragging their unexpected booty up to the castle while a force was swiftly raised to cut down any stragglers from Shirgir's retreating army.

Shirgir made the wrong call in abandoning his post with such urgency. When he reached Isfahan he found Mahmud II on the Seljuq throne, in an uncompromising mood. Responding to rumours that blamed the failed campaign on everything from military incompetence to secret Nizari sympathisers among Shirgir's staff, Mahmud had the general arrested, and then executed.

Meanwhile, the opportunistic Sanjar launched an invasion of Mahmud's new realm in the hope of seizing territory, or perhaps even the Sultanate itself. Sanjar has often been portrayed as the Nizaris' most implacable foe, the nemesis who opposed Hasan Sabbah throughout his reign and beyond. Yet the force he mustered against Mahmud included a number of Nizari warriors among its ranks. They may have been motivated by hard cash, a desire to ingratiate themselves with Sanjar or an attraction to any conflict that would promote division among their Sunni foes. It is impossible to be sure, but it does illustrate a more

A Mamluk warrior confronts a contingent of Assassins. *Author's collection*

The mythical Old Man of the Mountain indoctrinates his followers, while a trio of houris waits for them outside in his legendary pleasure gardens. *Mary Evans*

Above left: Crusader and Saracen clash at the Battle of Arsuf. The Assassins took advantage of local conflicts to establish themselves in hostile territory. *Dover Publications*

Above right: The legendary Saracen leader, Saladin, who survived three assassination attempts before making a secret pact with the Syrian Nizari leader, Sinan. *Dover Publications*

Right: The wholesale murder of prisoners of war outside the walls of Acre, ordered by Richard the Lionheart in 1191. Such war crimes were commonplace during the Crusades, putting the targeted murder policy of the Assassins into perspective. *Dover Publications*

The statue of Richard the Lionheart that stands outside London's Houses of Parliament. The English king is reputed to have employed the services of the Assassins to eliminate one of his enemies. *Georgia Woods*

Above left: An Assassin leader orders two of his followers to commit suicide, to intimidate a visiting dignitary. The Assassin stabbing himself is a fanciful detail. Some also maintain that enduring tales of Nizari devotees casting themselves from castle battlements are also just a fable. *Mary Evans*

Above right: The payment of tribute – protection money – by both Christian and Muslim leaders to their stronger neighbours was a central feature of the Middle Eastern economy in the Middle Ages. The Assassins exacted annual tributes from local lords fearful of assassination, but in turn paid tribute to the fighting monastic orders of the Knights Templar and Hospitaller. *Dover Publications*

Left: An Assassin stalks the Sultan's Court section of the Madrid Wax Museum. As Spain is the only European country with a significant history of Muslim domination, some have dubiously suggested that the Jesuit Brotherhood was inspired by the Assassins. *Author's collection*

Above left and right: Regarded as a hero in his Mongolian homeland, Genghis Khan, whose armies exterminated the Assassin communities of Persia in 1256, has been portrayed by Hollywood by a diverse selection of actors, including John Wayne (1956), Jack Palance (1961) and Omar Sharif (1965). The most recent depiction, the acclaimed film *Mongol* – first part of a proposed trilogy – was criticised by some for its sympathetic portrayal of a leader some condemn as a genocidal tyrant. *Author's collection*

Left: Russian nihilists plot an assassination. The movement's description of such acts as "the propaganda of the deed" was later taken up by anarchists and bolshevists, and has its roots in the methodology of the medieval Assassins. *Author's collection*

Above left: The slogan 'Marihuana: Assassin of Youth' was coined by Harry J. Anslinger of the Federal Bureau of Narcotics, who used the supposed historical link between cannabis and the Assassins in his 1930s campaign to prohibit the drug. The slogan was also an alternate title for this 1937 exploitation film. *Author's collection*

Above right: Arkon Daraul's 1961 *History of Secret Societies* introduced many hipsters to the Assassins. *Illuminatus!* co-Author Robert Anton Wilson said that it 'belongs in every conspiriologist's library'. The lurid cover gives an idea of its sinister, sensationalist tone. *Author's collection*

Left: The mysterious Knights Templar have become inextricably entangled in Assassin mythology. Here a Grand Master makes a heroic last stand against the Saracen hordes. The Order of the Knights Templar was also suppressed under accusations of perverse practices and devil-worship.
Dover Publications

Above left: The face that launched a thousand conspiracy theories: President Kennedy's head explodes on the cover of a Spanish comic based on the most infamous assassination of all time. *Author's collection*

Above right: The assassin assassinated: TV news footage of Lee Harvey Oswald's murder, by Jack Ruby, provides arguably the best-known image of the JFK assassination. It's replicated here for the Spanish conspiracy comic book. *Author's collection*

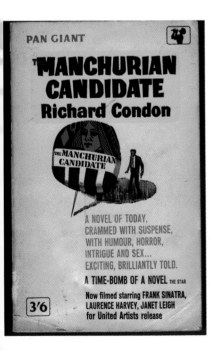

Left: The 1962 movie tie-in paperback of *The Manchurian Candidate*. The book is epigraphed by a quote that reads, 'Assassins were sceptical of the existence of God, and believed that the world of the mind came into existence first' – popularising the idea of Hasan Sabah as a nihilist philosopher. *Author's collection*

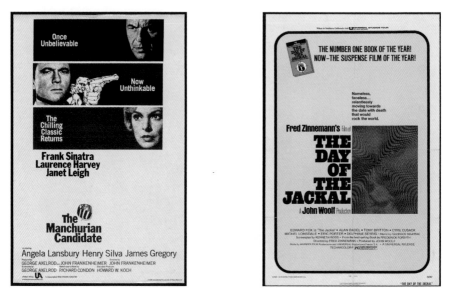

Above left: The mnemonic to murder: *The Manchurian Candidate* became a byword for the brainwashed 'trigger killer'. Its sleeper-assassin is activated by the Queen of Diamonds in the card deck. *Author's collection*

Above right: The Day of the Jackal was based on the numerous attempts to assassinate the French president, General De Gaulle, in the early 1960s. Its political hitman is the fictional assassin archetype: professional, cold, anonymous. *Author's collection*

Left: An Assassin makes an unsuccessful attempt on the life of Prince Edward of England, in 1272. Had he succeeded, the Prince would not have gone on to become King Edward, the Hammer of the Scots, his kingdom may never have been united and the whole course of European history might have changed. *Dover Publications*

complex relationship between the Assassins and some of the Seljuq warlords than might be supposed.

Mahmud eventually bought off the invading army by ceding territory to his slippery neighbour Sanjar, including much of that bordering upon regions occupied by the Assassins. And so a period of comparative tranquillity ensued for the previously embattled Nizaris. Pushed to the very edge of extinction by Muhammad Tapar's relentless war, the inhabitants of Alamut and Hasan's other communities enjoyed a lengthy breathing space, giving them ample time to restore their ruined lands and replenish their depleted spirits.

Inevitably, there was speculation as to why Sanjar was happy not only to tolerate heretics on his very doorstep but even to grant them financial support. Sanjar, however, was very much the cynical pragmatist. Anything that troubled Sultan Mahmud was fine by him, and little troubled Mahmud so much as the presence of Assassins throughout his realm, lying in wait for the secret order to strike.

Another theory gives a different motive for Sanjar's apparent complicity with his Nizari neighbours: 'Hasan Sabbah would send ambassadors to seek peace but his offers were not accepted,' according to the historian Juwayni.

'He then by all manner of wiles bribed certain of the Sultan's courtiers to defend him before the Sultan; and he suborned one of his eunuchs with a large sum of money and sent him a dagger, which was stuck in the ground beside the Sultan's bed one night when he lay in drunken sleep. When the Sultan awoke and saw the dagger he was filled with alarm but not knowing whom to suspect he ordered the matter to be kept secret. Hasan Sabbah then sent a messenger with the following message: "Did I not wish the Sultan well that dagger which was struck into the hard ground would have been planted in his soft breast." The Sultan took fright and from then on inclined towards peace with them. In short, because of this imposture the Sultan refrained from attacking them and during his reign their cause prospered. He allowed them a pension of 3,000 dinars from the taxes on the lands belonging to them in the region of Qumish and also permitted them to levy a small toll on travellers passing beneath Girdkuh, a custom which has survived to this day. I saw several of Sanjar's firmans [decrees] which had been preserved in their library and in which he conciliated and flattered them; and from these I was able to deduce the extent to which the Sultan connived at their actions and sought to be on peaceful terms with them. In short, during his reign they enjoyed ease and tranquillity.'

***

The ageing Hasan Sabbah appears to have known he was dying when he was stricken by a serious illness in the summer of 1124. He doubtless looked back on his career with a mixture of pride and frustration. Hasan had failed to topple either the Seljuq Sultanate or the Fatimid Caliphate, and if he had envisaged his own Nizari Caliphate presiding over the whole of Islam, such ambitions had proven to be pipe dreams born of religious fervour. But his revolution had survived for over three decades, a huge achievement considering the powerful forces ranged against his tiny army of fanatical devotees, sometimes numbering just dozens against armies of thousands. Perhaps he'd never anticipated victory in his own lifetime. After all, by his own insistence Hasan was only the representative of the coming Nizari Imam, preparing the way for the messiah who would lead his people to ultimate glory.

He had established Assassin enclaves in the Persian districts of Rudbar and Quhistan and the territory surrounding the castle at Girdkuh. It was a fragmentary kingdom, spread over thousands of kilometres, held together by a precarious chain of castles and sympathetic settlements. Missionaries had been despatched westward to Syria – where the chaos of the Crusades provided fertile territory for the Assassins' style of asymmetric warfare – and to the north – reaching the region that is now Georgia – and east, as far as the Indian subcontinent. Syria would become almost as significant as Persia in the history of the Assassins, the point where Europeans first encountered the sect. Georgia would later give the world Josef Stalin, the Soviet Union's man of steel, who some have compared to Hasan in terms of determination and ruthlessness. India would prove pivotal in the future of the Nizaris, nearly a thousand years on.

Meanwhile, Hasan had contributed to the deterioration of his principal foes. The Seljuq Sultanate would never enjoy the solidarity it had under Malikshah, due in no small part to the death of his right-hand man, Nizam al-Mulk, under an Assassin's blade. Similarly, targeted assassinations ordered by Hasan had ensured that the Fatimid Caliphate went into a terminal decline from which it would never recover.

Hasan Sabbah was buried near Alamut, his mausoleum becoming a place of pilgrimage for the Nizari faithful. On his deathbed he appointed his trusted commander, Kiya Buzurgummid, as his successor. Buzurgummid had seized the important Assassin fortress of Lamasar in 1096 and ruled the surrounding territory ever since, before being summoned back to Alamut to take the reins of power. He was, in modern parlance, a safe pair of hands, someone Hasan could comfortably entrust his legacy to – though the late Grand Master had also appointed a trinity of advisors to assist his successor.

Hasan's choice was soon tested as Sanjar once more re-entered the story. Ever alert for an opportunity, Sanjar evidently expected the Assassin succession to be accompanied by the same violent turmoil that characterised the handover of power in the Seljuq Sultanate, and he planned to profit by it. In the second year of Buzurgummid's rule, Sanjar sent two powerful forces deep into Assassin territory, carving a bloody swathe through defenceless villages, leaving a litter of butchered civilians in their wake.

It would ultimately prove another bloody exercise in futility. The power struggles that Sanjar had anticipated would divide his foe never happened. Hasan's choice of successor was accepted by his followers as holy writ, and the Assassins were soon able to turn the tables on the invading force. By now they were veteran guerrilla fighters, and Buzurgummid's men subjected their foes to a succession of ambushes, expertly employing the terrain and their superior morale to send Sanjar's army home with its collective tail between its legs. The seasoned Buzurgummid even managed to make modest territorial gains before Sanjar once more sued for peace.

When the vizier who had commanded one of Sanjar's armies, and had also been instrumental in advocating the invasion, returned home, he decided it might be politic to appease his master with a gift. Mindful perhaps of the fate that had befallen Shirgir upon his failure to capture Alamut, the vizier resolved to send his master two of his finest racehorses. So he sent for his most trusted grooms in order to discuss which of the horses in his stables might be most suitable. When the grooms arrived, any discussion of the matter was aborted when the vizier's supposed servants reached into their robes, drawing their daggers and stabbing the startled official to death.

The point had been very sharply made. Even Sultan Mahmud wondered if he might sleep easier if he made peace with Alamut and sent conciliatory messages to Buzurgummid, inviting him to send envoys to Isfahan. It did not go well. After an audience with the Sultan, the guards escorting the Assassin ambassadors were overrun by an angry mob and, in scenes reminiscent of the Isfahan masscares in 1101, the Nizari envoys were torn apart. Buzurgummid was outraged, demanding the perpetrators be brought to justice. Mahmud refused, wary of appearing to bow to the wishes of a heretic over the interests of his own people.

In frustration, Buzurgummid ordered an attack upon the town of Qazvin, his troops butchering some four hundred of the Sunni inhabitants by way of reprisal. It is an unusually ugly episode in the history of the Assassins, an example of the sect indiscriminately targeting innocent civilians rather than public figures. It also provides a particularly rare occasion when the tactics of the Assassins can be directly compared to the modern-day jihadist.

For his part, Sultan Mahmud felt obliged to retaliate with further futile military campaigns against the Assassins. But he was just going through the bloody motions.

The frequency of Nizari assassinations had declined during the latter years of Hasan Sabbah's reign, and did so still further under Buzurgummid. Some have interpreted this as a sign of diminishing religious fervour in the halls of Alamut, yet it might equally be the sign of success. A policy of assassination risks following the law of diminishing returns. The fear of assassination is at least as important a tool as the act itself in intimidating a political opponent, and most Nizari assassinations were acts of reprisal in response to enemy aggression, signs that the sect was under attack. Under Buzurgummid's leadership the Nizaris began minting their own money, exacting taxes and establishing tentative diplomatic relations with the governments of the region. The Assassins were experiencing a period of consolidation, transforming from a revolutionary movement into a state – albeit a highly unorthodox one, still regarded as a cancerous aberration by the majority of their Islamic contemporaries.

'Buzurgummid remained seated on the throne of Ignorance ruling over error until 9 February 1138, when he was crushed under the heel of Perdition and Hell was heated with the fuel of his carcass,' according to the Arabic chronicler Juwayni. This time the succession would follow the path of tradition, with the mantle of leadership passing to Buzurgummid's son, Muhammad. It was a significant departure from the policy of his predecessor, Hasan, who had gone so far as to execute his heirs.

The question of Hasan Sabbah's legacy has remained a perplexing issue over the ensuing years, centuries, even millennia, as a diverse gallery of characters have interpreted his mission as everything from a dark crusade that blighted history to a quest for spiritual enlightenment.

Does he survive in our culture as a terrorist prototype? A Persian nationalist? An unholy messiah? A pioneer of communism, or even a beat generation icon? Just what did the sect's founder actually preach? What was the appeal of his secret message that compelled his followers to court certain death, and his opponents to persecute the sect with almost unparalleled savagery?

IX

LOOKING AWAY FROM MECCA

The complacent spirit that crept into Alamut under Buzurgummid's rule appears to have taken firm hold under his son and heir, Muhammad. Hasan Sabbah's filial sacrifice had been in vain. The position of Grand Master would now pass from father to son, and while conflicts of succession never reached the disastrous pitch that they did among the Nizaris' opponents, subsequent generations would look back at the reign of their founder as a lost golden age.

Many Assassins had been born after Hasan's death. They made pilgrimage to his tomb, but the number of those devotees who had ever actually met their legendary founder dwindled. While most early Assassins had all of the fervour of the freshly converted, as time went on a growing percentage were Nizaris born and bred. It can only have diluted the sect's zeal.

Grand Master Muhammad I's reign began in 1138 with the murder of the new Abbasid Caliph, al-Rashid. Al-Rashid's father had met the same fate at the hands of the Assassins, three years earlier. The assassination was marked in the usual fashion, with seven days of celebration in Alamut and violent anti-Nizari riots in Isfahan. Other victims of Muhammad's Assassins include a Seljuq Sultan named Da'ud – though the days when one ruler could claim exclusive power over the whole Sultanate had passed – and a dozen lesser local leaders and religious dignitaries who had inspired his wrath.

However, Nizari history of the era suggests a movement losing its way. Assassinations were notably less common under Muhammad than his two predecessors and, while this does not inevitably denote waning power, other evidence paints a picture of a movement that lacked the passion and determination of its initial revolutionary stage.

Nizari records that once spoke of toppling empires and establishing a new world order were now crowded with reports of raid and counter-raid

– the same pattern of inter-tribal livestock theft and banditry that had characterised the region for countless generations. The Assassins were beginning to resemble any one of dozens of sects, clans and racial groups that made up the people of the medieval Middle East.

Yet the Nizaris were not accepted as simply another community. The leaders of the region of Manzandaran and the city of Rayy waged constant war on their Nizari neighbours. They beheaded every Nizari that they captured, using the severed crania to form pyramids of skulls – grisly monuments to the powerful hatred that Hasan's people inspired among their opponents. But in an era when politics was characterised by bloodshed, it seems implausible that the sect's infamy rested solely upon their propensity to assassinate opposing leaders.

Events have ensured that the doctrines of Hasan Sabbah remain swathed in mystery. According to eminent Ismaili historian Dr Farhad Daftary, the 'black legend' of the Assassins is a libel inspired solely by subtle doctrinal differences – significant to Muslim theologians, but blown out of all proportion for the purposes of propaganda. In conversation with the authors, the doctor described how the principle difference between Sunni and Shia Muslims hinged on 'the question of leadership. In terms of teaching they were the same. They differed on who was the right teacher within the community. A matter of genealogy, succession, leadership.

'The same applies to a large extent to the difference between the Ismailis and other Shia. So in fact the whole thing arose from the beginning, on the question of succession to the Prophet. It was a political issue, in a sense, who was to be the leader in the community after the Prophet. The Sunnis said, "Well, the community has to choose"; the Shia believed that the Prophet himself had appointed his son-in-law, Ali, called him under divine guidance to succeed him. So hence the very high reverence of the Shia for Ali. When, after a few generations, the family of Ali grew into a larger number, the Shia themselves could not agree as to who was the rightful leader after Ali. And that was the cause for a split within the Shia themselves.'

However, while he has a good claim to being the world's leading expert on the history of the sect, his career dedicated to studying the origins and legacy of the Nizaris, Dr Daftary is still handicapped by the same problems that face every researcher attempting to establish an accurate picture of their doctrines and practices. Hasan and his followers were, by necessity, highly secretive. 'They did not produce, like some preceding and later periods [in Ismaili history], a substantial literature – what they did produce, the bulk of it was destroyed by the Mongols in 1256,' concedes Dr Daftary. While they kept records of their creed and philosophy in Alamut's extensive library, in addition to 1256, as we shall see, there was at least one other occasion when it was purged of all texts that might be considered subversive or heretical. Other sources tend to come from contemporaries of the Assassins who were able to copy down passages of Nizari literature, though all are open to accusations of bias.

Such evidence is largely separated from Hasan Sabbah's sect by hundreds of miles, or even hundreds of years. Assassin doctrine seemed to change fairly radically during the sect's lifetime in Alamut, while the Syrian arm of the sect appears to have acted independently of Persia for a period, all adding to the problem of making any confident statements about their true credo. Compounding the mystery surrounding the hidden beliefs of the Assassins is the Islamic doctrine of *taqiyya* – the dispensation to hide or deny your true beliefs if faced by religious persecution. It was rejected by most Sunni Muslims, accepted with reservation by many Shiites and embraced by the Nizaris. Obviously, for any Assassin hoping to infiltrate an enemy community, *taqiyya* was essential dispensation, though at times the Nizari faith en masse appears to have adopted a policy of concealing their true beliefs under a mask of orthodoxy. The puzzle for many historians lies in identifying at which points the Assassin leadership were showing their authentic face, and when they were employing *taqiyya* for political reasons.

Speculation allows for radically differing viewpoints on the Assassins. The Austrian orientalist Baron Joseph von Hammer-Purgstall, who wrote the first Western book on the sect in 1813, *The History of the Assassins*, described them as a 'union of impostors and dupes which, under the mask of a more austere creed and severer morals, undermined all religion and morality; that order of murderers beneath whose daggers the lords of nations fell . . .'

By way of contrast, in 1938 F. A. Ridley wrote *The Assassins*, designed to refute Hammer-Purgstall's view: 'Fifteen centuries after Plato, Hasan Sabbah made a reality of the platonic dream, for he too recognised that in this harsh world the philosopher-king can flourish only behind insurmountable walls and that, for the few to be free to seek the truth, the many must be kept at bay by terror.' The two different authors brought very different agendas to the subject, for Hammer-Purgstall was a reactionary Catholic and Ridley a secular socialist.

Most commentators agree that the Assassins were an initiatory secret society, a hierarchical order wherein each new promotion entitled the member to both more authority within the sect and access to new secrets – bringing them closer to the total enlightenment promised to the inner circle. Various structures have been suggested over the years, with the number of ranks ranging from nine (common to previous Isamili initiatory orders) to seven (a number of special significance to the Nizaris). Edward Burman gives a plausible framework in his 1987 book, also entitled *The Assassins*, positing seven ranks which he further divides into four categories. At the top is the Imam, a position left empty since the murder of Nizar. Beneath that are the fully initiated – three categories of missionary ranging from the Chief Missionary or Grand Master (the post held by Hasan himself) down to his lieutenants, the superior missionaries and the ordinary missionaries. Below them are the partly initiated, also known as the Rafiqs. The uninitiated consist of the Lasiq or adherents (significant sympathisers) and the Assassins.

It is notable that the rank of Assassin lies at the very bottom of the ladder in both status and importance. On the face of it it seems strange that the members of the sect who attracted most notoriety – indeed, who established its name in the history books – should occupy the lowliest position in the pecking order. Yet in many respects it makes perfect sense, not least because the men expected to undertake suicide missions should be expendable members of the lower orders rather than experienced administrators, military commanders and religious dignitaries. (The same applies to modern suicide bombers, who are seldom the same people who plan the terrorist campaigns.)

The use of the term 'Assassin' also proves slightly awkward, as the vast majority of this rank never undertook assassination missions – they must have numbered thousands, while the rolls of honour seldom list more than a dozen or so successful assassinations under any given Grand Master. The majority of Assassins most likely operated as spies in enemy territory, worked Nizari land or defended the strongholds in times of need. Many accounts suggest that promising young men were recruited from surrounding territories by the Grand Master's representatives to receive specialist training, schooled in foreign languages and the skills of disguise necessary to infiltrate enemy camps and communities. Dr Daftary dismisses this as improbable, but this begs the question of how the Assassins were so successful in their infiltration techniques. Even in the absence of hard evidence, it seems reasonable to assume some kind of intensive training programme at Alamut and other significant Nizari strongholds, such as Masyaf in Syria.

The question of what other instruction or indoctrination may have taken place to prepare young candidates for suicide missions remains controversial. Many experts are now sceptical of the stories recorded by Marco Polo of secluded gardens, where drugged candidates were deposited to experience a literal taste of Heaven before seeking salvation by dying in the service of the Grand Master. There is palpably no such location that could have contained such a site, replete with fountains of wine and honey, in the ruins of the fortress of Alamut. ('Alamut' is often used locally to describe the surrounding valley, rather than just the castle itself, so it is possible, if still slightly fanciful, that we might find the original site of this earthly paradise further afield.)

Gardens are frequently used in Islam as a metaphor for Heaven (as they are in Christianity – Adam and Eve originally dwelt in a garden before their expulsion from Paradise). So it is unsurprising that Heaven was envisaged as a well-irrigated green idyll of sweet-smelling flowers and soft fountains, when so many lived on barren mountains or in bleak desert regions. Perhaps the stories of a Garden of Paradise at Alamut originated in the verdant vistas the Nizaris diligently cultivated in the land around the castles that they captured.

According to the legend, drug-fuelled journeys to Paradise were not the only techniques employed at Alamut to convince initiates that death held no sting. According to Arkon Daraul in *Secret Societies*,

> 'Hasan had a deep narrow pit sunk into the floor of his audience chamber. One of his disciples stood in this in such a way that his head and neck alone were visible above the floor. Around the neck was placed a circular disc in two pieces which fitted together, with a hole in the middle . . . "Tell them," commanded the chief, "what thou hast seen." The disciple then described the delights of Paradise . . . The effect of this conjuring trick . . . increased the enthusiasm for martyrdom to the required degree.'

Dr Daftary would doubtless dismiss this as yet another example of the black legend. And it's verifiable that history provides prolific examples of terrorists where no deceptions involving talking heads or narcotic-induced visits to Paradise are required to recruit those responsible. Current events offer chilling evidence that religious devotion alone is more than adequate. But the current 'War on Terror' has provoked renewed interest in the Assassins from those looking for the Islamists' spiritual forefathers. In *The Secret History of Al-Qaida*, for example, journalist and expert on radical Islam Abdel Bari Atwan includes a potted history of Hasan Sabbah's sect. 'There are obvious comparisons to be made with al-Qaida here,' he explains, 'in the emphasis on and power of allegiance and the desire for an effective use of martyrdom as a weapon in asymmetric war.'

Yet, as we have already suggested, portraying the Assassins as a medieval version of al-Qaeda is probably at least as misleading as it is illuminating. According to Richard Belfield in his book *Assassination*:

> 'Tempting though it is to argue that Al-Qaeda are the natural heirs of the Hashshashin there is a much better candidate: the Cosa Nostra in Italy. Both have members who are "soldiers" in civilian clothing and every soldier is both a spy for the organisation and, crucially, a killer. Initially, the Hashshashin (like the Cosa Nostra) began as outsiders with their heartland based deep in an impenetrable mountain range but soon became the dominant power, first in local and then in national politics. . . . Like the Hashshashin before them the Cosa Nostra have used the threat of assassination as effectively as the deed itself.'

Again, it is an analogy which has severe limitations, though it is not without merit. Like the Cosa Nostra (or Mafia), the Assassins employed fear as both a defence strategy against their foes in the establishment and as a crucial source of revenue. The Nizaris collected protection money from neighbouring states, whose leaders were fearful of the sect's infamous Assassins, and in its latter years appear to have undertaken assassinations for cash (just as it is alleged, for example, that the US Government covertly employed Mafia hit-men to silence troublesome foreign figures).

Yet financial gain was never the Nizaris' principal motive, as it is for the Cosa Nostra. Like al-Qaeda, the Assassins appear to have stuck to a revolutionary theological agenda throughout their existence, even if it was periodically eclipsed by more immediate concerns of survival. Al-Qaeda differ from the medieval Nizaris in structural terms – like the Assassins they appear to control an underground network of support, but they have yet to come anywhere near establishing the state-within-a-state commanded by the Grand Masters of Alamut.

(Some dismiss the idea of al-Qaeda as an organisation, claiming it as an invention of the American security services. The reality is that it is more of a concept that unites a diverse spectrum of Islamist radicals.)

While both Hasan Sabbah and Osama bin Laden seem to have shared extreme Islamic roots, in most other respects their agendas are profoundly different. At the very least they are separated by the division between Shiite and Sunni, the frequently bitter sectarian schism that has divided Islam for centuries. While al-Qaeda is a recognisably Sunni movement – albeit a highly controversial one vehemently rejected by many Sunnis – the Assassins belonged to a schismatic arm of the Shiite tradition, though the extent to which the teachings of Hasan expanded, adapted, or even rejected such roots is unclear.

In addition to being repudiated as heretics by their Sunni contemporaries, the inhabitants of Alamut were castigated by Shiite theologians, particularly among the Mustali and Twelver branches of the creed. A number of the most vitriolic anti-Nizari polemics of the day condemned the Assassins as worse than atheists, some going as far as to suggest that the secret revealed to those who reached the highest ranks was a denial of God. Present-day Ismailis reject this as poisonous sectarian slander, yet it is an accusation that bears further scrutiny.

'Nothing is true, everything is permitted' is the maxim associated in the West with the legend of Hasan Sabbah – though as ever, some question the aphorism's historical authenticity. According to one theory, supported by Arkon Daraul, the initiatory hierarchy of the Assassins systematised the conversion technique used to such devastating effect by their travelling missionaries. The method consisted of challenging and then destroying the subject's belief system, replacing it with that of the Nizaris. More controversially, it is also suggested that, once the subject accepted conventional Nizari doctrine, the next level was achieved when this, too, was deconstructed in favour of a mystical philosophy which dismissed conventional Nizari codes, such as Sharia law, as necessary only to guide the vulgar and simple-minded. At the end of this philosophical trail lay the revelation that nothing can be satisfactorily proven, that everything except the will, as moulded by the Grand Master, is merely an illusion. Nothing is true and thus there are no moral limits on behaviour beyond those laid down by a spiritual superior.

It all sounds a lot like the methodology of modern cults. In *Mystics and Messiahs*, Philip Jenkins describes cults as 'exotic religions that practice spiritual totalitarianism: members owe fanatical obedience to the group and to its charismatic leaders, who enforce their authority through mind-control techniques or brainwashing. According to the stereotype, cult members live separated from the 'normal' world, sometimes socially, in the sense of being cut off from previous friends and family, and sometimes also spatially, in a special residence house or remote compound. Other cult characteristics include financial malpractice and deceit by the group or its leaders, the exploitation of members, and sexual unorthodoxy.'

All other charges aside, the characteristics of a charismatic leader and a secluded location could certainly be made to fit Hasan Sabbah and Alamut.

In *Cults in Our Midst*, Margaret Thaler Singer and Janja Lalich define cults as groups

'who expose their recruits and members to organised psychological and social persuasion processes designed to produce attitudinal changes and to establish remarkable degrees of control by the group over these recruits' and members' lives. These cults deceive, manipulate, and exploit their members and hope to keep them for as long as possible.'

The authors describe them as commonly employing

'thought-reform processes. The originators of cults and thought-reform groups tend to conjure up coordinated programmes of coercive influence and behavioural control using ages-old persuasion techniques in order to change people's attitudes around a vast array of philosophies, theories, and practices.'

Just as one man's terrorist is another man's freedom fighter, so the difference between a cult and a religion is largely a question of perspective. Pretty much every one of the negative characteristics of a cult can also be applied to most of the world's major religions, which in turn have also had a hand in many of the world's most catastrophic conflicts.

But assassinations have also frequently been intended as precursors to secular revolution. Strong echoes of Hasan's supposed dictum – 'nothing is true, everything is permitted' – can be found in the nihilists of late 19th-century Russia. The nihilists became internationally notorious as anti-establishmentarians whose creed went beyond anarchism, after their assassination of Tsar Alexander II in 1881 (see Chapter Two). In another detail resonant of the medieval Nizaris, they referred to assassination as 'propaganda of the deed' – the symbolic use of violence to cow the establishment and inspire dissent among the masses.

The doctrine was controversial among the wider anarchist movement, some believing it counterproductive and unethical. It declined sharply after the Russian Revolution of 1917, which both eclipsed anarchism's significance as a revolutionary movement, and put in place a communist government more effective in crushing dissent than its Tsarist predecessor.

Some have also suggested close parallels between communism and the Nizari state established by Hasan Sabbah, as well as the dread of subversion engendered by his Assassins and the paranoid fear of communist infiltration experienced by America in the 'red scare' of the 1950s. While we have few details of their economic system, we do know that the Assassins divided the loot taken in raids equally among all participants, which was unusual. According to Dr Daftary, there was also a great deal more social equality and mobility in Nizari society than its Seljuq equivalent. All of the leading Nizaris were drawn from comparatively humble backgrounds, and everybody was expected to pitch in with public works projects routinely undertaken on Nizari land. Perhaps most intriguingly, some insist that *rafiq* was not a rank within the Assassin hierarchy but the term of address used between Nizaris, translating as 'comrade'.

Socialist author F. A. Ridley supports his thesis of the Assassins as proto-communists by quoting Dr H. F. Helmolt's *World History*:

'. . .the heresy of the Ismailians developed out of a mixture of Mohammedanism and various other beliefs of which perhaps the most important were the communistic doctrines of the Mazdakites. The doctrines of the Ismailians were gradually transformed into an esoteric system of beliefs, which, in the hands of the most intellectual of its adherents, approached pure nihilism – the conception that all things are indifferent, and hence all actions are permissible – while the bulk of the believers lived in a state of mystic respect for their still more mystic superiors and leaders.'

Mazdak was a sixth-century Persian social reformer and religious prophet, who preached an early form of communism before his sect was suppressed and followers massacred in 528 by adherents of the Zoroastrian faith. Pockets of this heresy survived, however, and, according to Ridley, blossomed under Hasan Sabbah.

Imagining Alamut as the heart of a socialist utopia overlooks some uncomfortable facts about both socialism and Hasan Sabbah. Hasan's severity had extended to the execution of both of his sons. As far as we know, nobody was assassinated on a whim, but some of those who he ordered to be killed were simply guilty of disagreeing with his beliefs. This was no benign philosopher-king.

Similarly, while socialism is fine in principle, communism has proven at least as repressive and open to corruption as the supposedly decadent systems of government it has overthrown. But Ridley wrote his book before the advent of the Cold War forced the West to face up to the reality of the Soviet Union as a ruthless dictatorship, and Stalin as a man capable of anything to retain power, including the death of millions of his own people.

Yet there are still today some citizens of the former Soviet Union who subscribe to the cult of Stalin, and more who would begrudgingly acknowledge his achievement in dragging his nation into the modern world while facing the mercilessly efficient Nazi war machine. Sometimes brutal times call for ruthless men – men like Josef Stalin, or perhaps Hasan Sabbah. Just as the Grand Masters of Alamut concluded numerous temporary alliances with avowed foes that seemed incongruous to outside observers, so Stalin would sign his infamous non-aggression pact with Hitler in 1939. In fact, an interpretation of Alamut as a prototype for Hitler's 'Wolf's Lair' control centre in Poland is at least as valid as idealising the medieval Nizari capital as some kind of communist utopia.

There are further intriguing suggestions in the account of the Assassins given by Jean de Joinville, the eminent French chronicler who encountered the sect in the mid-13th century:

'Whenever the Old Man of the Mountain went out riding, a crier would go before him bearing a Danish axe with a long haft encased in silver, to which many knives were affixed. As he went the man would continually cry out: "Turn out of the way of him who bears in his hands the death of kings!"'

The term 'fascism' derives from *fasces* – the Latin term for an axe, its haft bound with sticks, which was the symbol of power carried by Ancient Roman magistrates. Its symbolism of the strength of unified force was adopted by the various fascist movements that emerged across Europe in the 20th century. It is not so fanciful to take the rallying call of 'Believe, obey, fight' – as coined by the fascist leader Benito Mussolini –as a plausible summation of the doctrine of *ta'lim*, central to the teachings of Hasan Sabbah.

If we can be confident about anything concerning the dogma of Hasan, it is that obedience was at its core. While Sunni Muslim theologians generally allowed that consensus and reason could play a part in identifying the true path, their Shiite counterparts were inclined to emphasise divine inspiration as the only authentic route to righteousness. The Ismaili Shiites took this further, and Hasan in turn preached a philosophy that took this line of reasoning to its ultimate conclusion. The will of God – ultimate wisdom – is beyond the comprehension of ordinary mortals. Any attempt to appreciate the divine is futile. The only guide we can trust is the word of God's representative on earth – the Imam – hence unquestioning loyalty to his will is the only true path to salvation. Hasan was always adamant that he was only the Imam's representative, awaiting the advent of the true messiah who remained, for occult reasons, hidden or invisible. But during the reign of subsequent Assassin Grand Masters, this would change . . .

Under Muhammad, the Assassins took a backseat in the power politics of the Middle East. He was a competent but far from dynamic ruler, who successfully maintained the Nizari state without furthering the radical ambitions of the sect's founder. However, the revolutionary spirit was far from dead.

Conflicts between father and son are a recurring theme in dynastic history. The story of England's ruling houses is characterised by domestic tensions that have run out of control under the heady influence of power, where arguments over the breakfast table developed into situations that threatened the realm with civil war. During the period of the Crusades, the Plantagenet dynasty – under whose reign the English identity was established – constantly conspired against each other. The Georgian monarchs, who presided over the establishment of the British Empire in the 1700s, were also notorious for the dysfunctional relationships between the ruling sovereigns and their heirs. So it was with Muhammad and his son in Alamut, six centuries before.

Muhammad's son, Hasan, was everything his brusque, diligent father was not. Hasan was dynamic, charismatic and driven. He spent many hours in Alamut's legendary library studying the writings of his namesake, as well as the arcane texts that informed the sect's core philosophy. Hasan began to attract a following among the younger, more volatile denizens of Alamut, some of whom began to talk of him in the same breath as the sect's legendary founder. A few even began to wonder if this brilliant, magnetic young man might even be the coming Imam that the Nizaris had been eagerly awaiting for some 40 years, regarding him rather than his father as their true leader.

This was too much for the Grand Master to take. Whether or not Hasan had taken any part in spreading these rumours, they were undermining his authority. 'This Hasan is my son, and I am not the Imam but one of his missionaries,' he thundered to a public assembly, for the Imam had to be a direct descendant of Nizar to be legitimate. 'Whoever listens to these words and believes them is an infidel and an atheist.'

Muhammad backed up his outburst with action that proved he still had the iron ruthlessness required of an Assassin Grand Master. He identified 500 of his followers known to endorse his son as the predicted Nizari Imam; half were executed, with their corpses strapped to the backs of the other 250, who were driven out into exile.

Hasan evidently got the message, and kept his head low until his father died in 1162. When he finally ascended to the throne, the fledgling Grand Master, now in his mid-thirties, set about making his mark. Suggestions of his disdain for Nizari convention, even rumours that he had drunk wine, could not have prepared the faithful for the religious revolution that occurred under their new leader.

Hasan's declaration of *qiyama* – or the Resurrection – some two and a half years into his reign represents one of the most enigmatic and fascinating episodes in the history of the Nizaris, or indeed the entire Islamic creed. Its significance remains wide open to debate. Was it a radical change in spiritual direction for the Assassins, or simply an extension of previous policies? Perhaps Hasan II was simply opening up the cult's secret teachings, previously confined to the upper grades of the order. Certainly, the readiness with which his preaching was embraced throughout the scattered Assassin realms suggests that it cannot have been a total surprise to his followers.

***

The date had been chosen with great care. It was the 17th day of Ramadan, the month when good Muslims observed their fast, in the year 1164. It was also the anniversary of the death of the Imam Ali, some 500 years ago. Meticulous calculations by Hasan and his astrologers had determined a date blessed by the stars, with Virgo in the ascendant and the sun in Cancer. Just as much care had been taken laying out the pulpit in the valley beneath the castle of Alamut. Hasan gave precise instructions for the location of every one of the structures his carpenters industriously erected in preparation for the coming festivities. Around the pulpit, four great banners were raised to surround it; from one fluttered a white silken flag, from the others flags of red, green and yellow. Tables were aligned around the edge. Each detail, the tradesmen understood, carried vital occult significance that only the enlightened could comprehend.

Hasan's most entrusted chefs and servants were also kept busy, following his exact instructions under a pall of secrecy. Messengers had been sent to the far-flung states of Hasan's realm, travelling through hostile territory to deliver invitations to his commanders and governors, his priests and lieutenants, bidding them attend their Grand Master for a ceremony of crucial importance. And so they began to arrive, caravans of Assassin worthies snaking across arid deserts and winding mountain passes, wary of the hostile patrols who could count on a weighty bounty for taking the heads of such distinguished heretics. As they arrived, making camp in Alamut's fertile valley, the atmosphere of anticipation became tangible. Hasan, unlike his legendary predecessor and namesake, was a familiar face to many of the people of Alamut, but few had seen him for weeks, contributing further to the rumble of speculation that hummed throughout the valley.

When the ordained day came, Hasan's lieutenants marshalled the different delegations to their allocated positions facing the pulpit. Those from the northern territories were positioned to the front, those from the east to the right, those from the west to the left. The ceremony was as carefully choreographed as any military manoeuvre, with Hasan arranging human bodies and wooden constructions as carefully as an astrologer casting a chart. Once all were assembled a heavy silence descended. They waited until it seemed that impatience would overcome reverence.

Then the gates of Alamut opened. Hasan emerged at the head of a small entourage, but all eyes were fixed upon the Grand Master who made a stately descent towards the podium. His robes and turban were of a dazzling white, capturing the sun, making the man resemble an angel or a spirit to those who squinted up the hill to the approaching figure. Hasan had timed his approach exactly so that he reached his podium at the exact moment the sun reached its zenith in the sky.

It is at this point that a few of the assembled recognise the field has been laid out precisely so that all of his guests are facing away from the holy city of Mecca. But nobody says anything, as the magnetic presence in the pulpit draws himself to his full height and draws his scimitar, which catches the sun in a way that seems somehow unnatural. In a mesmerising voice, Hasan greets his three groups of guests, employing his sword to give emphasis.

'O inhabitants of the world, djinn, men and angels!' he stares skyward. 'The Imam of our times has sent you his blessing and his compassion, and has called you his special chosen servants. He has freed you from the burdens of the rule of Holy Law, and has brought you his Resurrection.'

The effect upon the assembled Assassins is electric. Breath freezes in throats, hearts hammer in ribs, eyes forget to blink. The time that the faithful have awaited for generations – the advent of their Messiah – is at hand. As their Grand Master elucidates the new dawn, his congregation imbibe each intoxicating sentence as if in a daze. He condemns those who will not see the truth as walking corpses, henceforth sentenced to living damnation, and exalts the devotees as avenging angels. The Sharia, once sacred, is now taboo. The saved need no such superstition, and the advocates of these obsolete laws shall now be put to bloody death, just as they once inflicted their violence upon those who transgressed.

Nobody can say how long Hasan's address lasts – a moment or a lifetime – but he reaches the end of his explosive sermon, bows humbly twice and motions for silk cloths covering the surrounding tables to be removed. If anything can complete the astonishment of the assembled Assassins, it is this: each table bows under plates of pork and jugs of wine.

All freeze. None are sure what to do – is this a test? Has their Grand Master gone mad, or is he divinely inspired? He walks calmly over to a table, pours himself a flagon of wine and impales a slice of pork upon the point of a knife, greedily devouring both. While across the Islamic world the faithful observe the fast of Ramadan in sombre silence, beneath lofty Alamut the Assassins feast upon the forbidden, accompanied by riotous laughter and the strains of harps and rebecks. The Resurrection has been ordained by the man some believe to be the True Imam, the divine messenger of God.

***

Nobody is quite sure what to make of Hasan II's Resurrection. It presents problems for experts like Dr Daftary, who claims that it was simply an admonition to pay closer attention to personal spirituality and that stories of the Assassins abandoning Sharia law are yet more hostile propaganda. Most experts agree, however, that something radically strange happened on that fateful day at the castle of Alamut.

The ease with which Hasan II's rejection of Islamic orthodoxy was absorbed suggests that his apparent repudiation of sacred law was not a total surprise for many of his guests. Most agree that Hasan II studied the theological dogma set down by Hasan Sabbah assiduously, but Hasan I exiled musicians and had his own son killed for drinking wine, all the while living an ascetic lifestyle himself. How could a revolutionary leader famed for singleminded devotion to duty have inspired the licence of the Resurrection?

The history of cult leaders is littered with self-styled messiahs who impose celibacy on their flock while sleeping with attractive young followers, gorging on rich foods as their devotees starve. If anybody had been in a position to lead such a double life – where outward austerity concealed a doctrine that forbade nothing to the enlightened – then it was Hasan Sabbah, concealed from all but his closest associates in Alamut for the last three decades of his life.

Might this explain the rumours that connect his sect with the consumption of narcotics? Such accusations are purely speculative, and it is certainly true that Hasan's philosophy focused on the concept of obedience to the sect's divine Imam. But Hasan II now seemed to be about to lay claim to that very position, where his word quite literally became sacred law.

Religions gradually breed anti-religions among the decadent and dispossessed. In Europe, the totalitarian rule of the Catholic Church inspired symbolic revolt among those who chafed under its oppressive influence. The Black Mass would be the most infamous of anti-Christian rites, born out of the court of the Sun King, Louis XIV, in 17th-century France. Wealthy women are alleged to have paid a defrocked priest and his fortune-telling accomplice to conduct abortions, peddle poisons and sacrifice living children in ceremonies courting the favour of demons.

Yet the roots of the Black Mass are less lurid. Early examples consist of priests employing the supposed power of the orthodox Mass to personal ends – cursing the living by naming them in masses for the dead or simply blessing crops or fishing nets for a fee. Stories proliferate of obscene parodies of the Mass conducted by medieval peasants, too impotent to openly oppose their religious oppressors and reduced to mocking the Church's most sacred rite in secretive feasts – reminiscent perhaps of Hasan II's transgressive Resurrection.

The satanic tradition – to which the rite of the Black Mass belongs – is one of the most complex minefields in religious history. Most Satanism is actually militant atheism in the garb of anti-religious theatre, and it is possible that Hasan II's Resurrection was a ritualised repudiation of the Islamic establishment that subjected the Assassins' community to decades of brutal repression. But it is also at least as likely that the more scandalous accounts of Hasan's new declaration were products of the hostile imaginations of the sect's foes. Most historians of the European 'witch craze' – the supposed satanic conspiracy that inspired the torture and burnings that claimed so many lives in the 15th and 16th centuries – now portray the 'witches' as the victims of mass hysteria, superstition and sadism, wholly innocent of any subversive activity.

Others paint a more complex picture. One enduring hypothesis is that many supposed devotees of the Devil actually adhered to ancient pre-Christian cults. Like the European witches of the Middle Ages and the Renaissance, the Assassins were also accused by their persecutors of indulging in sexual licence, extending to taboo activities such as incest. There it is evidence to support such slanderous accusations, but if, as F. A. Ridley suggests, the doctrines of Mazdak were absorbed into the Assassins' creed, then there is space for speculation. For in addition to advocating shared property, the Persian prophet also sanctioned free love. Hasan II's Resurrection may have sought to loosen orthodox Islam's puritanical attitudes to sex, only for its edicts to be blown out of all proportion by his opponents.

The veil of secrecy that surrounds the doctrines of the Assassins continues to invite speculation. While the sympathetic Nizari scholar Dr Daftary has performed sterling work in his efforts to dispel the sensationalist aura surrounding the Assassins, the sect's secrets remain an intriguing enigma.

Prototypical nihilists? Pioneering communists? Theological fascists? Enlightened atheists? Libertines? Puritans? Cultists?

All hats can be made to fit, due to the gaps in our knowledge. The villains of Baron von Hammer-Purgstall's diatribe against the evils of secret societies may just as easily be the heroes of Mr Ridley's salutation to the defence of enlightenment. It is the occult overtones of the sect's doctrines that have inspired the most interesting and enduring flights of fancy concerning the Assassins in the West.

One of Hasan II's first acts as Grand Master was to despatch his trusted friend Rashid al-din Sinan to Syria, with orders to reinvigorate the struggling Assassin presence in the region. Sinan was to prove the most influential figure in the history of the sect from a Western perspective, an enigmatic figure that bolsters the idea of Assassin Grand Masters as adepts of the black arts . . .

X

A THEORY ABOUT CONSPIRACIES

Two centuries before terrorist atrocities inspired authors and journalists to investigate the medieval Nizaris – searching for parallels between the Assassins and terror groups like al-Qaeda – the sect had sparked a wave of interest, courtesy of what we now call 'conspiracy theories'.

The French Revolution of 1788-9 is widely regarded as the painful birth of the modern age, an explosion of violent radicalism that sent shockwaves across the map of Europe as commoners beheaded aristocrats upon the 'National Razor'. The destruction of centuries-old political and religious institutions sent spasms of panic and paranoia across the Continent, as European governments dreaded a bloody chain reaction that would engulf them all.

For some reactionary commentators, the conventional explanations for the Revolution – of poverty and hunger among the lower orders, alongside the decadence of the aristocracy and the ambitions of the middle classes – were not sufficient to explain the profoundly bloody shock that turned French society upside down. They searched for alternative reasons, identifying sinister figures behind the scenes, manipulating events to their own occult ends. This vortex of political paranoia was the cradle in which the first influential modern conspiracy theory was born.

The French Republican experiment was effectively brought to an end by Napoleon, who seized power at the head of the army in 1799 and was declared emperor in 1804. The year before he took power, Napoleon led an invasion of Egypt. Alongside his army, the military general also took 167 scientists and scholars with him.

In Egypt, despite being heavily outnumbered, Napoleon successfully defeated the Mamluk forces, descendants of the power that successfully tamed the Syrian Assassins nearly 500 years before. (As an interesting aside, the use of hashish was so ubiquitous in Egypt at the time that

Napoleon felt the need to ban it.) Napoleon's invasion was only a qualified military success at best, but his scholars brought back material which ignited an interest in the Middle East among European intellectuals, blossoming with the burgeoning academic discipline of orientalism in the 1800s. The heady blend of paranoia inspired by the French Revolution combined with the freshly budding academic interest in the Islamic world to inspire the first scholarly debates on the Assassins in modern Europe.

The history of the medieval Assassins had not been wholly ignored in preceding centuries. In 1594 a French court official named Lebey de Batilly penned a short book on the sect, doubtlessly inspired by his own turbulent times. For the previous king of France, Henry III, had died at the hands of an assassin in 1589. The murder has strong echoes of numerous similar Nizari plots, its perpetrator a religious fanatic who posed as a messenger with an important private communiqué for the King, using the ruse to get close enough to draw a knife and stab his target in the stomach before guards killed him where he stood.

De Batilly's master, Henry IV, was also the target of several assassination attempts, also reminiscent of Nizari murder missions. If de Batilly intended his brief study of the medieval Assassins as a cautionary tale, it was ultimately a futile one, for in 1610, Henry IV was murdered by another knife-wielding religious fanatic.

In 1697, the Assassins took their place in Bartholome d'Herbelot's *Biblioteque Orientale*, a pioneering work of orientalism cramming a summary of Western knowledge on Islamic history, art and religion into four volumes. In 1751, Emile Falconet wrote a dissertation on the sect, which became the basis for Edward Gibbon's condemnatory coverage of the Assassins in his epic *Decline and Fall of the Roman Empire*.

In 1806, Simone Assemani, an Italian professor of oriental languages, contributed an article to a journal in which he argues that the term 'Assassin' came from a mistranslation of the Arabic for 'men from the mountains'. Perhaps in part by way of response, three years later the French orientalist Silvestre De Sacy delivered a paper on the subject to the Institut de France, later published as a monograph, in which he argued persuasively that it actually derived from the term for 'hashish user'. Fascinating as these theses may have been, they were all very much academic works aimed at a specialist audience. It would take a more passionate author, with a more emotive prose style and the willingness to take a controversial line, to pen a work that would bring the Assassins to the attention of the general public.

The History of the Assassins by Austrian orientalist and aristocratic adventurer Joseph von Hammer-Purgstall – published in 1818 and translated into English in 1835 – is as much a pioneering work of conspiracy theory as a history of the Nizaris. Hammer-Purgstall makes no bones about the aim of the book, to 'show the disastrous influence of secret societies and the dreadful prostitution of religion to the horrors of unbridled ambition'. In doing so, the Austrian draws from the many hostile accounts of Hasan Sabbah and his followers, then weaves the Assassins into the centre of a web of secret conspiracies that have eaten away at the fabric of Western society ever since. His book helped establish a place for the Assassins in future works of alternative or revisionist history, an area that has become a multimillion-dollar publishing phenomenon in recent decades.

One alternative historian influenced by Hammer-Purgstall was the French Catholic priest Augustin Barruel, who, in 1797, published his *Memoirs Illustrating the History of Jacobinism*, while in exile in England. His book, which blamed an anti-Christian conspiracy for the French Revolution that had led to his exile, went through several expanded editions, gradually growing into the mother of all conspiracy theories. Later editions contained increasing elements of anti-Semitism and, under the influence of Hammer-Purgstall, roped the Assassins into his ancient, global network of unholy secret societies, led by the enigmatic Illuminati. Among those who read the book was the poet Percy Shelley, who in 1814 began a work entitled *The Assassins*. He never completed it, but the fragments that survive illustrate that the Romantic poet's sympathies were very much with the anarchic Assassins. Most of Barruel's readership, however, shared his reactionary sentiments, and the book's pernicious influence spread worldwide among paranoid conservatives.

Cult novelist and veteran conspiracy theorist Robert Anton Wilson – who mixes a healthy dose of scepticism and humour into his numerous perceptive works on paranoia politics – notes in *Everything Is Under Control*:

> 'A large part of this Fu Manchu-style mythos quickly infested New England and some Federalists, especially among the clergy, used it against Thomas Jefferson, whom they claimed acted as the Illuminati's top man on the then-new US government . . . The whole Barruel Jewish-Masonic-Arab conspiracy appeared occasionally among the 1840s anti-Masonic Party in this country [America], and has influenced

all right-wing politics in Europe ever since, including Italian Fascism and German Nazism . . . A very unsanitary version, including the anti-Semitism, motivates a great deal of "militia" activity.'

Of course, by no means all conspiracy theorists are right-wing, and just as many have entered the fray with a leftist agenda. Many such theorists involve the Jesuits in their speculative conspiracies. (Barruel was a Jesuit – so might his conspiracy theory itself be part of a conspiracy?) Some orientalists have also drawn secret comparisons between the Jesuits and the Assassins. According to F.A. Ridley,

'In the history of secret societies, Ignatius Loyala [founder of the Jesuits] and Hasan Sabbah probably represent the two greatest names. The personal resemblances between these two great conservative masters of counter-revolution is, indeed, extraordinary, and no less is the phenomenal resemblance between their two famous orders. So great in fact is this far-reaching resemblance that I have elsewhere styled the Jesuits as "the Assassins of Christendom". As we shall see presently, the term "Assassins" is not to be understood in a merely figurative sense!'

Both orders, he observes, operated primarily via a policy of covert religious conversion in enemy territory and followed a doctrine of fanatical loyalty to their respective leaders. Both used this loyalty to compel lowly members to undertake suicide missions, using stealth and disguise to get close enough to powerful opponents of the order to murder them. (Both Henry III and Henry IV have plausibly been identified as the victims of Jesuit plots.) However, Ridley concedes that the geographical and historical distances between the organisations – Persia's Assassins had been suppressed some 250 years before the foundation of the Jesuits in Spain – makes any direct link between them an improbable leap of logic. Rather more likely is that organisations with similar ends are inclined to evolve via similar means.

Other theorists have proposed that the Assassins established the prototype for all future Western secret societies after Europeans first encountered them in the Holy Lands. According to the eminent Indian Muslim historian and politician, Syed Ameer Ali,

'From the Ismailis the Crusaders borrowed the conception which led to the formation of all the secret societies, religious and secular, of Europe. The institutions of Templars and Hospitallers; the Society of Jesus, founded by Ignatius Loyola, composed by a body of men whose devotion to their cause can hardly be surpassed in our time; the ferocious Dominicans, the milder Franciscans — may all be traced either to Cairo or to Alamut. The Knights Templar especially, with their system of grand masters, grand priors and religious devotees, and their degrees of initiation, bear the strongest analogy to the Eastern Ismailis.'

**

The role of secret societies in human history is an accepted part of modern cultural discourse. Frequently cast into the ghetto of ridicule by the term 'conspiracy theory', both the wildest and most seemingly credible of these theories are therefore rendered harmless. As the most ardent theorists have pointed out, there is no need for midnight arrests or staged 'accidental' deaths when you are safely lumped into the same crackpot entertainment bracket as tabloid newspapers claiming to find Luftwaffe bombers on the moon.

As popular narratives explaining the often wayward paths of human history, many conspiracy theories make a lot of sense. As historical texts in themselves, they tend to throw up more questions than they answer. Almost inevitably, the Assassin cult of Hasan Sabbah has played a significant part. This besieged and marginalised Muslim sect became, according to popular legend, the allies and confidants of the elite of the Crusader forces during the 12th century.

However unlikely this may seem, there are a number of historical studies which hint at an alliance or at least an understanding between the Assassins and the Knights Templar – a secretive order of warrior monks regarded as the Pope's shock troops, adorned in the white mantle with red cross that still visually represents the Crusades. Their combination of religious mysticism and martial violence may explain how they became conflated in the popular imagination with Muslim suicide squads, who should have been their natural adversaries.

In the Order of the Temple's two-century tenure in the Holy Land, from the 12th to 14th centuries, some claim that the knights of the Order cultivated an altogether more cosmopolitan society than those of their

Crusader contemporaries who returned home (or perished in combat). Inevitably, over a succession of generations, those Crusaders who chose to make their homes in the Holy Lands assimilated some of the local culture, if only by a process of cultural osmosis. For obvious military reasons, much of the castles of the monastic fighting orders were on the frontline between the Islamic inhabitants and Christian conquests. According to conspiracy theorists, the Templars absorbed many of the customs, industry, science and art of both the Islamic and Judaic cultures of the region, which led to radical changes in the Order's secret doctrines. Certainly, the Templar custom of growing beards, like their Muslim foes, and the large number of their brethren fluent in Arabic was the subject of gossip among those less than sympathetic to the Order.

This may explain why, from the days of Arnold of Lubeck and Marco Polo onwards, some historians have speculated that the Order of the Knights Templar and the Order of Assassins came to an early accommodation. It has even been claimed that Richard the Lionheart, royal champion of the Crusades, initially acted as intermediary between the two warrior sects. Another version of the story goes so far as to portray the Templars as wholly modelled on the Assassins, borrowing everything from the ranking system to the uniform colours of Hasan Sabbah's secret society (some claim that Nizari ritual dress consisted of white robes, trimmed with red shoes, sashes or caps). It is certainly true that aspects of the two organisations – secretive initiatory religious orders that relied upon powerful strongholds to exert their influence – offer obvious parallels.

But as the Assassins fade from scholarly history, wiped from the page by the hordes of Genghis Khan, it is the Templars who go down in Western folklore as the shadowy secret society, initiates privy to forbidden knowledge, willing to go to extremes to influence events. As with the Assassins, however, their legend has long outlived the power of the ill-fated Order itself.

The righteous Knights of the Temple, the battle-hardened paladins who fought and often died in the name of Christianity, would be demonised by their own religion in a manner far beyond that suffered by Hasan's order. The destruction of the order – although popular legend insists it survived down the centuries in a number of clandestine forms – can be attributed to the French King Philippe IV, or 'Philip the Fair', as history has christened him.

It is a safe bet that Philip's 'fairness' pertained to his good looks rather than fair-mindedness. Envious of the now-affluent Order to whom he owed money, and who were imperious enough to reject his request to join them, he embarked on a campaign of vilification and revenge.

Accounts and accusations of Templar rituals, which involved stamping or spitting upon the sacred cross and repudiating the name of Christ, would condemn them in the God-fearing culture of the Middle Ages. At best, they were accused of similar heresy to the Cathars – who believed that all matter was sinful and only the spirit was pure – at worst they were condemned as devil-worshippers who adored a mysterious cat, or an entity called Baphomet that appears to have been a severed head. (The name later became most closely associated with depictions of the Devil featuring a goat's head and legs.) The charge sheet was also dominated by accusations of ritualised homosexuality.

From our perspective, one of the more intriguing accusations which led to the downfall of the Templars refutes those theories that suggest the Order was in cahoots with the Assassins. According to this charge, the Grand Master of the Assassins, Sinan, sent a message to the Crusader King of Jerusalem, Amaury I, offering to convert to Christianity. Amaury was overjoyed at the prospect and enthusiastically accepted. The Knights Templar did not share his enthusiasm and ambushed the Assassins on their route home, butchering the Nizari envoy – much to the fury of the King, who apologised to the Assassin Grand Master and had the Templar responsible arrested. However disingenuous the offer of conversion may have been, it still looked bad for the Templar cause in Europe, having violently terminated negotiations with a potential ally who would have been an invaluable addition to the Christian fold.

Some believe the Templars were motivated by naked greed – another charge routinely levelled at the Order in its latter years – as it is said they feared that the new alliance might endanger the annual tribute they received from the Assassins. While the Assassins boosted their exchequer by collecting protection money from neighbouring princes, the Knights Templar did the same to the Assassins – as did the Templars' rival monastic military order, the Hospitallers of the Order of St John. As both the Templars and Hospitallers were ruled by elected Grand Masters, not hereditary rulers, they were not vulnerable to the Nizari threat of assassination. Kill one Grand Master and they will simply elect another, so the Assassins evidently thought it prudent to pay off the most fearsome fighters on the Christian side.

During the Ninth Crusade, Louis IX of France was approached by an Assassin delegation who demanded tribute on behalf of their master. The Grand Masters of the Templar and Hospitaller orders warned them off and the Assassin Grand Master changed tack, instead offering a plethora of gifts to the French monarch. It has also been suggested that the Templars convinced the Grand Master to abort an earlier plot to assassinate Louis. Whatever the true relationship between the Templars and the Assassins, it is clearly more complex than the official version (implacable opponents) or the enduring accusation (covert allies).

How seriously the more colourful charges of Satanism and ritual sex against the Templars should be taken remains a debatable point. They would have been far from the first all-male institution to harbour a gay element, and the denial of certain Christian symbols does not automatically equate with devil-worship. (For example, the Cathars denied the cross because they believed that Jesus, as a being of pure spirit, could not physically have been crucified.) But it is clear that – as their Ismaili defenders would say of the Assassins – Philip IV's religious propaganda campaign against the Templars had made them the stuff of black legend. In March 1314, the Grand Master of the Order, Jacques de Molay, was put to death by slowly roasting over a fire for his supposed blasphemies. And so the Knights Templar, like the Assassins, suddenly vanished from official history. But it is here that the legend truly begins.

De Molay was said to have issued a curse from his dying lips as he was immolated in the flames, that both King Philip and Pope Clement would join him in death within a year. Sure enough, history shows that both were dead of unspecified medical causes in mere months of the Templars' extermination. Adding to their growing myth, a gruesome piece of folklore emanating from the late 12th century was further embellished: according to the newly popular version, a necrophilic nobleman who fathered a magical child by raping the corpse of his dead lover was actually a Templar. (In 20th-century pop culture, the Templars received their ultimate macabre accolade – portrayed as a cult of vampiric walking corpses in the Spanish horror movie series that begins with Amando de Ossorio's *Tombs of the Blind Dead*, 1972.)

But it is in the belief in secret societies – of manipulative elites privy to hidden knowledge – that the legacy of the Knights Templar truly survives. This is verifiable fact, inasmuch as the original structure of the Templars as an elite Catholic brotherhood inspired the formation of the first Freemasonry societies, unified by London's Grand Lodge in 1717. In a sense, the Masons are the classic secret society, deriving their odd Masonic rites (secret handshakes and funny aprons) from the ritual trappings of the Catholic Church – still powerful, but mostly elbowed into second place by Protestant Church-State alliances in Western

Europe after the Reformation. Despite this, lodge membership purportedly has no prescribed theology apart from a devotion to God, the brotherhood (no ladies allowed, I'm afraid, madam) and good works in the community.

In practice, modern Masonic societies seem centrally concerned with offering each other advantages in business – which all seems innocuous enough, though it makes something of a mockery of the idea of a 'free' market. However, high-ranking policemen within the brotherhood have been a thorn in the side of investigative journalists for years. Suggestions that fellow lodge initiates may have less to fear from the law than the vulgar masses are as persistent as they are frequently denied.

But to a certain Western mindset – principally that reared on the Protestant work ethic and the belief that individuals should profit solely from their own efforts – there is something inherently sinister about any group that wilfully sets itself apart and hides itself away from mainstream society.

Eighteenth-century Britain, a hard-drinking libertarian society on the brink of imperial dominance, was overrun with clubs with their own panoply of rituals, ranks and occultic ephemera. It was a golden age for British freemasonry, but there were also exclusive clubs dedicated to everything from political radicalism to farting. In some respects these were manifestations of the intellectual Enlightenment, organisations that fostered free thought and free speech, unfettered by the arcane diktat of outdated ethics and old-fashioned orthodoxies. Inevitably perhaps, those that challenged religious taboos were among the most notorious.

In 1721, King George I issued an edict outlawing those clubs that 'in the most Impious and Blasphemous Manner, insult the most sacred principals of our Holy Religion, Affront Almighty God Himself, and Corrupt the Minds and Morals of one another.'

The undoubted target of the monarch's sanctimonious wrath was the club led by one Philip, Duke of Wharton, a young aristocrat who was as impetuous and volatile as he was talented. His secretive fellowship, which became popularly known as the Hellfire Club, attracted a congregation of society swingers who appear to have engaged in covert blasphemous rites. The extent to which this was a serious anti-religious organisation or simply unholy horseplay remains unclear. But the scandal precipitated the downfall of Wharton, also an active freemason, whose star swiftly fell. He died an effective exile in 1730. However, the enigmatic Hellfire tradition did not die with him and similar impious clubs erupted across the British Isles and Ireland, to the scandal of polite society.

The most notorious was founded by an affable aristocrat named Sir Francis Dashwood. It may or may not have been known as a Hellfire Club, but the members preferred to call themselves the Knights of Saint Francis. They included a roll call of the most talented and privileged rakes of the day, who attended regular secret meetings to indulge in mysterious rites, rumoured to be unholy orgies with prostitutes dressed as nuns. (Their motto was *Fay ce que voudrais* – 'Do as thou wilt', which may carry a faint echo of 'Nothing is true, everything is permitted' for those of a conspiratorial frame of mind.)

Many historians dismiss Sir Francis' occult order as a sort of Georgian Playboy Mansion with playful Pagan overtones, but it included many of the most influential figures in British politics during a pivotal point in world history. Britain's American colonies were approaching open revolt, and many of the politicians who were publicly opposed over how to address the issue were meeting privately at Dashwood's notorious club.

It also welcomed some eminent guests, not least the official representative of the American colonists, Benjamin Franklin. Franklin, an active freemason and later signatory of the Declaration of Independence, was also rumoured to have been involved with a Hellfire Club in his native Pennsylvania. But did his networking play any part in the foundation of the world's most powerful nation? 'If people knew of the role the Hell Fire Club played in Benjamin Franklin's structuring of America, it could suggest changes like: "One nation, under Satan", or "United Satanic America",' according to 20th century occultist Anton LaVey. (As the founder of the Church of Satan, LaVey may be forgiven for a certain bias.) Most find the concept of Benjamin Franklin – his humble portrait enshrined on the hundred-dollar bill – an unfeasible candidate for a disciple of the Devil. As we shall see, however, conspiracy theorists continue to find evidence for their beliefs in the US currency.

Which brings us back to Abbe Barruel, who, among the bewildering network of groups he claimed were plotting the downfall of Christianity, conflated the Assassins with the ubiquitous Illuminati. Formed in 1776, the year of the Declaration of American Independence, by a free-thinking Bavarian theologian named Adam Weishaupt, the organisation's aim was to spread revolutionary thinking among the West's existing Masonic lodges. While it's disputable as to how much revolutionary fervour this may actually have inspired in the world (speculation about the Illuminati's role in the French Revolution seems to be without much foundation), the Illuminati have become a perennial presence in modern-day conspiracy theories.

In the present-day USA, Freemasonry is also conflated in certain mindsets with both the Illuminati and the Knights Templar, all of whom are seen as surviving into modern times in underground cabals, despite whatever the 'official version' says, and as propagating subversive occult doctrine, whatever their Christian origins. Even the dollar bill – an all-American symbol if ever there was one – has been said by ardent conspiracists to contain a portrait of Weishaupt, rather than George Washington, while its emblem of an eye in a pyramidal triangle is purportedly a Masonic/occultist symbol – regarded in much pop culture as the symbol of the Illuminati.

(It actually bears more resemblance to the Eye of Horus, a piece of Ancient Egyptian lore appropriated by Aleister Crowley – which presumably also drags his occult lodge, the Orientalischer Templer Orden, into the whole deal.)

Modern America is the spiritual home of conspiracy theory. While much of its discourse may be marginal, it is *only just* outside the parameters of what it is now accepted truth in popular culture. Its constructed narratives – often inherited, or passed on to, or embellished by, others who think similarly – make sense to the believer of the hidden, secret or occult dynamics of history, and the times that we are living in.

Left-of-centre conspiracists exhibit a fearful distrust of establishment politics that ties together events like the Iran-Contra weapons scandal of the 1980s, the alleged importation of cocaine by the CIA and even the mysterious death of newspaper magnate Robert Maxwell in the early 1990s into one tidy paranoid package. The 'Octopus' conspiracy, as it has become known, places at the centre of all these events the dissemination of computer software by the CIA which ostensibly allows its overseas users to spy on others – while in fact allowing the US intelligence services to keep the software's users under surveillance, extending their tentacles worldwide.

It may seem like a usefully pat scenario, until perhaps we consider the investigative journalists who subscribed to its veracity, all of whom seem to have either died suddenly of unexplained causes or else fled the country. On this basis, jailhouse philosopher Charlie Manson may have been right when, in one of his moments of acute lucidity, he described paranoia as a heightened form of awareness.

More *outré*, perhaps, is the belief that the political elite of the US conduct obscene occult rituals at their annual meetings at Bohemian Grove in Monte Rio, Northern California. Essentially a Masonic lodge whose rituals hark back to Pagan, rather than Catholic, traditions, its membership has included most of the Republican presidents of the past century, and even a few of their Democratic counterparts. It has also become the centre of one of the most extreme but potent conspiracy theories of recent years.

In July 2000, Texan radio personality and documentary maker Alex Jones took covert film of an odd quasi-Masonic ceremony called 'the Cremation of Care'. According to him, the ritual was an 'ancient Canaanite/Luciferian/Babylon mystery religion ceremony', symbolising sacrificial murder. (He also identified the Lodge's emblem, the statue of an owl, as representing Moloch – who was indeed the false god of Middle Eastern Pagans, according to the Old Testament, though he is usually described as a Minotaur entity with the head of a bull.) British journalist Jon Ronson later incorporated Jones' footage into his TV series on conspiracy theories, *Secret Rulers of the World*. Ronson's view was that, while the rite was admittedly bizarre, he perceived nothing inherently satanic or frightening about it.

But the Bohemian Grove conspiracy has become an article of faith among a number of Americans. Some on the left perceive it as evidence of an all-powerful occult cabal containing members of the Republican Party. On the religious right, it is seen as proof that the political establishment are responsible for some of the worst atrocities committed in the USA, allegedly including satanic ritual murder and child abuse.

(It may seem strange that some ultraconservatives should condemn a club belonged to by both the Presidents Bush, senior and junior, but, due to factors like refusing to condemn an openly gay politician among their ranks, there are some who regard the Bushes as just not conservative enough.)

Two years after Jones shot his film, an ex-serviceman named Richard McCaslin was apprehended in the grounds on the dawn of the lodge's annual meeting. While it was believed he had no prior mental health issues, he was carrying enough weapons for a small militia, including an MK1 automatic assault rifle. He had, he said after surrendering, come to kill anyone he believed to be engaging in ritual child abuse.

And at the centre of all this, according to the copious website exposés of the Bohemian Grove conspiracy, are the Illuminati – surviving well into the 21st century, comprising America's political elite and hell-bent on undermining Christianity in the USA.

***

'The secret practices of the Ismailis were *secret!*' asserts Dr Farhad Daftary, spokesman for the Ismaili creed, of the beginnings of the Assassin-Templar legend. 'You do not find these tales in contemporary Muslim sources, who were equally for their own reasons hostile towards the Ismailis, but they never felt the need to explain or to talk about the secret practices. So why did the Crusaders, who remained very ignorant about basic facts of Islam and its subdivisions in terms of various religious communities? In fact they were not even able to identify correctly who the Ismailis were.'

So it is with the modern-day conspiracy theorist. Elaborately imaginative hypotheses are spun around the basis of what is supposed to be hidden, and may never truly come to light. The theories are often constructed purely on the basis of a willingness to believe, with little or no verifiable evidence. But then the world's great religions have very similar foundations.

Ultimately, to the believer, the conspiracy theory closes the gaps in knowledge and understanding, and makes sense of the chaos of existence. It is very easy, perhaps facile, to dismiss the true believer on the basis of a lack of empirical evidence. In the extremely improbable instance that all secrets, all subterranean activity, suddenly became visible to the inquisitive eye, it's likely the reality would be very different from the conspiratorial hypothesis. What is far from certain is that it would be any less frightening. For conspiracies permeate every era of human history, but by their very nature they remain secret, unknowable.

It also raises the basic question of what constitutes a conspiracy. We are all, ultimately, in a minority of one. One man's sinister conspiracy is another's legitimate association of the like-minded. One might easily define civilisation itself as a conspiracy – the imposition of order by a self-appointed elite, employing arbitrary and covert force.

Most conspiracies only appear to be conspiracies from the outside. No sane government or organisation operates with a policy of blanket disclosure, any more than any of us welcome a life devoid of privacy. But then governments throughout history have challenged the rights of their citizens to privacy, whether justified by the activities of al-Qaeda today or by those of the Assassins in the medieval world. Can secrecy be wrong when privacy is a right?

Paranoia-as-a-form-of-awareness is something of a mantra among conspiracy theorists. Statistically speaking, someone out there is out to get each and every one of us. So how do we react? 'They who can give up essential liberty, to obtain a little temporary safety, deserve neither liberty nor safety,' according to Benjamin Franklin, which seems a fine philosophy. But there again, it does come from a member of the Hell Fire Club . . .

XI

THE ASTROLOGER, THE GOLDSMITH
AND THE ALCHEMIST

Much of what we think we know about the Assassins in the West comes from the sect's interaction with the Crusader states in Syria. While the title or nickname of the 'Old Man of the Mountain' is routinely employed to describe Hasan Sabbah, it also refers to Rashid al-din Sinan, Grand Master of the Syrian Assassins. It is also almost certainly a mistranslation of 'Sheikh al-Jabal' that confuses the Arabic 'sheikh' – which means a tribal elder – with the term 'old man'.

When Hasan II despatched Sinan west from Alamut in 1162 it was not simply as a reliable religious representative to impose his new doctrine of the Resurrection on the sect's western territories. Hasan clearly felt the Syrian Assassins required some inspirational new leadership, and Sinan was the man for the job.

Syria must have looked like a promising prospect when Hasan Sabbah first sent his missionaries and Assassins about 60 years earlier. It had many similarities to his Persian field of operations, where the Assassins enjoyed notable success. Like Persia, Syria was characterised by plains broken up by inhospitable mountain ranges which encouraged a number of religious and political dissidents to take shelter there, making for an unruly and independent-minded population.

If anything, Syria's power structure was even more brittle than that of Persia, as it represented the frontline between the Seljuq Sultanate and Fatimid Caliphate, and was still reeling under the hammer blow of the Crusader invasion. However, Hasan Sabbah's agents met stiffer resistance in Syria than Persia, most likely because their appeal to Persian nationalism could be a liability in a primarily Arabic region. For some reason, the Syrian Assassins would also follow a subtly different stratagem to their Persian counterparts, favouring infiltrating cities over capturing easily defended strongholds.

The Assassins' earliest conflicts swiftly involved them in the complex and volatile politics of the region. It was these aspects that may have made it an easy target for the Christian invaders, with feuds and follies frequently taking precedence over wider interests. The situation of the time reads like a tale taken straight from *The Thousand and One Nights*: At the time of the First Crusade, Syria was dominated by two fortified cities, Aleppo and Damascus, ruled over by the brothers Ridwan and Duqaq. But fraternal feeling was in notably short supply. In the chronicles of the day, Ridwan reads like a pantomime villain from a particularly grim production of *Aladdin*. Small, slender and severe, he was an unsettling presence who dabbled in witchcraft. When he ascended to the throne of Aleppo in 1095, he had two of his younger brothers strangled. Only Duqaq escaped, taking refuge in Damascus where the garrison offered him the crown. In his way, Duqaq was almost as bizarre as his older brother – an impetuous, shrill, fragile young man with an explosive temper. He was also understandably somewhat paranoid.

Ridwan was happy to do anything he could to feed that paranoia, including inviting the newly arrived Assassins to make their home in Aleppo. They were led by a Persian Nizari who they referred to as the Physician-Astrologer – the two trades were not unrelated in those days – though whether this reflected his cover story or his original calling is unclear.

Welcoming such heretics within the city walls was a deeply unpopular decision among Aleppo's population, but Ridwan did not regard rulership as a popularity contest. If anything, he appeared to collect enemies, such as Janah al-Dawla, ruler of the city of Homs. Janah had once been Ridwan's guardian, and was now well-regarded as one of the few Muslim leaders to forsake local squabbles in order to mount an effective resistance to Crusader expansion. Ridwan hated him.

The opportunity to use the great city of Aleppo as a base was too good an opportunity to pass over. The Physician-Astrologer thanked his host in the only way he knew how. The Arabic chronicler Ibn al-Qalanasi describes the scene as the ruler of Homs attended the city's mosque on 1 May 1103,

> 'surrounded by his principal officers with full armour, and occupying his place of prayer according to custom, [Janah] was set upon by three Persians belonging to the Batiniya [Nizari heretics]. They were accompanied by a sheikh, to whom they

owed allegiance and obedience, and all of them were dressed in the garb of ascetics. When the sheikh gave the signal they attacked the emir with their knives and killed both him and a number of his officers.'

The sheikh was almost certainly the Physician-Astrologer. The murder had its desired effect – many of Janah's supporters fled the city, creating a power vacuum in Homs, though it also dealt a blow to any co-ordinated Muslim response to the Crusade.

It was the first example of an Assassin's blade coincidentally serving the Crusader cause, but it would be far from the last. It is easy to see how some might infer a clandestine understanding between the Nizaris and the European invaders under such circumstances.

Like modern terrorist groups, the Nizari revolutionaries required chaos to survive, and anything that maintained a state of conflict at the expense of their established rivals furthered their cause. The assassination of the Emir of Homs also cemented their relationship with Ridwan. Though the Physician-Astrologer himself died shortly afterwards, his successor, Abu Tahir (known as the Goldsmith), was welcomed with open arms by the ruler of Aleppo, if not by his subjects. Chroniclers of the day claim that Nizaris began to infest Aleppan society at every level with their host's blessing. From their new Syrian base of operations, the Goldsmith set about establishing Assassin bases in suitable nearby strongholds, settling upon the castle of Afamiya. Afamiya had been taken from Ridwan by an Ismaili loyal to the Fatimids named Khalaf, and seemed to be an ideal target. The ensuing drama would lead to the first significant contact between the Assassins and the European invaders.

***

Abu Tahir spent months preparing the expedition. First, missionaries were sent to the districts surrounding Afamiya, probing for weaknesses, preaching the gospel of Hasan Sabbah and soliciting support among the surrounding tribes. His agents told him that Khalaf was an impudent, conceited ruler who enjoyed little affection from his own people; that he was a proud lord, a brigand who revelled in plunder and pleasure but had little time for either religion or his people. The Goldsmith saw that the circumstances were ideal to plan his strike, and sent word to his missionaries to prepare all fresh converts for action, as Khalaf was soon to become another sacred victim in the cause of their Grand Master. Preparations were quietly made in Aleppo for the campaign and a force assembled, but this was no invading army of thousands. Six men walked out of the gates leading a horse and a mule, the latter carrying upon its back the arms and armour of a Crusader which the Goldsmith had bought from an Aleppan merchant.

The small group wended their way to the gates of Afamiya, cogs in a plan which they were resolved to carry out or else die trying. Everything happened as Abu Tahir had told them it would. As they approached the towering walls of Afamiya, the sun was dipping beneath the distant mountains and the gates were closed. A sentry hailed them from the walls. 'Who approaches?'

'We have come here to enter your master's service,' responded the Nizari who strode to the front, Abu'l-Fath. 'We found a Frankish knight and killed him, and we have brought you his horse, mule and armour.' The Assassin waved his arm to indicate the two beasts behind him, burdened with Christian steel. While a quartet of guards remained on the walls overlooking them, one disappeared. The six Nizari agents waited in the fading light as the gates slowly creaked open.

Again, it was just as the Goldsmith had predicted. The six men were greeted as conquering heroes by the garrulous Khalaf, who insisted that they eat with him that evening. They feasted that night with the commander of Afamiya, a battle-scarred bear of a man, who wanted to know where they had come from, how they had heard of him, and – in particular – how they had bested the Christian devil. The Assassins gave their carefully rehearsed replies, calculated to flatter their effusive host.

Curiosity about the fearsome Christian invaders burned in many hearts. Who were these fierce strangers, with their golden hair and pink complexions? Barbarians? Cannibals? Ogres? Hate and fear gave any account of these foreign monsters a special fascination.

The trophies taken from a slain infidel clearly delighted Khalaf. How could he reward such valiant warriors, wondered the warlord, clasping two of them in his arms, as morning approached. With feigned reluctance, Abu'l-Fath finally suggested that perhaps they might be permitted a house within the walls. 'Choose it, and it is yours,' laughed Khalaf, the words that sealed his fate.

The Assassins selected a humble dwelling that backed onto the castle walls. In the following days they began industriously chipping at the mortar that held together the stones of the outer wall with tools they had brought with them from Aleppo. Eventually their labours bore fruit, and they loosened enough masonry to chisel an inobtrusive portal to the outside world.

Abu'l-Fath slipped through the gap under cover of darkness, to contact the Assassin missionaries hiding in nearby villages. A host was assembled of tribesmen newly converted to the Nizari faith, armed with swords and spears. In the small hours of the morning they filed silently towards moonlit Afamiyah, guided wordlessly to the tiny gap in the walls by Abu. One by one they slipped through, where the waiting Assassins directed them in threes and fours to where the castle's sentries might be found, as an orgy of butchery began.

The first scream that tears the night makes Khalaf start in his sleep; he rolls over, shakes his head, then struggles to his feet as he sees a figure looming in the doorway. 'Who dares enter my private chamber?' he roars, his voice betraying both rage and fear. As his eyes adjust, he identifies his intruder as Abu'l-Fath, with three other erstwhile guests filing in behind him. All four have daggers drawn.

'We have come to take possession of this castle in the name of our Lord Abu Tahir,' announces Abu, as calmly as if he were discussing the weather.

Khalaf fumbles by his bed for a weapon, calling for his guards. But his guards are dead, and his hand finds the hilt of a knife too late. Abu bears down upon the big man, burying his own blade with practised precision into his target's soft gut. Adrenaline and warrior instincts kick in as Khalaf manages to shoulder his assailant to the ground; with blood pouring down his legs he runs for the door to the tower. But he's not quick enough, and another Assassin intercepts him with a knife blow to the kidney. It sends Khalaf tumbling to the cushioned floor, a giant halo of crimson growing around his twitching form.

By the time the sun rises over Afamiyah, it is in the hands of the Assassins.

***

When word reached Abu Tahir of the conquest he was overjoyed, immediately relocating the Syrian Nizari nerve centre to Afamiyah. It may have been premature, as he was not the only local leader who had cast an acquisitive eye over the castle. Shortly after the Syrian Assassins took possession, they experienced their first encounter with the Christian invaders, in the shape of an army led by a knight named Tancred – a burly figure, not without charm, but with a strong ruthless streak. Tancred had led the successful Crusader assault on Jerusalem seven years before, for which he was rewarded with the Principality of Galilee, and had been expanding his territory ever since.

When he reached the walls of Afamiyah, Tancred introduced the defenders to an Assassin he had captured – Abu'l-Fath's brother. He offered to exchange his captive's life and retreat peacefully in exchange for a hefty amount of gold, in the first of many examples of bribery replacing conflict in relations between the Nizaris and the European invaders.

A panicked Abu Tahir agreed, as it dawned on him that the castle was ill-equipped to resist a prolonged siege by a determined foe. Tancred's first expedition seems to have been a reconnaissance mission, for just months later he was back and this time he would not settle for protection money. The Goldsmith was obliged to offer an unconditional surrender, ceding the castle and all of its wealth to Tancred. In exchange they were allowed to return to Aleppo with their tails between their legs, with one exception. Tancred was courting the good favour of Khalaf's brother, and so the Assassin Abu'l-Fath was tortured to death.

The situation in Aleppo was tense. After being soundly defeated by Tancred at the Battle of Artah in 1105, Ridwan also found himself paying protection money to the fearsome Crusader, sending him an annual tribute of 20,000 dinars and ten of his finest horses. This, in turn, was exacted from Aleppo's hard-pressed taxpayers, who were becoming increasingly incensed by the steady tide of Muslim refugees arriving in the city with tales of Crusader atrocities. The only cheering news for Ridwan was that his hated brother Duqaq had died of disease in 1104, after a series of his own humiliating defeats at the hands of the European invaders. His place was taken by Tughtigin, who deposed Duqaq's heir in a palace coup.

The Aleppan attitude to the Assassin presence in their city had not softened, while the Nizaris responded in their habitual fashion of silencing their most vocal critics with a knife blade. Resentment simmered and increasingly boiled over into vigilante action directed at the unwelcome guests. Meanwhile, Abu Tahir's attempts to secure another fortress as a refuge for the sect in Syria met with mixed success at best.

The parlous situation in Syria, where the Crusaders appeared to be expanding their realm unchecked, had not gone unnoticed in the Seljuq capital of Baghdad. Sultan Muhammad was still, in theory, ruler of the entire sultanate, but in practice many local leaders paid him no heed unless it suited them. A holy war against the fledgling Crusader kingdoms would not only address the threat of the Christian cuckoos in the Palestinian nest, but give him a chance to reassert his authority over the Muslim leaders of neighbouring Syria, such as Ridwan.

The Sultan appointed a seasoned commander named Mawdud to lead the jihad, who was then Governor of Mosul, a city he had captured for the Sultan in 1109. Mawdud began his campaign in 1110, with an army composed of contingents from several local Muslim leaders, and led sorties deep into Crusader territory. The following year he arrived at the walls of Aleppo where, much to his chagrin, Ridwan forbade him entrance. The Damascan ruler Tughtigin proved more hospitable, and joined the jihad in its third year. The tide appeared to be turning as the combined forces of Mawdud and Tughtigin defeated the Crusader King of Jerusalem, Baldwin I, at the Battle of Al-Sannabra. But, before the Saracens could press their advantage, disaster struck in the streets of Damascus, just outside the Umayyad Mosque.

'When the prayer was over and Mawdud had performed several supplementary devotions, they both departed, Tughtigin walking ahead out of respect for the emir,' reports one Arabic chronicler, quoted in Amin Maalouf's *The Crusades through Arab Eyes.*

'They were surrounded by soldiers, guards, and militiamen bearing arms of all varieties; the slender sabres, sharp épées, scimitars, and unsheathed daggers gave an impression of thick undergrowth. All around them, crowds pressed forward to admire their arsenal and their magnificence. When they reached the courtyard of the mosque, a man emerged from the crowd and approached the emir Mawdud as if to pray to God on his behalf and to ask alms of him. Suddenly he seized the belt of his mantle and struck him twice with his dagger, just above the navel. The *atabeg* [governor] Tughtigin took a few steps backwards, and his companions quickly surrounded him. As for Mawdud, who never lost his head, he walked as far as the north gate of the mosque and then collapsed. A surgeon was summoned and managed to suture some of the wounds, but the emir died several hours later, may God have mercy upon him!

'The murder stopped the jihad in its tracks. There are no prizes for guessing who was in the frame for killing the Seljuq general, as it was a classic Assassin hit. But it was not so clear who might have put them up to it. Tughtigin lost no time in identifying Ridwan as principal author of the atrocity. It is an indication of the complexity of the corrupt politics of the day that not everybody bought this story. Some whispered that Tughtigin himself had orchestrated the assassination of his erstwhile comrade-in-arms, to protect Damascus from domination by the Sultan. Subsequent events suggest this may not be too far-fetched. Baldwin I sent Tughtigin a message that suggests he shared these suspicions, simply reading, "A nation that kills its leaders in the house of its God deserves to be annihilated."'

Regardless of who was responsible, the Assassins had little time in which to feel satisfied at their audacious act. Before the end of the year their Aleppan protector, Ridwan, fell ill and died, and their precarious position in the city looked worryingly exposed.

Ridwan's successor, Arp Arslan, was a chip off the old block, a teenager with a stutter who some have depicted as something of an Arabic Caligula, opening his reign with a programme of executions. He initially followed his father's policy regarding the city's Nizari contingent, but, after he received a message from Sultan Muhammad urging him to exterminate them, he began arresting the heretics. Angry mobs formed in the streets of Aleppo to hunt down the unwelcome guests, in scenes that recalled the bloody purge of the Assassins in Isfahan twelve years earlier. Many were lynched, others threw themselves from the city walls rather than be torn apart by the enraged Aleppans. A few Assassins were spared by sympathetic neighbours, and a number escaped. Abu Tahir was not among them. Those who survived the brutal pogrom scattered — many, it was said, to Crusader territories.

A new Grand Master was duly despatched from Alamut, named Bahram, who was known for his obsessive secrecy, maintaining a notably low profile even by Assassin standards. He offered a deal to Tughtigin similar to that which his predecessor had enjoyed with Ridwan, and the Assassins were soon installed in Damascus, much to the dismay of its citizens. Their new host even offered the Nizaris an official embassy, which some sources describe as a palace.

From there Bahram continued his predecessor's policies of attempting to acquire isolated fortresses to act as strongholds for the sect, while employing the knife to eliminate or intimidate their most influential opponents. Meanwhile, Sultan Muhammad, understandably dissatisfied by the outcome of his first jihad, raised another mighty army to march against the infidel.

This time they encountered an even more dispiriting response from the Muslim princes they proposed to liberate from the Crusader threat. Once they reached Syria, the Sultan's army was confronted by a combined force consisting not only of Crusaders but Saracen troops from Aleppo and Damascus, and even a contingent of Assassins. Stalemate ensued, until their commander despaired of ever imposing the Sultan's authority over such a treacherous land.

It is said that Muhammad washed his hands of the whole affair in disgust, at this point. If Damascus and Aleppo would rather ally with infidels and heretics than risk acknowledging him as overlord, then to hell with them! Meanwhile, the man believed to be the ringleader of the massacre at Aleppo received Assassin's justice, butchered with his two sons as he crossed the River Euphrates.

As the presence of Assassin troops in the host that repelled the Sultan's jihad suggests, the Nizari presence was now sufficiently solid to try to advance the cause militarily. However, pitched battle was never the sect's strong suit, and in 1128 the elusive Bahram was killed in a skirmish with a neighbouring tribe, enraged by the assassination of one of their chieftains. As a brutal reminder that the Assassins faced bitter opposition not just from the Seljuqs to the north, but also from the fading Fatimid Caliphate to the south, Bahram's ceremonial ring, head and hands were hacked off and despatched as a gift to the delighted Caliph in Cairo. The Nizaris responded by assassinating the Caliph two years later.

The year 1128 was notably ill-starred for the Syrian Nizaris. It was the year Tughtigin expired. In a repeat of the Aleppo massacre of fifteen years before, after a brief interlude, the wrath of the Damascan populace was unleashed upon the city's heretic population. The resultant carnage was even more intense, with thousands – some Arabic commentators improbably claim tens of thousands – murdered in one awful night, and by the morning, 'the dogs were yelping and quarrelling over their limbs and corpses.' To cap this obscene episode, those regarded as the foremost Assassins were dragged onto the city battlements and crucified, as macabre testament to what most Muslims felt about the heretics in their midst.

Bahram's successor, Ismail, was not among them. At the time he was safely ensconced in Banyas, one of the fortresses the sect had successfully captured. Tughtigin's successor, Buri, who was responsible for the massacre of the Assassins, was more than a little nervous, and took to travelling everywhere in armour, surrounded by a heavily armed escort. It was to no avail. He was duly attacked by two Assassins and wounded in the neck and hip. He survived the assault but died within a year, when the wound on his hip reopened and became infected.

It was perhaps an indication of the waning vigour of the Syrian Nizaris that these killers were despatched from the sect's Persian HQ of Alamut. Ismail proved a less than inspirational leader. He despaired of the defence of Banyas and gave it to the Crusaders, retiring to Crusader territory where he suffered an ignominious end, expiring of dysentery in 1130. The sect was quite clearly in crisis, requiring a change of policy and an infusion of new ideas if it was to survive in the brutal arena of Syria.

In the ensuing decades the Assassins shifted their focus, from the power politics surrounding the opulent city states of Damascus and Aleppo to the inhospitable mountains dividing central Syria. They had allowed themselves to become too comfortable, and it was time to get back to their roots. A period of quiet consolidation followed, where Syrian Grand

Masters carefully eschewed the sinister flamboyance of their predecessors in favour of patiently acquiring castles that were easily defensible and set in inaccessible locations, rather than possessing any obvious tactical significance.

Using subversion, coercion, force and simple purchase, the Assassins regrouped in locales where they were less likely to attract the attention of the region's major powers. Their most significant acquisition was the capture of the formidable fortress of Masyaf in 1141. Masyaf would become Syria's equivalent of the legendary Alamut, an unassailable bolthole in which Assassins could be trained and dispatched to promote the cause, an imposing stone symbol of Nizari power in the region. But now that Syria had its Alamut it also required its own answer to Hasan Sabbah to preside over it. He arrived in the shape of Grand Master Hasan II's childhood friend, Rashid al-Din Sinan, who reached the region in 1162.

Sinan had arrived in an ambivalent capacity. He appears to have been principally entrusted with announcing Hasan II's new Resurrection doctrine to the sect's Syrian communities, but was almost certainly also there as a troubleshooter. Just as the Seljuq Sultans experienced problems maintaining control over their supposed underlings, so the large distances and hostile territory that divided Alamut from Masyaf invited dangerously independent thinking. When Sinan arrived in Syria the Assassin leadership was fast approaching crisis point. After Grand Master Abu Muhammad died he was succeeded by a candidate named Masud, without any consultation with Alamut. Masud was duly stabbed while getting out of the bath, in a conspiracy involving Abu Muhammad's nephew.

It is here that Sinan appears to have taken charge. Speaking with the authority of Alamut, he had Abu Muhammad's nephew executed but pardoned the other conspirators. He then took the reins of power and announced the Resurrection, condemning all outsiders as the walking dead and absolving the faithful from the bondage of Sharia law. Orthodox Muslims in the surrounding area were horrified, some insisting that the doctrine sanctioned unbridled sexual licence and deified Sinan as a god, but, as in Persia, the Assassins themselves appeared to accept the Resurrection with little resistance.

Sinan was a leader of great charisma, intellect and vitality whose achievements rival those of the sect's founder. Like Hasan Sabbah, he set about fortifying the castles that the Assassins already possessed with great vigour. But Sinan faced different challenges and needed to adopt different strategies if he was to wage an effective asymmetric war in late 12th-century Syria. The volatile, fragmentary political situation needed to be exploited successfully if the Nizaris were to thrive among so many powerful enemies. For, as Sinan entered the arena, the political map was in a state of violent flux.

The Seljuq Syrian territories had fallen under the rule of the Zangids, a Turkish Sunni dynasty who were pursuing the kind of vigorous war against the Crusaders that had previously been so conspicuous by its absence.

Their current leader, Nur al-Din (later known in the West as Nureddin), had ambitions of uniting all of Islam beneath his banner and driving the infidels into the sea. Faced with such an implacable and able opponent, the Crusader warlords despaired of expanding north or east and their acquisitive eyes turned south to the wealthy Fatimid Caliphate, now decadent and unstable, a fruit ripe for the plucking. But Nur al-Din had come to much the same conclusion, and the 1160s saw a military game of cat and mouse between the Zangid and Crusader forces, struggling for control of Egypt. Nur al-Din's general, Shirkuh, ultimately prevailed, delivering a stinging defeat to his Christian rivals and entering Cairo in triumph in 1169. He then promptly died. The man appointed as his successor as Governor of Egypt was his nephew, the young Saladin.

At this time, Richard, heir to the English throne, was barely five years old. In the ensuing years, Saladin would emerge from beneath Nur al-Din's shadow to become the champion of Islam (or at least Sunni Islam), while Richard would take up the cross to become history's most famous Crusader King. The clash between these two larger-than-life monarchs would come to embody the Saracen-Crusader conflict in Western legend, symbolised as a duel between two legendary warlords.

In this over-simplified picture, Sinan lurks in the background, a shadowy presence that touched the life of both men, a master manipulator – even, some said, a magician – who influenced events with his own subtle sorcery. In the ongoing quest to unify Islam, Saladin encountered the Assassins long before Richard first set foot on Middle Eastern soil in 1191. But Sinan was far from inclined to bow beneath Saladin's banner of a unified Muslim world. One of Saladin's first acts upon taking control of Egypt had been to suppress Ismaili worship in Egypt, executing the Fatimid Caliph. While the Assassins had been no friends of the Cairo Caliphate, Sinan had no wish to join the Caliph as a victim of this dynamic new Sunni champion of orthodoxy.

Saladin's former master, Nur al-Din, died in 1174, clearing the way for his upstart protégé to make a play for power. Saladin did so with a combination of diplomatic finesse, apparently sincere piety and military genius that left most of his opponents struggling for a response. But not the wily Sinan, who proved a worthy opponent. The Assassin leader set about establishing a network of alliances designed to fortify his precarious kingdom, establishing links with the embattled Crusader states and Zangid rebels in Aleppo and elsewhere. Sinan also needed to thwart any attempt to re-establish the unified Sunni Sultanate, shattered by his spiritual forefather Hasan Sabbah's murder of Nizam al-Mulk, the sect's first assassination. In short, Saladin had to die. It was time for Sinan's Assassins to do what they did best.

As described in Chapter One, Saladin survived three assassination attempts, the last of which occurred when the Saracen leader finally decided to attack the problem at its source and besiege Sinan's headquarters at Masyaf. Saladin would abandon the siege under mysterious circumstances in 1176. Some Ismaili historians suggest this reflected not only the leader's unwillingness to live under the constant threat of an Assassin's dagger, but an impressive display of sorcerous power on Sinan's part. Less fanciful accounts suggest successful mediation between the two leaders by interested parties, while military historians point out that Saladin had other fish to fry, with fresh Crusader aggression demanding his urgent attention. But the fact remains that Saladin – a devout Sunni – thereafter left the heretical Assassins in peace.

Sinan has been the subject of numerous tales that depict him as an accomplished sorcerer. Dubious accounts of conjuring tricks involving fake severed heads aside, there is little of biographical note to identify the ascetic Hasan Sabbah as educated in the occult arts. But 'occult' is a very flexible term. It literally means 'hidden' and most of the Assassins' world could be filed under such an adjective. Astrology and numerology – the occult properties of numbers – almost certainly figured in Assassin doctrine. The number seven was of special significance, as another name for the Ismailis was the Seveners – a reference to the sect's view of the order of sacred succession from Muhammad, successive prophets occurring in cycles of seven. The Assassins are also supposed to have had seven ranks, and the celebrations following a successful assassination are invariably described as occupying seven days and seven nights. Yet such numerological observances or superstitions scarcely qualify for the more colourful images popularly associated with occultism.

Sinan, however, has enough of a reputation to place him among the motley ranks of history's occult masters. When Crusader chroniclers describe the Old Man of the Mountain employing witchcraft to mesmerise his followers, they are unquestionably referring to Sinan.

Aside from the disappearing acts, spells to immobilise his opponents and astral projections recounted in Nizari accounts of Sinan's response to Saladin's siege of Masyaf, other stories suggest the Syrian Grand Master had a habit of answering questions that people passing beneath his window had only thought. Intriguing tales of Sinan addressing animals as if they were reincarnated people – he identifies a bird as Hasan Sabbah, a snake as a dead traitor to the sect – suggest the doctrine of transmigration of souls, reincarnation of a dead spirit passing into a living body. This is not part of any orthodox Islamic creed, but certain sources claim it as a feature of Assassin heresy. As one medieval Christian chronicler observed, it may also offer an alternative explanation as to why the Assassins were willing to undertake suicide missions. If a noble death leads to reincarnation at an elevated rank, it represents a powerful incentive to die in the service of your spiritual superiors.

Back in the pragmatic realms of Sinan's struggle to survive, some have suggested the Syrian Grand Master's popularity started to strain relations with his theoretical superior in Persia, particularly after his boyhood friend, Hasan II, died in 1166. Others suggest Sinan began operating an independent policy to that of Alamut, and that Hasan II's successor, Muhammad II, despatched Assassins to cut short his reign.

If so, they were unsuccessful. Sinan's ability to survive in such circumstances, while also keeping Saladin and the Crusaders at bay, was remarkable. He seldom used assassination against the Crusaders themselves, preferring diplomacy or other avenues. For successfully infiltrating a Christian environment would prove far more of a challenge for his Arabic and Persian Assassins than a more familiar Muslim equivalent. The exception that proved the rule – the assassination of Raymond, Count of Tripoli, which happened for reasons unknown a decade before Sinan reached the region – had far-reaching repercussions for all parties.

The immediate Christian reaction to the murder was a riot, where every non-European who could be found by the citizens of Tripoli was seized and killed. The implacable Knights Templar mounted a more calculated response, launching raiding parties from their castles into Nizari territory, raising hell in reprisal for the murder. The Assassins were no match for the elite corps of the Crusaders in open battle, and quickly offered to pay an annual sum of 2,000 dinars to their Templar neighbours by way of compensation. As to why the Templars deserved compensation for the death of the Count of Tripoli, some Christian commentators believe that it confirms the Order's reputation as cynical and grasping.

The ease with which the supposedly inflexible champions of Christian orthodoxy made peace with their heathen foes also damaged their image, fuelling the rumours that suggest the Knights enjoyed a secret alliance with the Assassins.

After capturing Egypt Saladin's forces had marched northward, carrying everything before them. They had soon engulfed Damascus and Aleppo, and it was during this Syrian campaign that Sinan sent his Assassins on the three unsuccessful attempts to kill Saladin described in Chapter One. The surprise accord between the two leaders in 1176 represented a huge relief for the Syrian Nizaris and a nightmare scenario for the embattled Crusader states. Saladin began closing a vice on the infidel territory, squeezing them from both sides with the immediate aim of recapturing Jerusalem, ultimately wiping the Crusader principalities off the map of the Middle East.

The bigger picture was reflected in microcosm on the plains of Hattin in the summer of 1187, near an extinct volcano now located in modern-day Israel. The Crusaders had pooled all of their forces in a bid to deliver a knockout blow to the Saracens, effectively betting everything on one roll of the dice. It came up snake-eyes for the Christians on that burning hot July day, as they were brilliantly outmanoeuvred by a Muslim foe who concentrated on denying his opponents access to fresh water. By the morning of the battle, many of the Christian soldiers were literally dying of thirst. They could see fresh water at the bottom of the hill on which they were encamped, and so a desperate *ad hoc* downhill charge began into the Saracen ranks. Despite fighting bravely, the demoralised, dehydrated Crusader force was doomed. The defeat broke the back of Christian military power in the Middle East and opened the way to Jerusalem, which Saladin took just months later after a short siege. At this point he seemed unstoppable but success appears to have encouraged a little complacency in Saladin, while in far-off Europe the fall of Jerusalem galvanised righteous zeal in many a Christian heart. A new Crusade would soon be afoot.

Saladin had assumed the remainder of his campaign would prove little more than a mopping-up operation. He turned his attention to besieging the port of Tyre, which had welcomed many of the survivors of the disaster at Hattin. While its situation made Tyre easy to defend, the defenders' morale was broken and its disheartened leaders were preparing to surrender. The arrival of an obscure Italian noble named Conrad of Montferrat changed everything. A colourful character and able warlord, Arabic chroniclers described Conrad with begrudging respect as, 'a devil incarnate in his ability to govern and defend a town, and a man of extraordinary courage'. He made his name in the defence of Tyre, reinvigorating the garrison and organising a fightback, successfully crippling Saladin's inadequate navy. By 1189, the Crusader forces had regrouped and surrounded the port of Acre, which Saladin had captured from the Christians just two years before.

Saladin's army arrived to surround the besiegers, creating a siege within a siege, but reinforcements were arriving from Europe all the time. This co-ordinated effort to retake Jerusalem was later referred to as the Third Crusade, led by the English king Richard the Lionheart and his French counterpart and rival Philip II. It was significant that they crusaded together, as if only one had gone forth the other may have taken advantage of his absence to invade his opposite number's realm. For the Christian forces in the Middle East were just as prone to internecine fighting as their Muslim opponents, as future events would soon demonstrate.

A third junior partner came in the shape of Leopold of Austria, a cousin of Conrad of Montferrat standing in for the Holy Roman Emperor's brother, who had drowned en route. When the Crusaders finally prevailed over Saladin's relief force, Conrad placed his cousin's banner over the walls alongside those of Richard and Philip. Richard gave a classic demonstration of his fiery temper when he contemptuously tore it down – a ducal banner had no place alongside the royal standards of England and France. It was a petulant episode that would ultimately cost him dear.

Under the vociferous command of King Richard, the Crusaders once more began to turn the tide. He delivered a body blow to Saladin at the battle of Arsuf in September of 1191, giving a virtuoso display of the Crusaders' mounted charge and earning Saladin's respect. A series of negotiations and exchanges ensued, with displays of chivalric sentiment between the two contrasting sharply with their ruthlessness on the battlefield.

Perhaps the most bizarre proposal was that Saladin's brother should marry Richard's sister, sharing the crown of Jerusalem. Much to Richard's surprise, Saladin agreed, but Richard deferred, saying his sister had point-blank refused to contemplate wedding a Muslim. Questions over the crown of Jerusalem threatened to aggravate rivalries in the Christian camp, as two competing candidates for the position emerged. It was a moot point – there was no Christian kingdom of Jerusalem to speak of – but the issue brought tensions to a head, which the wily Sinan identified as an ideal opportunity for the Assassins to ferment turmoil in the region.

Richard's favoured candidate was Guy of Lusignan, but everybody else thought Guy had forfeited any right to rule after a disastrous performance at Hattin and losing Jerusalem to Saladin. Conrad of Montferrat was still the hero of the hour but no friend of Richard's. As Conrad was a relative of both Leopold of Austria and Philip II of France, however, the English King was obliged to reluctantly concede. But Conrad was only able to enjoy his new status for four short days, before a duo of Assassins dressed as monks fell upon him in Tyre. There are conflicting versions of events, but one suggests that an Assassin was captured and, under torture, confessed that King Richard had commissioned Sinan to order the assassination.

Other theories said that Saladin – anxious to eliminate a Crusader commander – had entreated Sinan, also requesting the murder of Richard who would prove too difficult a target. In reality, it's likely that Sinan had ordered the murder of his own volition – in revenge perhaps for Conrad's casual murder of the crew of a Nizari ship – though the possibility of causing chaos among his rivals always appealed. By both assassinating a rival and using the murder to sow dissent among his enemies, Sinan killed two birds with one stone.

By the autumn of 1192 time was running out for Richard, and Saladin knew it. King Philip of France had headed home over a year before; it piled on the pressure for the English monarch to secure his own kingdom, amplified by daily reports from London entreating his return, warning that his younger brother, John, was plotting against him. Without ever seeing Jerusalem, Richard was obliged to sign a humiliating treaty with Saladin before setting sail for Europe. He was apprehended while crossing the lands of Leopold of Austria, who remembered his humiliation on the battlements of Acre with stinging rage and imprisoned Richard under the charge of commissioning the murder of his cousin, Conrad of Montferrat. It would be well over a year before Richard successfully secured his release, at a price in gold that practically bankrupted England. Meanwhile Saladin, his health failing, died of a fever soon after Richard's departure, with many honours to his name but his ultimate goal unfulfilled.

Sinan died around the same time, and could also look back over his life with a mixture of pride and disappointment. He had steered the Syrian Nizaris through difficult times, facing two of the medieval era's most fearsome warlords, perhaps even making covert alliances with them both. But the Assassins were still effective outcasts, pariahs who existed on a knife edge. Saladin had not ultimately achieved his aim of uniting

Islam under a Sunni banner, but his efforts had demonstrated that such a thing was possible.

If a subsequent ruler was able to achieve this dream, the Assassins would be back where they started a century before. Without an inspirational leader like Hasan Sabbah their days would surely be numbered. But there was cause for cautious optimism. In the wake of Saladin's death his empire was caught up in the inevitable succession struggles, while the new Grand Master successfully agreed a pact with Conrad of Montferrat's successor, Henry of Champagne.

But a storm was slowly building in the Far East of such unparalleled violence that, in retrospect, no preparation for its advent seems adequate.

XII

FROM ALAMUT TO MANCHURIA

If drugs were used to programme an Assassin to kill, that was only part of the homicidal equation. As we have seen, whether in fact or myth, hashish was a component part of a watershed experience which would be recalled whenever the agent was required to sacrifice his life, or the life of another, for the greater good of the Ismaili creed. The memory of Paradise was a trigger, a mnemonic to holy murder. It is a pattern of motivation and control that many tried to re-interpret or replicate throughout the 20th century, in their attempts to describe or to initiate the perfectly wound-up clockwork killer. On our side of the millennial divide, there are many who believe that they succeeded.

To those with any working knowledge of the traditions associated with drug use, the idea that a chemical substance alone could be an agent of mind control was always a dicey proposition. This is demonstrated by the charismatic pastor of an American religious sect, who made an altogether more prosaic use of drugs.

In the 1950s, James Warren Jones had been a young ideological socialist and opponent of racial segregation in his native Indiana. Relocated to San Francisco in the 1960s, he embarked on a wilfully provocative campaign to rid California of the last vestiges of segregationist bigotry. As the Revd Jim Jones he also founded his People's Temple, an avowedly communistic Christian sect that took its inspiration as much from Karl Marx – that old materialist denouncer of religion as 'the opium of the people' – as from the Gospels.

It was a courageously radical theology, particularly in the great nation that continues to insist that Jesus – the heretic lay rabbi who insisted his followers give up all worldly possessions – was some kind of prophet of free enterprise and private property. With his open-doors policy toward the African-American dispossessed and the white poor of Northern California, he also drew support from such liberal sources as Jerry Brown,

Governor of California, and Harvey Milk, the now iconic gay Mayor of San Francisco who was assassinated by a colleague and who, even towards the end of Jones' apocalyptic ministry, described him as 'a man of great character'.

It was this great character, imbued with a larger-than-life ego, which pushed the Revd Jim toward ever greater messianic heights. According to his wife, Marcy, 'Jim used religion to get some people out of the opiate of religion.' In other words, the Kingdom of Heaven was a lie, but if people looked to Jim Jones as their messiah he could offer them Heaven on Earth. Fuelled by an increasing intake of hallucinogens, barbiturates and amphetamines, Revd Jim also began to espouse the apocalyptic theology that characterises radical new religions. For Christianity too began as a doomsday cult, prior to its reinterpretation by St. Paul, and Jesus had preached that the end of the world was at hand – not in the third millennium or at some unspecified date in the future, but back then, two thousand years ago.

Preparing for the nuclear Armageddon that he'd first predicted would occur on 15 July 1967, the Reverend and his flock decamped in the mid-1970s to a piece of land the Temple purchased in Guyana, which he humbly christened Jonestown. It was here that the congregation were indoctrinated in the ways of socialistic living and marital fidelity, while their messianic pastor demanded the sexual attentions of their women and men alike. They were force-fed a diet of utopian ideology and drug-fuelled paranoia, with the movie *Executive Action* as a tract of faith – a briskly efficient thriller written by Temple lawyers Donald Lane and Mark Freed, showing how JFK was supposedly assassinated by right-wing conspirators, the kind of enemy Jones warned the congregation that they faced.

Both the paranoia and the apocalyptic visions would have their apotheosis. The Revd Jones sought to control renegade members of his flock by dosing them with downers – barbiturates like Valium and Demerol. Like his formerly idealised society, the Soviet Union, he treated would-be emigrants as dissidents and put them under the chemical cosh. In 1978, complaints by concerned family members would lead to a congressional investigation, and the skies would fall in upon Heaven on Earth.

When a delegation led by Congressman Leo Ryan visited Jonestown on 17 November of that year, Jones' paranoia and grandiose visions hit danger levels. Neither Ryan nor four of his colleagues would make it home, gunned down by the Temple's faithful guards at the nearby makeshift airport. Back at the Temple's tiny citadel-compound, Jones urged his nearly thousand-strong flock to join him in an act of 'revolutionary suicide'.

In the 1980s, a recording of the Jonestown mass suicides would be disseminated by underground sources (such as England's occult countercultural group, thee Temple ov Psychick Youth). Titled *The Last Supper* and of rough audio quality, Jones can be heard in it extolling his flock to partake with him of cyanide-laced Flavor Aid grape drink, while a young woman argues against him and dozens of distressed young children bleat pitifully in the background. But this was the only way to *save* the children, Jones insisted, from the fascistic enslavement that was surely coming. 'You can go down in history, saying you chose your own way to go,' preached their charismatic leader. But when nine hundred dead bodies, including the Revd Jones himself, were found lying in Jonestown, it became clear the choices were made by only one man.

Jim Jones had done his best to reshape and mould the psyches of his devout flock, few of whom had the willpower to resist his final destructive implorations. Drugs, however, paid a purely secondary role in it. True, he had weakened their will with powerful depressants like Thorazine – just as bludgeoning Largactyl was routinely administered in Soviet psychiatric institutions (and not a few American counterparts). But the real influence lay in their constant dogmatic indoctrination, with Jones – who increasingly left the teaching to his lieutenants as he withdrew into drug addiction – basing his utopia on the communist North Korean model of eight hours work/eight hours education per day for every citizen.

Compounded by a sense of geographical isolation and constant warnings about a fascist threat from without, Jones' very blunt techniques harked back to the reports of brainwashing of American soldiers during the Korean War. As with his political radicalism and religious fervour, it had its origins in the early 1950s of his youth.

***

It was researchers acting on behalf of the US government to counter the communist foe who developed the most radical theories about the mind as a malleable tool. While Soviet Russia had a head-start with the association and aversion therapy of behavioural psychologist Ivan Pavlov, the secretive nature of Soviet society meant that much of their post-Pavlovian research into mind control would remain unknown. (Aversion therapy is now often used in US psychiatry, for example, among convicted paedophiles who volunteer to receive a mild but painful electric shock on viewing pictures of children. But its most famous instances are still the stuff of classic speculative fiction, in Aldous Huxley's *Brave New World* and Anthony Burgess' *A Clockwork Orange*.)

It is only in the post-Soviet era that former communist intelligence operatives have felt at liberty to talk about matters such as mind control and 'remote viewing' (i.e. ESP). 'You can hardly imagine the warfare that broke out in this area in the first half of the last century,' claimed former KGB general Boris Ratnikov in December 2006. 'It would hardly be an exaggeration to say that sometimes real "astral battles" took place,' he contended, before testifying to such unsubstantiated techniques as a psychic scanner that could supposedly detect images in a subject's mind.

But it was in the new consumerist utopia of 1950s America that mind-control experiments would be best documented. Allen Dulles, the first director of the newly formed Central Intelligence Agency (CIA), may have warned in 1953 about Soviet 'brain perversion techniques . . . [in which] the individuals so conditioned can merely repeat the thoughts which have been implanted in their mind by suggestion from outside,' but the Agency's subsequent activities make clear that this was an ideal to which they too aspired.

'I find it extraordinary that you have two views saying essentially that the mind is a mechanism,' says *Welcome to Mars* author Ken Hollings of the newborn religion of Scientology and the concept of brainwashing, 'and once you approach it as a mechanism it's very easy to tinker with it, rework it. I suppose the other part of the triangle would be that Alan Turing publishes his first document on the notion of the "Thinking Machine", in the summer of 1950 in *Mind* magazine.

'So they are all proposing that there is a relationship between the mind and technology, the mind and machines, which had not been completely articulated before. It is very interesting that it all happens in a very, very short space of time in 1950, and you find the idea playing out throughout the decade.

'There was a really fascinating guy who has the unique distinction of being one of the scientists who actually scared the CIA in terms of the project he was putting forward. He was one of two guys working in sensory deprivation for the National Institute of Health in the US, the other was John C. Lilly. Lilly was actually developing a float tank, and he experimented quite a lot on himself. The idea was that if you could kind of isolate the mind from sensory inputs, what would it do? Would it become more suggestible, would it crave any kind of stimulus to the point where it would just accept anything?

'It was a case of, "Let's unplug the mind and see what it'll do.",', continues Hollings. 'Maitland Baldwin – the other guy that the CIA was interested in – was an army psychologist who developed some basic ideas in group therapy. If you ever want to find the model for Burroughs' Dr Benway in *The Naked Lunch*, it's this guy. He wanted funding for an experiment in which he was going to put a subject in a padded, soundproofed box, and was occasionally going to feed him gruel through a slot. Basically he was going to keep him there "to the point of termination", which is the phrase that he used. In other words he's going to wait until the guy is just a breezeblock, with lard for brains by the end of it. He put in his proposal, "It is ultimately possible that the subject might suffer some mental impairment as a result of this experiment." Just a tad! The CIA rejected this project with a rather terse note, in which the guy that turned it down made the recommendation that perhaps the field operative who suggested this experiment should go in the box first. Baldwin was actually too weird for the CIA.

'This was one way of doing it, describes Hollings. 'There was also a psychologist in Canada who was doing some work for their defence board, who ran some very interesting experiments early in the decade. He was using headphones and fake glasses, there would be cardboard tubes on the arms so the subjects could not actually touch anything. If they were fed anything it was just a kind of tasteless peplum. Their one stimulus was that they would be played bits of music occasionally through the white noise. The suggestion was made to them that they might be interested in occult matters of any kind – ESP, flying saucers. Science students were running this experiment, and they did notice a small but appreciable rise in the number of students taking out books on occult or spiritual matters. So there was a certain pause for thought – but this was at the end of seventy-two hours of lying in a room, with many of them hallucinating wildly.

'That was "sensory dep", the idea that you actually broke someone down, or you disconnected the mind from the outside world to see what it would do.'

The other psychic experiments of the time were designed to gauge the controlling potential of various psychoactive chemicals – in particular LSD, the new wonder drug synthesised from the wheat fungus ergot which, in its raw form, may have granted St John the Divine his visions of Hell in the New Testament's Book of Revelations. The prototype for all subsequent experimentation came with the US Navy's 1947 Project CHATTER, in which test subjects were dosed with the similarly profound hallucinogen mescaline, to test its worth as a 'truth drug'. While the will of the bewildered and tripping subjects was observed to be weakened, the researchers had little success in directing it towards any more practical end.

That did not deter the CIA from engaging in its own long-term psychedelic experiment, starting in 1953. Chemist Sidney Gottlieb was granted a mandate by the Agency's new director, Richard Helms, to acquire enough acid (then produced legally) to blow the mind of every living person in the USA. 'This stuff is dynamite!' enthused Helms, sensing the covert warfare potential of a chemical that completely distorted a subject's sense of reality. He immediately sanctioned Project MKULTRA, which would carry out 149 experiments in mind control using the drug.

The trouble with dosing people with acid under such experimental circumstances is, of course, that they will react according to their own state of cognition combined with the external stimuli of the time – that is, if you trip someone out in an environment which makes them at all unsure or apprehensive, you can virtually guarantee a profoundly negative psychological experience. As the astute little trickster Charlie Manson would become aware in the late 60s, the positive effects of LSD depend almost entirely on the trip occurring in a benign environment with trusted peers.

But of course the CIA took few such precautions. One of their subjects, Dr Frank Olson, threw himself out of a hotel window after being unknowingly spiked with the stuff, believing he had become permanently insane. Incredibly, this did not stop the US Army's Chemical Corps from testing massive doses of LSD and mescaline on their own unwitting soldiers. Over a thousand would develop severe psychological or neurological problems as a result, while a number would also attempt suicide.

'It goes back to this very mechanistic view of the mind: that it is in essence a tape recorder: if you know how to work the switches you know how to work the mind,' considers Ken Hollings. 'You find people experimenting with drugs like LSD and amphetamines or barbiturates or whatever, and becoming increasingly frustrated. Because no effect ever seems permanent, it never does the same thing twice, you cannot repeat the experiment in a useful way with another party. And it's almost like they are throwing their hands up, saying, "This drug's too unpredictable, we cannot do anything with it." Rather, to the contrary, the mind itself is too unpredictable!'

While the Chemical Corps were considering releasing hallucinogenic gases on unsuspecting American civilians, to test how drugs might incapacitate an enemy in combat, it is to be assumed that they had given up on LSD as a tool of mind control. The CIA's Project MKULTRA would continue for years, but if, as has widely been hypothesised, one of the objects had been to turn an individual person into a living weapon, a 'trigger killer', then on that level it had certainly failed. For the brutal practice of brainwashing, as practised by the Far Eastern communists, had used the most basic techniques to break someone down emotionally and then building them back up again.

'It was not any kind of complicated affair involving drugs, or sensory deprivation, or hallucinations, or film loops and tapes, or anything like that,' agrees Hollings. 'They would basically just take their subject and tell them the same story over and over and over again, in shifts so that there was very little sleep. But essentially they are just being asked to tell the same story so that there are no minor variations. By the time they've got their subject saying, "Yes, I am a counter-revolutionary, I am a terrible person," then they go through the whole story *again* and interpret it in terms of what would be the correct way to behave, what would be in line with the People's Revolution? So it was a very slow, painstaking Q&A, basic police-interrogation techniques but pushed to the extreme.'

Brainwashing as a concept in pop culture is epitomised by crime fiction author Richard Condon's 1959 novel, *The Manchurian Candidate*. So effective was its exaggeration of the treatment believed to have been meted out to GIs in the Korean War that its title has become a byword for mind control, and belief in the pre-programmed assassin.

Resistance to an all-enveloping international conspiracy is seen through the eyes of good soldier Captain Ben Marco, but the anti-hero of the novel is brainwashed assassin Sgt. Raymond Shaw – winner of the Congressional Medal of Honour for saving his comrades, the torn figure at the centre of a fragmented reality. For his heroics never really took place and, despite his fellow soldiers' strangely involuntary claims of love and affection toward him, he is a cold fish with a demeanour suggesting 'someone might just have opened a beach umbrella in his bowels'.

Back in Tungwha, a province of the sub-Arctic Chinese region of Manchuria, the Red Chinese had taken the Koreans' brainwashing techniques through several evolutionary leaps: 'the battalion had completed a two-storey, twenty-two-room structure with a small auditorium. The building was called the Research Pavilion and had some one-way transparent glass walls.'

Inside this place the Korean captive Shaw is 'built' into a trigger killer by Professors Yen Lo, from Red China, and Berezovo, from the Pavlov Institute in Moscow. His brainwashing runs fundamentally deep, leaving him aware of his fragmented consciousness but powerless to disobey the mnemonics that have been placed within. Beyond the factual realms of the North Koreans' harsh interrogation techniques, this mythical form of brainwashing combines hypnosis, drugs and Pavlovian autosuggestion that turns Raymond almost into a science-fiction automaton.

The American agent pulling the trigger when he returns home is his own shrewish and overambitious mother. In an oedipal twist, her lifelong browbeating of him is as profoundly damaging as the communists stealing his mind. Personified by the symbol of the 'Red Queen', the Queen of Diamonds in a pack of cards, her suggestion that he play a little solitaire is the behavioural trigger that sets Raymond on his mission. Just as Pavlov's dog was conditioned to associate the sound of a bell with food, Shaw, an altogether more complex living organism, is instilled with the playing-card signal that triggers the assassin within.

Shaw's mother is also remarried to a McCarthyite politician named Johnny Iselin, whose winning shtick is to smear seemingly half of the US Congress as communists. It sounds like a classic reds-under-the-bed Cold War scenario, but Condon's narrative is far less pulp-ish and more subtly satirical of its era. Mrs Iselin is no undercover commie but a woman so monstrously ambitious she would make a power play on behalf of her ideological enemies, and destroy her son's mind into the bargain. She also has an apocalyptic ambition to realise the puritan dream of the Founding Fathers in blood.

In screenwriter/producer George Axelrod and director John Frankenheimer's classic 1962 screen adaptation, Condon's sardonically paranoid narrative is de-kinked and made more linear. Where the movie matches the novel is in its *Twilight Zone*-ish surrealism. The brainwashed GIs believe they are in the genteel presence of the Ladies of the Garden of New Jersey, when they are really surrounded by their Red Chinese captors flanked by images of Stalin and Chairman Mao. Nearly 50 years on, the scenes where Shaw is instructed by Yen Lo (whom he addresses as 'Ma'am') to strangle one of the privates who supposedly went missing in action and to shoot another point-blank through the head are still monochromatically chilling. The victims' passive acceptance of their fate (*all* the GIs have been brainwashed) goes far beyond anything either the KGB or CIA are known to have achieved in all their years of messing with the human mind.

('The brain hasn't just been washed,' jokes Yen Lo, 'it's been dry-cleaned.')

In a climactic screen dream now touched by the taint of history, Shaw battles with the burden of his ultimate mission: to assassinate a presidential candidate with an army sniper's rifle. In the movie version, the presidential nominee's speech – 'Nor would I ask of my fellow American in defence of his freedom that which I would not willingly give up myself' – has probably intentional echoes of President John F. Kennedy's 1961 inaugural speech: 'And so, my fellow Americans, ask not what your country can do for you, but what you can do for your country.'

In fact, the film's headlining star, Frank Sinatra (Captain Marco), had been a part of the highballing elite in the heady days of JFK's Camelot, partying at the White House in a hedonistic style that suggested the President may have been just a little more self-serving than his words let on. ('I was Frank's pimp and Frank was Jack [Kennedy]'s,' Sinatra's fellow 'Rat Pack' member Peter Lawford later boasted.) It was also Sinatra who brought *The Manchurian Candidate* to the production executives at United Artists, having optioned the novel to further his acting career.

(In 2004, a team of producers including Sinatra's daughter Tina would remake the film for the hi-tech age and the Iraq War era, their assassin programmed by a microchip in the brain. With the nightmare US demagogue/communist conspiracy made obsolete by the course of history, co-writer Daniel Pyne explained, 'Corporate totalitarianism was the new philosophy that was scariest,' and Manchuria Global is the name of the corporation seeking total power in the USA. It is also the narrative's central flaw – in the age of G. W. Bush, why would a multinational have to go to such lengths? Could they not just get a few of their people into the administration?)

As screenwriter Axelrod reminded Ol' Blue Eyes, many years later, 'The President said, "What are you going to do next?" You said, "*The Manchurian Candidate*." He said, "Great, who's going to play the mother?"'

Jack Kennedy, the youngest chief, was hip to pop culture, though his response to the film version was not recorded for posterity. Within just over a year, however, the end sequences of the film would play like a strange black and white portent, and the popular myth would be born that Sinatra had withdrawn it from distribution.

***

The most influential film on the subject of assassination is not *The Manchurian Candidate*, but a piece of gaudily coloured amateur footage shot in Dallas, TX, on the sunny midday of Friday 22 November 1963. A local clothing manufacturer named Abe Zapruder had taken his cine-camera to film the presidential motorcade that came to town and, in so doing, recorded modern history in its most bloodily iconic form.

As the President's open-topped Lincoln glides steadily from Elm Street down into Dealey Plaza, the crowds that line the streets to greet him grow thinner but goodwill still seems present in the multitude. Texas is often renowned as a redneck state, and there are many who would regard Kennedy as a 'communist', much like the hyperbolic smears of Mrs Iselin in Condon's novel. But the good-hearted and well-scrubbed of Middle America have turned out in throngs, as have black Americans who believe a president who supports the civil liberties unions is definitely on their side.

With JFK and his glamorous (and much cheated-upon) wife Jackie in the back, the middle seats of the slow-moving limo also contain John Connally, Democratic Governor of Texas, and his wife, Nellie. Kennedy raises his hand to wave at the crowd, a moment frozen in time.

The visual history of the assassination has since been slowed down, enhanced, freeze-framed, to the point where everyone who has ever looked at a TV screen since that day has become one of millions of witnesses to the murder of John F. Kennedy. Initially, federal investigators feared that they had little photographic evidence, but Zapruder's cinefilm would soon be sequestered into evidence and then become a raw building block of belief, a foundation on which much dogged research and heartfelt fantasy would rest.

With the first shot, coming from the direction of the Texas Book Depository, Kennedy is hit in the throat. He grips onto his wound as the second shot follows in quick succession, less visible but hitting him in the back.

The flickering, obscured frames of cinefilm are stretched out into slow motion to witness what occurs in the next few seconds. With the third shot the back of the President's head explodes in a blurry focus, fuzzy rivulets of red flying off into infinity. Jackie Kennedy, hysterical, is by this time clambering out of the back of the limo. Governor Connally will later say she was screaming for help. Unkind observers suggest she is trying to save her own pampered ass. It does not seem too fantastic to consider that, in her anguish and panic, she is trying to retrieve a small piece of her husband's brain that has been blown out of his head.

The President was pronounced dead at a local hospital within the hour, becoming the fourth US President to die by assassination. A shocked world held its breath; many feared all-out war with the USSR, assuming that the Reds had to be involved in the assassination. But on a local level, in the streets of Dallas, a more microcosmic drama was playing out.

Lee Harvey Oswald was a malcontent young man who had never found his place in the world. Aged 24, he was now working at the Texas Book Depository, but a chequered life had also seen a teenage stint in the US Marines before embracing Marxism. He defected to the Soviet Union in 1959, hoping to become a part of the great communist utopia, but seemingly led just as marginalised an existence among the Russians (many of whom seem to have distrusted his motives). In 1962, the year that *The Manchurian Candidate* came to the screen, he was allowed to return to the US with a young Russian wife and two infant children.

Life was not good for Oswald, even before that fateful afternoon. By the time the Feds and the local police came to the book depository, from whence they had traced the trajectory of the bullets, he was nowhere to be seen but had left a bolt-action rifle behind. When the cops overpowered and arrested him in a local cinema, he was also arrested on suspicion of killing a local patrolman, who had been shot dead with a handgun 45 minutes after the President's assassination.

Within a couple of days Oswald, too, would pass out of history and into iconography. With the television cameras on him as he is readied for transfer from the police cells to the county jail, he is approached by a burly stranger who is apparently unimpeded by the cops. Jack Ruby, a Dallas nightclub owner, draws a handgun and pumps bullets into Oswald's torso at point-blank range before surrendering himself to the surrounding police.

Oswald's agony also remains frozen in time, on black and white stock more professionally shot than the Zapruder film. It is this that allows him to pass posthumously down the decades as the second victim of the alleged Kennedy assassination conspiracy. (The unfortunate slain cop, J. D. Tippitt, is largely forgotten.) Suddenly everything smells rotten. It seems that Ruby has been allowed to assassinate the assassin, and there has been more than one gun and one pair of hands behind the killing of the President.

The possibility that Jack Ruby was just a local doofus, who thought shooting the man who shot the President would make him a hero, seems admittedly slight. (This, however, is what Ruby claimed.) It soon became common knowledge that his nightclub had been frequented by local Mob boys, and 'the Mafia killed JFK' – on account of his Attorney-General brother Robert's campaign against organised crime – became one of the longest standing and most popular theories surrounding the President's death. Ruby himself would die of cancer after four years in prison – by then, according to his attorney, subscribing to an insane theory of his own that all of his fellow American Jews were being brought to Dallas for extermination.

All the disquiet that was felt about the death of Kennedy continued to build from this point. The September 1964 conclusion of the official governmental commission, adjudicated by Senator Earl Warren, that Oswald had acted alone as the sole assassin was treated sceptically and became itself, over time, 'proof' of an establishment cover-up.

Exhaustive research into the JFK assassination became the province of investigator and obsessive crank alike. Conclusions were many and most seemed credible: it was the Mob. It was the right wing of the Republican Party in cahoots with reactionary businessmen. It was the CIA, alarmed that Kennedy's foreign policy was starting to go leniently on the Soviets and the Cubans. (This only really holds up if you discount the fact that JFK had already sent 16,000 US military 'advisers' to aid South Vietnam. Some of his liberal admirers continue to insist he would never have allowed the situation to escalate to war, unlike his successor Lyndon Johnson.) It was Castro's Cuban agents, in retaliation for the attempted Bay of Pigs invasion. It was the anti-Castro Cuban exiles, incensed that Kennedy refused to sanction all-out military action. It was the FBI, whose deviant cross-dressing quasi-fascist director, J. Edgar Hoover, despised the Kennedys and their liberal-pinko politics.

Many of these theories began to cross-pollinate, with, for example, explanations of how the CIA and the Mafia worked hand in hand. The 'ghost at the feast' in all of this remained Lee Harvey Oswald – who was, according to the varying scenarios, an entirely innocent man who had been elaborately set up to take the fall; a 'patsy' who had taken part in the assassination as part of a two (or several)-man team, and was silenced before he could talk; or else someone else entirely, a shadowy double agent posing as the left-wing dissident Oswald and part of a wider and more grandiose conspiracy.

At least some of this seemed to be borne out by a Select Committee of the House of Representatives in 1979, which overturned part of the Warren Commission to the extent that it accepted the likelihood of two gunmen. This was largely due to disagreement about whether Oswald could have fired the third shot from his position in the book depository, and reports that some witnesses may have seen or heard a second gunman from the now-famous 'grassy knoll' close to where the motorcade was passing.

By now, the consensus wisdom that JFK was killed by a far-reaching conspiracy was enshrined in Western culture. As a kid in 1977, one of your co-authors delighted in a sleazy Spanish comic book purporting to tell the 'truth', filled with bullets, blood and as many boobs as an orgy at Camelot: 'A young journalist who is now one of the most important representatives of the United States press, whose name we are not permitted to divulge, let us have his report of the dramatic events which culminated in the assassination of John Kennedy and his brother Robert. We have used the actual names of persons involved wherever possible in order to further authenticate our story even though this may incur some risk on our part.' (Only two of the six issues were translated into English – maybe the CIA got 'em after all.)

On a more serious level, Richard Condon returned to conspiracy fiction with *Winter Kills*, a viable representation of the kind of military-political complex that might have killed John, and later Bobby, Kennedy. Don De Lillo's haunting 1988 novel *Libra* presented a literary imagining of the working of Oswald's mind, presenting him as the assassin but placing him at the centre of historical events he can neither fully comprehend nor control.

In 1991, Oliver Stone's much-trumpeted movie *JFK* synthesised a hybrid of Dallas District Attorney Jim Garrison's pursuit of what he regarded as a cabal of right-wing conspirators, as told in his book *On the Trail of the Assassins*, with Jim Marrs' consideration of the various conspiracy theories in *Crossfire: The Plot that Killed Kennedy*. (Garrison was played in the film by Kevin Costner, Mr Middle America himself. The only public servant to secure a prosecution connected to the Kennedy case, he took New Orleans businessman Clay Shaw to court on conspiracy charges in the late 1960s. Garrison insisted Shaw was one of several conspirators from a neo-fascist gay network, but the defendant walked.)

Stone's heavily detailed movie made headlines worldwide, delighting conspiracy theorists and enraging the conservatives who derided them.

(For this writer's money, the more economic thriller *Executive Action* – an article of faith for Revd Jim Jones – is more chilling, making good use of the Zapruder footage.) On closer examination, it does seem that Stone elaborated on some of the events in Garrison's investigation, making the links between them more concrete to the extent where the film became fictionalised. But then by now fiction, legend and myth were playing as profound a role as any verifiable fact.

It all gave a deeply paranoid but seemingly substantial sense of *us* being unwittingly manipulated by the covert actions of *them*, who we were powerless to control. Even the writer who may be modern crime fiction's apogee, James Ellroy, got in on the act with his millennial *American Tabloid* and *The Cold Six Thousand*, the first two thirds of the mooted *American Underworld Trilogy*. Never in thrall to JFK's liberal canonisation (Ellroy used to proclaim himself 'the white knight of the far right'), he puts us on either side of the assassination's historic watershed, with its antecedents and after-ripples seen through the eyes of well-connected thugs. When asked if he believed this was a realistic scenario, Ellroy tipped himself the nod; when pushed on whether he believed it actually happened, he shrewdly responded that it cannot have done, 'I made it up.'

But, as Ken Hollings remarks on the secular belief system of JFK theories,

'I get very frustrated, or slightly annoyed, by the kind of rational spoilers who see in conspiracy theory some blind groping for comfort. That somehow it explains the world when it does not explain anything. I'm sorry, but I do not feel more comfortable in a world in which it's possible that the Mafia, Cuban revolutionaries, the Soviets, the Freemasons, *all* conspired to kill John F. Kennedy. This does not make me in any sense more comfortable about *anything*.'

***

If old Frankie had truly felt regretful about his involvement in *The Manchurian Candidate*, after hearing of the fate of his good friend Jack, it may have been because of the subsequent twists their friendship had taken. When the President became a recurring tape loop of history that bright November day, Sinatra was filming *Robin and the Seven Hoods*, a musical comedy pastiche of gangsterdom in Prohibition-era Chicago. It was almost a coy parody of the social interconnections between the crooner movie star and the young President.

For the Kennedy clan retained stubborn Mob connections all throughout their brightest star's 46 years of life. Their patriarch, Joe Kennedy, had made his first fortune as a bootlegger during Prohibition; during his son's presidential campaign it is widely believed he called in Mob favours to help swing certain key states. In the Camelot years, Frankie introduced Jack to a good-looking brunette named Judith Campbell, who was screwing Chicago Mafia don Sam Giancana at the same time as her liaison with the President.

Ms Campbell would die young in circumstances that have aroused suspicion ever since, and it takes no great leap of the imagination to see that Giancana was pissed at the Kennedys for their congressional war on organised crime – for biting the hand that fed, in effect.

It was these factors that, by November 1963, had caused a rift between Kennedy and Sinatra, and the latter's drift rightward to the Republican Party. For all the hindsight resonance of *The Manchurian Candidate*'s climactic scenes, if Sinatra thought the programmed 'trigger killer' scenario had any relevance to JFK's death he never publicly articulated it.

In fact it is only in the wilder theories of conspiracists – the type that have proliferated since the birth of the Internet – that the idea of Kennedy's killer as an automated 'sleeper' has gained ground. But in the years following the JFK assassination, the concept became common currency when it was attached to other historical homicides.

The first of these is seen by many as a continuation of the original tragedy, though it has a dynamic all of its own. Just after midnight on the early morning of 5 June 1968, Robert Kennedy (now the Senator for New York) had taken the podium at the Los Angeles Ambassador Hotel. Aged 42, he was aiming to fill his late brother's shoes by becoming the second Kennedy to win the Presidency of the United States.

Despite a warm response from the crowd, Bobby would not even begin his campaign speech. Hit by three bullets, in the head, chest and neck, it was the brain injury that would end his life a little over 24 hours later. Five other people on the stage were also hit by stray shots.

From the moment of the assassination there seemed little doubt as to who was responsible. A 24-year-old Palestinian immigrant named Sirhan Sirhan was overpowered and arrested at the scene. Witnesses stated that he defiantly proclaimed, 'I did it for my country . . . I love my country.' Apparently appalled by Kennedy's now-traditional US liberal support of beleaguered Israel over the dispossessed Palestinians, it may have been no coincidence that Sirhan chose to act on the first anniversary of Israeli victory in the Six Day War.

It seems merely one of history's tenuous ironies that, at the time of his campaign, Bobby Kennedy was staying at the house of John Frankenheimer, director of *The Manchurian Candidate*. But events would suggest a chillier resonance.

Despite the apparent incontrovertibility of the facts, Sirhan would claim at trial that he had no recollection of the events that led to his arrest. More problematic were the ballistic reports, which suggested the fatal head wound was inflicted by a shot fired from behind the presidential nominee, whereas Sirhan approached Kennedy from in front of the podium.

No credible second gunman has ever been identified. Sirhan was initially sentenced to die in the gas chamber, but his sentence was commuted to life when the State of California briefly declared the death penalty unconstitutional. To this day he remains incarcerated, unlikely ever to be paroled.

Doubts as to Sirhan's level of culpability were cited by a psychiatrist acting on his legal behalf, stressing that the voices the killer claimed he heard in his head were a symptom of schizophrenia. To more esoteric cultural commentators this meant something else altogether.

Arch conspiracy theorist Alex Constantine has propagated an alternative cultural history of the USA, based on the premise that the CIA mind-control experiments begun with MKULTRA have been adapted and mutated but never discontinued. In wilfully alarming works such as *Psychic Dictatorship in the USA* and *Virtual Government: CIA Mind Control in America*, he posits the contention that both Oswald and Sirhan were 'hypno-patsies', their will and consciousness reshaped by the Agency to direct them to kill the Kennedys. Classically earnest in its cultural paranoia, it is the kind of stuff that is all too easy for non-believers to attack.

Harder to dismiss, perhaps, is *BLUEBIRD: Deliberate Creation of Multiple Personality* by psychiatrist Colin A. Ross M.D., who indirectly supports Constantine in all but his most extreme contentions. According to Ross's research, purportedly supported by access to government files under Freedom of Information laws, MKULTRA researcher Dr Ewen Cameron succeeded via a combination of LSD and hypnosis in 'wiping' one female depressive subject's personality entirely (as per Hollings' tape-recorder analogy). This in turn led to the more sophisticated Project BLUEBIRD, and more finely-honed mind-control techniques that could be utilised by the intelligence agencies.

And so the accusations and counter-accusations accumulate. To most, ex-Beatle John Lennon's murder by shooting at the Dakota apartment building in New York City, on 8 December 1980, was a grotesque outgrowth of fan culture. Mark Chapman, the bespectacled doughboy who pumped five bullets into Lennon, was an inadequate personality who, it seemed, both over-identified with and wanted to usurp his idol. His fragile psyche and self-esteem may have been damaged by experimentation with the psychedelic drugs the more robust Lennon once popularised. ('We must always remember to thank the CIA and the army for LSD,' Lennon said in his final *Playboy* interview. 'They invented LSD to control people and what they did was give us freedom.') Chapman's personal bible was J. D. Salinger's *The Catcher in the Rye*, the novel of archetypal American adolescent alienation, with a narrator who saw himself as living in 'a world of phoneys'. To the confused Chapman, the formerly messianic Lennon now seemed to be just one more such phoney.

Three decades on, Chapman remains in a prison cell where the carrot of parole is occasionally dangled in front of him. His claim at the time of the murder, that he heard a voice in his head compelling him to, 'Do it, do it!' would seem to be a possible onset of schizophrenia – or maybe just the inner voice of his own will, imploring him to continue with the action he had already decided upon.

Others perceive unseen hands at work. British lawyer Fenton Bresler, in his book *Who Killed John Lennon?*, points his finger at the FBI, who tried to have Lennon extradited as an undesirable alien in 1971, and, of course, at CIA mind-control experiments. The fact that Lennon had been granted a Green Card to remain in the USA in 1975 and had been politically (and mostly musically) inactive for years is apparently a mere red herring – as is the FBI's written assessment that he was adjudged back in the early 1970s to be too full of narcotics to be a political threat to anyone.

'Anybody who thinks that Mark Chapman was just some crazy guy who killed my dad for his personal interests is insane, I think, or very naïve,' announced Lennon's musician son Sean early in the third millennium. Bresler's hypothesis that Chapman was a CIA 'hypno-patsy' was based in part on the military background of the killer's family, his acquisition of rounded bullets (which explode inside the body on impact) and the alleged claim by a behavioural scientist that he was now capable of creating a 'Manchurian Candidate' for the CIA. For the term had now passed out of fiction and pop culture to become a metaphor for what the unseen powers are technically capable of.

All of this may or may not be vulnerable to rational analysis. These days, however, as Ken Hollings explains, the US military-industrial complex is capable of creating an artificial killing environment utilising much more consumer-friendly means than drugs or hypnosis:

'In Fort Seal, Ohio, they've been developing something called JFETS – which stands for Joint Fires and Effects Training System. It is a prime example of what the academic Tim Lenoir at Sanford University, in his essay "Theatres of War", has called 'the military-entertainment complex'. It is a completely immersive audiovisual environment, with huge plasma TVs and sound systems. It allows people to interact with attack and defence scenarios, mostly sited in Iraq.

'So in other words,' describes Hollings, 'if you want to know how to deal with someone who's shooting at your border patrol, you can go in a room and act out different versions of this scenario. And "scenario" is the right word – you're literally working through a movie set. The kind of young soldiers that are being trained on this are the kind who've grown up with Imax, 3D movies, video games, incredibly sophisticated sound systems. They are learning how to fight using them, how to coordinate themselves in these environments. What's interesting is that a similar kind of environment is also being used for therapeutic purposes for soldiers suffering from post-traumatic stress disorder. In other words it gives them the opportunity to *relive* the experience, in the hope that they can experience catharsis.

'So the illusion is a weird form of Paradise. It is possibly not one that Hasan-i-Sabbah would recognise, but in a strange sort of way they are recreating the Garden for those who are going to go and fight in Baghdad. We haven't moved very far away.'

***

When Lee Harvey Oswald returned to the USA, his solitary nature led him to visit movie theatres alone. Indeed, he would ultimately be arrested for the killing of the President at one such. He would walk daily past the Palace on Elm Street, close to Dealey Plaza, where *The Manchurian Candidate* played in late 1962. We do not know if he took in that particular film, but the testimony of his widow Marina about the frequency of his visits to the movies suggests he would have done so.

In cultural historian John Loken's 2000 study, *Oswald's Trigger Films*, he posits that the mnemonic for murder came from outside – from the world-changing acts of the assassin onscreen – but that it awakened something deep inside the frustrated young ex-Marine and political idealist: the need to step forward to take his place in history.

It is an arresting hypothesis, one that can never be proven or disproven – as with most of the JFK conspiracy theories, now that any means of objectively testing them is fading into history. Most intriguingly, it is one of a number of studies that have come full circle, rejecting the absorbing chimera-chasing of the more popular theories to arrive back at a reductive proposition: Oswald acted as a lone assassin, playing purely to a personal agenda.

This has been the rigidly held viewpoint of many establishment conservatives for decades, but in the mid-1990s it began to be articulated by less dogmatic voices – such as journalist Gerald Posner in the optimistically-titled *Case Closed*, or, perhaps most significantly, by Norman Mailer in *Oswald's Tale*. Mailer, the great but sometimes overrated old man of American letters, had been granted access not only to the Warren Commission's body of evidence on the gunman but also to a proportion of the material gathered by the Kremlin, both at the time of Oswald's defection and the moment of his posthumous infamy.

Mailer had often delighted in his image as a rare blood-and-guts liberal, the *bète noir* of American conservatives. He began his massive study in the belief that what he found would bear out his own suspicion that the ex-Marine had been used by a wider conspiracy. Instead, as he seemed happily surprised to admit, he came to believe that, 'Lee had the character to kill Kennedy and that he probably did it alone . . . it is too difficult, no matter how one searches for a viable scenario, to believe that others could have chosen him to be the rifleman in a conspiracy.'

So are Oswald's cultural descendants, his illegitimate sons, not the conspirators or 'hypno-patsies' of popular legend but an altogether different breed of assassin?

In the decade following the Kennedy assassination, Arthur Bremer, an alienated 21-year-old from Milwaukee, Wisconsin, wrote in his diary of his ambition to 'to do SOMETHING BOLD AND DRAMATIC, FORCEFULL & DYNAMIC, A STATEMENT of my manhood for the world to see.' Just like Lee Harvey Oswald.

Bremer became obsessed with committing a political assassination, and stalked President Richard Nixon at Republican Party conventions. He was frustrated in his aim to get close enough to shoot Nixon, blaming anti-Vietnam war protesters who attracted TV and press cameras, and found he could get closer to Governor George Wallace of Alabama. Wallace was on the campaign trail to secure the Democratic Party's presidential nomination, a 'pork-barrel Democrat' who defied opposition to the South's old racial segregation laws. He announced his running on the day Bremer was warned by the concerned mother of a girl named Joan that she would inform the police if he continued stalking her.

On 17 March 1972, Wallace was gunned down by Bremer at a rally in Maryland. He survived, but was paralysed by spinal injuries up until his death in 1998, spending much of the rest of his life building bridges with the African-American people he had alienated. Bremer was sentenced to 53 years in prison, a sentence he is still serving out. In 1973, extracts from his personal diary were published under the title *An Assassin's Diary*, despite his failure to actually kill anyone.

When screenwriter Paul Schrader wrote his masterwork, *Taxi Driver*, in 1972, he was living in the same state of near-madness as his title character – driving aimlessly around Los Angeles with a handgun in the glove compartment. Adding to his edginess was his other source of inspiration, the news story of Arthur Bremer.

In the completed 1975 film *Taxi Driver*, Robert De Niro would portray Travis Bickle, a New York cabbie descending into homicidal madness. When he changes his target from a politician to the pimp exploiting a child prostitute, it makes Travis into an accidental hero. Schrader had made his taxi driver a former US Marine, just like Lee Oswald.

But the parallels with Bremer are most striking. Bremer pestered a girl for dates only to repulse her with his fixation on pornography, as with Travis and Betsy (played by Cybil Shepherd) in the film. When it was clear he had no chance with the girl, Bremer turned his search for self-esteem into a search for an assassination target – Travis turns his attention to the presidential candidate Betsy works for, substituting the plan when he becomes conspicuous in the crowd, as with Bremer and Nixon.

Schrader made Travis's ultimate act of violence redemptive, rescuing a child prostitute named Iris (Jodie Foster) from her pimp. In the world beyond the movie screen, the irony of a psychotic becoming a hero by default was lost when it connected with another obsessive psyche.

Taxi Driver is an iconic film, entwined with the events that both inspired and followed it. It was seen many times by an unbalanced young man named John Hinckley, Jr, who developed a delusional obsession with young actress Jodie Foster and bombarded her with letters. As with his counterpart, Mark Chapman, he also felt a strong sense of identification with the narrator of *The Catcher in the Rye*. Ironically, it has also been suggested that Chapman's killing of Lennon, which apparently upset Hinckley greatly, may have been one of the factors that finally led him to act.

When his obsession hit crisis point Hinckley chose the same form of expression as Travis Bickle and Arthur Bremer – keeping a diary that told of his attempts to assassinate President Jimmy Carter, and then the new president-elect, Ronald Reagan. Hinckley's eruption into the world was announced in a letter: 'Jodie, I would abandon this idea of getting Reagan in a second if I could only win your heart and live out the rest of my life with you.'

Like Bickle and Bremer (and even possibly Oswald), the politics of his target were of no significance, switching from the liberal Carter to right-wing conservative Reagan out of expediency. On 30 March 1981, at the Washington Hilton Hotel, Reagan and his advisers were attending a political meeting. In the conference hall, John Hinckley opened up with a handgun containing customised 'devastator' bullets – like the exploding ammunition used by Travis in *Taxi Driver*. Though he was surrounded by secret service agents, Hinckley was not overpowered until he had fired off all six shots. The sixth hit the President, passing through his lung and necessitating an emergency operation for the seventy-year-old man, while his press secretary, James Brady, suffered brain damage and was forced to live out the rest of his life with impaired motor functions. (Brady also became that rarest of political animals, a Republican advocate of gun control.)

Hinckley was found not guilty of attempted murder in 1982 by reason of insanity (a verdict which outraged much of the American public), and committed to a psychiatric hospital. His trial featured a screening of *Taxi Driver*, and reluctant testimony from a traumatised Jodie Foster. In recent years, he has won the right to attend private dinners with his wealthy family – in stark contrast to Bremer's treatment – and a pen-pal girlfriend, while he has often composed disturbing, stream-of-consciousness writings for US underground publishers. (Pieces of his work were featured in Adam Parfrey's classic millennial anthology, *Apocalypse Culture*.)

In the aftermath of the turbulent 1960s, political assassination was no longer solely the domain of terrorists or hitmen but also, post-Kennedy assassination, of deranged gunmen who equated infamy with celebrity and felt that, in order to know that they truly existed, they had to *act*.

'There's a wonderful statement from the painter Robert Rauschenberg,' observes Ken Hollings. 'He's referring particularly to Warhol's shooting, which took place in the same weekend as Bobby Kennedy's. Rauschenberg said, "This is the new medium." This is the new communication network.'

(Andy Warhol survived his shooting by radical psycho-feminist Valerie Solanas, founder and sole member of SCUM [the Society for Cutting Up Men], but suffered from his injuries for the rest of his life.)

The bastard sons – and even daughters – of Lee Harvey Oswald are not the idealists and conspirator Assassins of Hasan Sabbah, but a phenomenon befitting their times. The all-American assassin is the lone killer who heralded an age of ego-driven, apolitically-motivated assassination.

XIII

THE OLD MAN OF THE MOUNTAIN

A congregation of sorry souls languish in a Genoese gaol. It is 1298, and these men are victims of the constant feuding between the Italian city states, captured during a skirmish between Venice and Genoa, awaiting the wheels of diplomacy to turn far enough to open the heavy prison doors and let them go home. The days drag, boredom is compounded by the buzz of flies, the oppressive heat and the stench of human waste that clouds their claustrophobic chambers. The men try to pass the time by exchanging stories that will allow their imaginations to take them briefly beyond the walls, to happier times and places.

Nobody can take them further than a Venetian merchant called Marco. His tales are so fabulous that his fellows soon nickname him Marco Million – for no journey in his stories is ever less than a million miles, no sum less than a million in gold. Yet Marco insists that his stories are no mere fables. The fabulous places he describes, the incredible people, the amazing adventures, have been seen with his own eyes on long journeys east with his father and uncle. One man pays special attention, a writer of romances from Pisa named Rustichello. Even in gaol it is possible to find little luxuries and, with a modest bribe, Rustichello secures paper and pens. He encourages his friend to recount his experiences in order, carefully transcribing them into French, his pen scratching away over the long, oppressive days and chilly, candlelit nights.

On one such night, Marco describes a place they passed while traversing the Persian lands, where, they were told, once had lived a man they called Aloodin in the local language, who others called the Old Man of the Mountain. There he built the most lavish gardens the world has ever seen – every form of flower and fruit grew there among gilded palaces and fountains of wine, milk and honey, while beautiful maidens sang like angels and played enticing melodies. So wondrous were these gardens that the Saracens thereabouts believed them to be the gardens of Paradise described in their holy book. Yet the Old Man did not use this wondrous place for pleasure, but for more sinister ends.

The garden's entrance was guarded by a castle so strong that none could penetrate it. He would invite boys of 12 years old who he adjudged to be of special courage to his court. The Old Man would give them a hashish potion to drink, and have them borne to his garden where they might experience every wonder that it offered. When he required somebody to undertake a mission for him, he would drug the strongest of these young men once more and have him taken from the garden. When he awoke he would be dismayed to have left the garden, which the Old Man told them had been Paradise itself. But, if he died doing the Old Man's bidding, he would return. So none of his agents held any fear and would kill the Old Man's foes, craving the embrace of death and a return to Paradise.

Some who listened to Marco's tales snorted with disbelief; others laughed, and some listened in rapt attention. Once the Venetian and Rustichello were released from captivity, it seemed that the whole world would be enrapt by the book they called The Travels of Marco Polo, The Book of Marvels *or simply* The Million. *Once he returned to Venice Marco never left the city again, but married, had children and lived a prosperous life. Others read his book and it fed their dreams, hungry to experience wonders of their own. One such was a man from Genoa named Christopher Columbus; the many hours he spent poring over Marco's book, carefully inscribing his own notes in the margin, planted the desire to plan his own voyage, which he would undertake in the year 1492 . . .*

***

Marco Polo might be described as an early Orientalist in both senses of the term. For in addition to describing the scholarly study of Middle and Far Eastern culture, orientalism is also used as a term for artists and composers who choose the 'mysterious East' as their subject, resonant with images of harems carpeted with silk pillows and turbanned potentates drawing lazily on hookah pipes. The term may also carry more negative overtones, stereotyping Asian cultures as alien and exotic in a fashion that is at best patronising and at worst perpetuates imperialist ideas. In his 1978 book *Orientalism*, the left-wing Palestinian-American academic Edward Said argues that the West's fantastic-romantic depictions of the Middle East encourage 'subtle and persistent Eurocentric prejudice against Arabo-Islamic peoples and their culture' which emphasise difference and encourage cultural conflict. Perhaps. But the West's fascination with the Orient, which Said condemns, does at least contain a powerful element of appreciative curiosity, which opens a crucial window for mutual respect. This has been conspicuously absent in contemporary dialogue between the 'decadent' West and Middle Eastern idealogues.

Other commentators have criticised Marco Polo's famous memoirs. Polo was recalling a journey he had undertaken some 30 years before he committed it to paper, and the date he would have passed through Persia was around 15 years after the Assassin sect had been successfully suppressed in the region. Dr Farhad Daftary dismisses all of the early European accounts of the Nizaris in a similar fashion, writing in his book *The Assassin Legends* that 'medieval Europeans learned very little about Islam and Muslims, and their less informed knowledge of the Ismailis found expression in a few superficial observations and erroneous perceptions scattered in Crusader histories and other occidental sources.' In conversation with the authors, the doctor elaborated on his view regarding Polo's famous account, suggesting that it was based upon hearsay heard *after* his expeditions. He also points out that the term 'Old Man of the Mountain' may have been used by the Crusaders to refer to the Assassin leader in Syria, but was not used for his Persian superior in Alamut.

'I do not doubt the fact that he went to China, because a book was written not so long ago even questioning his trip,' he told us. 'That's not under question, what is under question is whether Marco Polo himself had heard [his tales of the Old Man at first hand], because he breaks out the account of his travels at one point, and then he claims to have heard these stories from reliable sources in Iran, as he was passing through eastern Iran on the Silk Road to central Asia. And then he inserts this account, exactly what we find in the earlier European sources who have not gone to Iran. We also find some additional embellishments, the so-called secret garden of Paradise appears for the first time in Marco Polo's account.'

The doctor points out that Juwayni, one of the most authoritative contemporary Islamic sources on the Nizaris, who witnessed the destruction of Alamut in 1256, makes no mention of any garden in his descriptions of the castle (though, as we have suggested, the garden need not have been in the castle itself).

'This Old Man of the Mountain that Marco Polo is referring to was a very austere, pious man,' the doctor adds. The same Muslim sources of the period relate that he was so severe that he had only two sons and had both of them executed – one for having been accused of drinking wine, the other one had been implicated in a murder which later proved false. Now, a man who kills his own son for having drunk wine, how could he have created this garden with wine and houris [young women] and so on? So the conclusion is that Marco Polo could not have heard these stories in Iran, because these stories up until his book have never been mentioned. He must have heard them in Europe when he got back from his seventeen-year journey. These tales by that time had become extremely popular in Europe, so this section, which is completely out of context, could have been inserted either by Rustichello or by Marco Polo himself later when he revised his account, to enhance the interest in the work.'

Dr Daftary is right in that most sources identify Hasan Sabbah as a stern, ascetic figure, who does seem an unlikely architect for a decadent pleasure garden. Equally, however, later Islamic accounts accuse Hasan's successors of indulging in forbidden pleasures, particularly Hasan II, who is accused of endorsing wine-drinking. Such accounts come from sources hostile to the Nizaris, of course, and hence can plausibly be challenged but not automatically dismissed. For even if we accept that Hasan led an exemplary life of abstinence, it is no reason to automatically assume that such a tradition remained unbroken among those who succeeded him. While nobody would suggest that the Aga Khans – official modern descendents of the Imams of Alamut – are guilty of any of the blasphemies that the medieval Nizaris were accused of, more than one member of the dynasty has been deemed to be a playboy.

The question of the relationship between the Aga Khan and the Grand Masters of Alamut became the subject of an extraordinary court case in 1866, presided over by Sir Joseph Arnould, Chief Justice of Bombay. The background to the case takes us back to the period between the suppression of the Assassins in the 13th century and the resurgence of the Nizaris in the early-1800s.

The intervening centuries provide a challenge for the historian, as the cataclysm of genocide that overtook Alamut in 1256 encouraged many of the surviving Assassins to defensively adopt *taqiyya*, the defensive policy of denying your true beliefs to avoid persecution. The sect effectively went underground, though it was later claimed that an heir of the final Grand Master of Alamut survived the holocaust. Many Nizaris migrated east, eventually establishing communities in India where they became known as the Khojas. The next Nizari Imam would resurface on the world stage in the late-18th century, as wealthy governor of the Persian city of Kerman. It was his grandson who was given the title of Aga Khan in 1818 by the Shah of Persia, after his father was killed by an angry mob, purportedly for his support of the tyrannical Shah, though there may well have been a sectarian aspect to the violence.

The cordial relations between the first Aga Khan and the Shah did not last, however, and the Aga Khan became the focus of a series of rebellions against the Persian monarch. In 1841, he fled the country and headed for India, by now a nation with a large Nizari population, ruled by a British Empire which was then at war with Persia. The Aga Khan offered his services and those of his Nizari devotees to the British Empire, and the British – recognising the value of a friendly Islamic religious leader – willingly accepted.

But there were a couple of complications with this arrangement. For one thing, the Aga Khan proved every bit as crafty and charismatic a diplomat as any of his medieval predecessors, and those British officials who expected to be able to exploit the Nizari Imam often found the tables turned upon them. For another, far from everyone was convinced that the Aga Khan truly *was* the authentic descendant of the imams of Alamut – not least India's Khoja community, a significant number of whom refused to acknowledge the Aga Khan as their new leader, some even insisting their faith was Sunni in origin. There was much at stake, not only the leadership of the Khojas but also a large amount of money, as the Imam demanded a tithe from the faithful. Things came to a head in 1850, when four dissidents were murdered by Khan loyalists over the dispute. In a detail suggestive of the old days, the Aga Khan reportedly comforted the relatives of the murderers after they were executed for the attack by reassuring them that the killers would go straight to Heaven.

The violence did not silence the Aga Khan's critics, who accused him of being a retrogressive influence and using the tithes he received to finance a lavish lifestyle, rather than for the benefit of Islam or the Khoja community. If the Assassins had been a proto-communist movement, then clearly something had changed. In 1866, it was resolved to decide the issue once and for all in a court of law. Over 25 days during April and June, Chief Justice Arnould listened to complex arguments from historians and genealogists concerning the merits of the Aga Khan's claim. The judge ruled in his favour, which must have come as a surprise to some, not least because there are occasions during the turbulent history of the Nizari Imamate when substantiating an unbroken bloodline demands certain leaps of faith.

Hasan Sabbah was always adamant that he was not the Imam, merely his representative. The idea that the Grand Master of the Assassins *was* actually the Imam first surfaced with Hasan II, who it was asserted was actually a descendant of Nizar, brought secretly to Alamut and presented as Grand Master Muhammad I's son until the time was ripe to reveal his true lineage. It was denied angrily by Muhammad, and some might wonder if Arnould's decision had as much to do with politics as history or genealogy. If so, this at least was surely an authentic echo of the leadership of Alamut, for plots and deals were the essence of its diplomatic world and covert alliances the cement that held the Nizari state together.

Whatever sceptics may feel about the decision, it officially sanctioned the Aga Khan's claim thenceforth. It is also worth noting that, had Hasan Sabbah intended the leadership of his sect to be meritocratic then the Aga Khan fulfilled that demand, achieving a position of great influence largely by his dynamism and force of personality. His successors proved loyal friends of the British crown, raising forces to fight at their side in several major conflicts and being feted in return in European high society. They also managed to counter many of the criticisms levelled at the first Aga Khan for neglecting his duties as a Muslim religious leader, as several of his successors were active in promoting Islam internationally while campaigning for a more tolerant, progressive vision of the faith.

Which is not to say the dynasty turned their collective backs on the privileges of wealth. It is difficult to imagine Hasan jet-setting to the French Riviera, or having four wives including two glamorous French brides, like the third Aga Khan. (His ill-fated son married the Hollywood sex symbol Rita Hayworth in 1949.) In 1937, Aga Khan III was elected President of the League of Nations, perhaps the most prestigious position in international politics of the day. It was a *haute monde* world of dinner-jacketed glitz and chauffeur-driven privilege that seems a long way from the austere stone chambers of Alamut of 800 years before. It was too far away for some, who were re-evaluating Hasan Sabbah's legacy from an entirely different angle . . .

***

'The order of Assassins was formed in Persia at the end of the eleventh century. They were committed to anyone willing to pay for the service. Assassins were sceptical of the existence of God and believed that the world of the mind came into existence first, then, finally, the rest of creation.' – *Standard Dictionary of Folklore, Mythology and Legend.*

Thus runs the epigram to Richard Condon's paranoid classic *The Manchurian Candidate*. In setting a historical context for the fiction that follows, Condon was subscribing to what today's spokesman for the Ismaili faith describes vociferously as myth and legend. It is certainly true that the idea of the Assassins as killers-for-hire in the modern sense is open to question; the belief that they formed an unlikely alliance with the Knights Templar little more than misty rumour.

The existential depiction of Ismaili belief found its way into late 20th-century counterculture, however. The idea of worldly reality created solely in the human consciousness, with no assistance from an almighty God, is as great a heresy to Ismaili Muslims as to any of the father religion's other devotees. It is in the legends surrounding 'the Old Man of the Mountain' (the generic name popularly attributed to both Hasan and his disciple Sinan) that this most alluring myth seems to have its origins. The romantic inference is that, if Hasan truly did indoctrinate the Assassins using hashish as part of the process, then their world was one of smoke-wreathed dream and mystery, where nothing could be said to be truly as it appeared.

The Assassins emerged in a most unexpected and unorthodox form in France during the 1840s. Like its medieval inspiration, the Club des Haschischins had its secret initiatory ranks and its secluded headquarters. But the latter was an upper floor in the Hotel Pimodan on the Ile de St Louis in Paris, while the former were drawn from the most fashionably outrageous bohemian artists and authors of the era. Affairs were presided over by their 'Prince' or 'Sheikh' of Assassins – in fact a doctor named Jacques-Joseph Moreau de Tours – who administered hashish in a paste form to be consumed by his novitiates and initiates.

Moreau appears to have been inspired by Silvestre De Sacy's pioneering 1809 paper on the links between the Assassins and the drug – then still very much an unknown quantity in Europe,– to investigate its effects on a scientific level. His willing guinea pigs were no doubt intrigued by Marco Polo's descriptions of visions of Paradise, or perhaps Joseph von Hammer-Purgstall's book which linked the Assassins with anarchistic rebellion, first published in French in 1813.

It was not a particularly *secret* society, as its leading light, Theophile Gautier, published a luridly entertaining description of a typical meeting, where attendees experienced the mind-altering effects of a heavy dose of cannabis, in an 1846 magazine article. Gautier was a popular author and the avuncular forefather of the scandalous decadent movement. Other members included the famous novelists Alexandre Dumas and Honore de Balzac and Gautier's celebrated protégé Baudelaire, the definitive damned poet, who would later write an influential essay on the drug. Some of them would even dress the part, adopting elements of Arabic dress or curved daggers emblematic of the kind of orientalism which Edward Said loftily condemns as cultural insensitivity. Dumas was partially inspired by his experiences to write *The Count of Monte Cristo*, which features an episode drawn almost verbatim from Marco Polo's account of the Old Man of the Mountain.

Mike Jay includes the society in a significant section of *Emperors of Dreams*, his survey of drugs in the 19th century. He suggests that the article Gautier penned about the Club des Haschischins

> 'subsequently became a myth almost as well-entrenched as the Assassin legend it gleefully plagiarises and debunks . . . The demi-monde of 1840s Paris which it conjures brings together a set of lifestyles, attitudes and causes which were probably never combined before but have spontaneously replicated themselves ever since: long hair, outlandish dress, radical politics, getting up late and staying up all night, sexual libertinism, heavy drinking and, of course, a voracious curiosity about drugs.'

It is in the legendary maxim, 'Nothing is true, everything is permitted,' that Hasan escapes his own austere historical persona and becomes a late 20th-century hipster. Indeed, there are persuasive arguments that suggest the maxim may actually have originated with the post-war beat generation of writers, rather than with Hasan on his death bed, as the legend suggests.

Its suggestion of living in a hash-drunk dream, a truly subjective reality, contains a paradoxical discipline all of its own: the Assassin initiate must not only determine his own course of actions without moral guidance, but must also interpret the amorphous fabric of an unfixed reality itself. It has apparently little to do with the more fundamental interpretation of Islam that contemporary Muslim scholars might attribute to Hasan.

Indeed, the idea may have its origins not with the Assassins themselves but with their opponents within the wider Islamic faith. In his essay on the origins of the phrase for the Disinformation.com site, Brian D. Hodges cites a translated quote from *Radd-i-Rawafid*, an anti-Shia polemic by the Sunni Imam-i-Rabbani. According to this rhetoric, the worst heresies were encapsulated in the Ismaili sub-sect, whose beliefs were described thus: 'one does not have to go into trouble by worshipping . . . they quote the thirteenth *ayat* of *Hadid sura*, which points out the wall between the people who are in Paradise and those who are in Hell. They say, 'There is no *haram* (prohibited). Everything is *halal* (permitted)."

This is not a philosophical statement but an accusation by the dominant strand of Islam against one of the faith's smaller sects. It is inarguable that most (if not all) Ismailis would see it as a gross slur, but in a modern age of cultural uncertainty and personal exploration it had an appeal all of its own. It would take a quite different kind of cultural dissident to make the concept stick.

Enter William S. Burroughs: heir to the American adding-machine fortune and drug addict; a widowed homosexual and father of one; a gun enthusiast who accidentally shot his wife dead; social libertarian, literary experimenter and originator of his own surrealistic conspiracy theories.

In his novels of fragmentary, SF-tinged parody and grotesque sexuality, Burroughs struck imaginative blows against the various forms of social control he despised. On the completion of his first great literary nightmare, *The Naked Lunch*, he short-circuited his creative process and threw open the doors to randomness and chaos by adoption of the cut-up technique. An innovation of his close friend, the artist Brion Gysin, the cut-up involved just that: the cutting up of phrases and passages of text on paper (whether the author's own or derived from other sources) and their random reordering to arrive at new meanings and senses, a truly uncontrolled stream of consciousness.

It is in the cut-up novels that followed *The Naked Lunch* that Burroughs seems to take scissors and paste to the anti-Ismaili propaganda of *Radd-i-Rawafid*, arriving at the phrase soon assimilated by the beats and later countercultures.

'Burroughs certainly used the phrase, 'Nothing is true, everything is permitted,' a lot,' acknowledges Ken Hollings, an admirer of the late author-iconoclast, 'and even if it isn't attributed to Hasan-i-Sabbah then I think we can offer it to Uncle Bill.'

The ghostly figure of Hasan himself also became a recurring phantom throughout most of the writer's body of work. In *The Naked Lunch*, the semi-autobiographical narrator Bill Lee (the name formerly used by Burroughs to disguise the thinly-veiled self-portrait in his early-1950s novel, *Junky*) 'is himself an agent, representing Hassan I Sabbah, the master of the assassins.' Lee also describes himself as 'working for an outfit known as Islam Inc.', and the fractured hallucinatory narrative plays out in a mythic North African no-man's-land called Interzone.

(While Burroughs enjoyed the tolerant indifference shown to his sexual and narcotic predilections in the Moroccan city of Tangiers, it is hard to imagine devout Muslims appreciating this backhanded compliment. However, among the rapid-fire nightmare imagery, he describes how, 'Arab rioters yipe and howl, castrating, disembowelling, throw burning gasoline . . .' While the author may have seen the Islamic heresy of the Assassins as a radical challenge to the dead hand of Western materialism, it seems he had few illusions about its host culture.)

In a paranoid dystopia where every briefly glimpsed figure is an agent of some corporate body or conspiracy, this is the first of Burroughs' literary appropriations of the Assassins as part of his war against control – while controlled themselves by the guiding words of Hasan, they are necessary agents of chaos, hacking away at the parameters of what is real and what is permitted.

In *The Ticket that Exploded*, the second of the image-laden quarter begun by *The Naked Lunch*, one character rants about, 'The "Hassan i Sabahs" from Cuntsville USA backed by yellow assassins who could not strangle a hernia'; the novel closes (or rather disintegrates) with the accusation that 'Hassan' works for Naval Intelligence. Reference is made to selling the 'Garden of Delights' (i.e. Paradise, Jinna) as just another junky commodity, and for the first time the phrase, 'Nothing is true – everything is permitted,' appears.

In fact, this may be the first appearance of the phrase anywhere in recorded history. In appropriating the Assassins for the purposes of his own dense, modern myth-making, Burroughs seems to have posthumously and mischievously pinned the quote on Hasan Sabbah.

'And then Burroughs adds this essay, "The Invisible Generation",' observes Hollings of the later epilogue to *The Ticket that Exploded*, 'which I think was originally published in '66 by Los Angeles Street Press, and this is one of his first attempts to work out how he can use tape recorders in order to change the nature of reality, to change the course of events.' In matching sound recordings with the workings of the human psyche, Burroughs is both precursor and echo to Hollings' reflections on the uses of 1950s consumer technology in his *Welcome to Mars*.

'He uses this phrase which I think sounds like it's a direct reference back to the Assassin myth: "The Invisible Brothers invading the present time." Because Burroughs is fascinated by how the tape recorder can be used to bring bits of the past into the present. In this polemic he puts forward a very simple idea: what we see is to a large extent influenced by what we hear. In other words, take footage of people running for a bus, add machinegun fire and you've got Petrograd, you've got a little revolutionary scene going on, and this is where Hasan-i-Sabbah's statement becomes important.

'Because it's a short hop, skip and a jump from starting riots in "The Invisible Generation" to the far more strenuous, muscular statement in "Electronic Revolution",' extrapolates Hollings, 'which I think dates from about 1970-71, at a time when he's in interviews saying, "Illusion is a revolutionary weapon." In other words, the spell that you're able to create using a tape, cutting up taped messages etc, shatters consensus reality. But when he's asked about what he means, Burroughs actually inverts Hasan-i-Sabbah's statement and says, "Whatever is true is not permitted."

'If you live in a definite universe, of definitely defined things, your options for action are simply reduced. The establishment likes things to be definite, likes them to be true, likes reality to be real, because the more they can do that the less and less choice we have as individuals. This is how I tend to interpret, "Nothing is true, all is permitted" – there are no checks and balances, there are no restraints on our behaviour, should we choose to follow that course. Burroughs seems to be getting ready to pick up a stengun and join the Baader-Meinhof Gang at this point.'

In *Nova Express*, the last book of the quartet, Burroughs speaks apocalyptically in the voice of his mythically re-imagined Hasan: 'I Hassan i Sabbah *rub out the word forever* . . . Cross all your skies see the silent writing of Brion Gysin Hassan i Sabbah,' he continues elliptically, conflating the name of the magus who drew the author into the Assassin legend with the Assassin leader himself. But the materialist-addicts of Burroughs' modern nightmare will not reject Western materialism in favour of mystical asceticism: 'NO HASSAN-I-SABBAH – WE WANT FLESH – WE WANT JUNK – WE WANT POWER.'

In a 1970s work, *The Wild Boys*, Burroughs describes how, 'The old phallic gods of Greece and the assassins of Alamout [sic] still linger in the Moroccan hills like sad pilots waiting to pick up survivors.' In 1981's *Cities of the Red Night*, the first instalment of his final trilogy of novels and his most accessible work, the ghosts are still there: 'the spirit of Hassan I Sabbah, Master of the Djinns,' is a guiding force once again; the final citation, "Nothing is true. Everything is permitted." The last words of Hassan i Sabah, Old Man of the Mountain,' may have been written with a knowing smile, as what had by now passed into popular mythology was actually a cut-up phrase of Bill Burroughs.

As persistent and recurrent as the figures of Hassan and the Assassins are in Burroughs' work, the obsession was introduced to him by Brion Gysin. A painter/occultist/all-round dilettante, Gysin had a huge influence on Burroughs via (among other things) his creation of the cut-up. The couple first met in Tangiers, where Gysin was working as a restaurateur, but would not become friendly until they hooked up in the American artistic expatriate community of Paris. It was in Morocco that Gysin developed the sensibilities that would infect his more famous friend.

'I think that Gysin, of the two, was the more steeped in Muslim and North African lore,' observes Ken Hollings. Indeed, of the two it was Gysin who would visit the castle at Alamut – remarking on how it would be impossible for the grounds to contain up to two hundred people, as in the Assassin legends.

'I think it's interesting that, at the Café of 1001 Nights, Gysin had a tape recorder and was recording the musicians in the club. He was cleaning out the flue in the kitchen area of the restaurant and he found this sort of nest of bits of broken mirror and charms and animals and paper. And inside there's this magic square with a message: "May Massa Brahim leave this place as the smoke vanishes up the chimney," or words to this effect. It is a spell that's been put there to drive him out of the restaurant.

'Within weeks he has rendezvoused with Burroughs at the Beat Hotel in Paris, where he discovers the cut-up technique, having sliced through the papers. Burroughs is in the room downstairs finishing *The Naked Lunch*. What I find interesting about this spell,' elaborates Hollings, 'is that it connects to the ethnographic, cantering, ritualistic culture that Gysin was recording in Tangiers, and the notion that the spell was going to make him disappear. It seems very similar to the actions of the tape recorder that Burroughs first describes in "The Invisible Generation", cutting silence into crowd scenes. In the final part of the essay he talks about cutting everyone into thin air. So these ideas of tape-recording invisibility and somehow magicking someone out of existence seem very close to the Old Man of the Mountain appearing out of nowhere. Somehow the Assassins are not stoppable, they are "the Invisible Brotherhood invading present time".'

In Gysin's own later essay about developing the cut-up technique, he describes a scene in Paris: 'I look around at the pictures which [Bill] was the first to dig: "See the silent writing of Brion Gysin, Hassan-i-Sabbah, across all skies!" I write across the picture space from left to right . . .' The words were cut up and reused for Burroughs' *Nova Express*, and an ancient Islamic sect leader became the ghost in the machine for technological civilisation's discontents.

***

"'Thus it was that when the Old Man decided to send one of his Assassins upon a mission, such as to have a prince slain, he would send for one of these youths and say, 'Go thou and kill, and when thou returnest, my angels shall bear thee into Paradise. And shouldest thou die, nevertheless, I will send my angels to carry you back into Paradise.'" They enjoyed their work.' – Turner, played by Mick Jagger, quoting from *The Travels of Marco Polo* in Donald Cammell and Nicolas Roeg's film, *Performance* (1970).

When Bill Burroughs came to London in the late 1960s, he found himself one of the grand old men of a psychedelic counterculture that had less to do with hippie egalitarianism than old-fashioned British elitism. In the more salubrious parts of central and west London, drug-addicted dilettantes, art dealers and aristocrats mixed with the new aristocracy of 'Swinging London' – beat groups in general, but the Rolling Stones in particular.

Fed by similar narcotics to the 1950s beatniks (cannabis and opiates, occasionally cocaine), but with an infusion of LSD and other hallucinogens, the chicly decadent neo-hippies of Kensington and Chelsea were suitably steeped in mysticism and occult lore. Hailing from a similarly esoteric but more studied older generation, Californian art filmmaker Kenneth Anger had also come to London. A gay aesthete raised among the film community, Anger was the author of the celebratedly bitchy history *Hollywood Babylon* and a devotee of Aleister Crowley, the 'Great Beast'. He was also the auteur behind the *Magick Lantern Cycle* of short films.

Anger's Crowleyite Luciferianism – a dualistic synthesis of the world's great monotheistic and Pagan religions with antichristian ritual – was gaudily illustrated in his films. As the old man of Luciferian aesthetics, he also found himself a godfather to *Performance* writer/co-director Cammell, an actual 'godchild' of Crowley's whose father had been an associate of the great provocateur-antichrist.

'It is very interesting that *Performance* is part of that kind of cultural armoury,' observes Ken Hollings, 'that set of references that places Burroughs in Duke Street, and [art dealer] Robert Fraser – who was arrested with Jagger, who was himself interested in Africa and Muslim cultures and ended up in India – with Kenneth Anger. Anger, who was also handled by Fraser at that time, was in the background, offering advice or trying to impress an influence on this movie.'

Performance was shot in 1968 but not released by the nervous Warner Bros studio until late in 1970. The years have been kind to it while many better received pop-art hybrids of the time have dated horribly. Its sensual hybrid of sex and violence, of drug visions and psychosis, remains timeless, reflecting the clash between two 1960s countercultures at once fascinated with and distrustful of each other: organised crime and the nouveau-decadence of the rock aristocrat.

Chas Devlin, a London enforcer impressively played by upper-class actor James Fox, is on the run after taking gang boss Harry Flowers' directions to intimidate a former friend too far. Killing as an act of revenge, the vicious Chas is both a maverick and a hunted man, imbued with a sadistic sensuality he does not really comprehend.

When he holes up at the Notting Hill abode of retired rock star Turner – its décor pitched somewhere between Kasbah and whorehouse – the two of them collide in a joint performance that goes 'all the way to madness'. Mick Jagger had recently completed *Beggar's Banquet* with the Stones, the album that features the classic, Anger-influenced 'Sympathy for the Devil'; while *Performance* lingered in the can, Jagger would adopt the androgynous, Luciferian Turner as his late-1960s stage persona.

Such fluidity of identity is the film's central theme. Dosing Chas with magic mushrooms while his bisexual girlfriends apply rouge and mascara to the gangster, Turner catalyses a transfer of personalities that reaches apotheosis in the film's final scenes – where Chas shoots Turner point-blank through the head, only for Turner's face to appear in lieu of that of Chas as his fellow gangsters drive him away to be killed.

And of course, amidst the heady mix of psychedelic psychodrama and hip occultism, Turner evokes the legend of the Assassins.

'Whenever Hasan-i-Sabbah's name is mentioned these days,' remarks Hollings, 'I do tend to think about the note that Chas leaves at the end of *Performance*, on the bedside table: "Gone to Persia. Chas." I think it seems entirely appropriate that Chas himself of course is an assassin, is the "performer".' In fact the charismatic Chas is modelled on an authentic London gangland figure of the 1960s, maverick gunman Jimmy Evans. In acting autonomously as a killer, in effectively becoming an assassin, he is condemned by a London underworld that held torture, disfigurement and intimidation in common currency but frowned on the unnecessary attention attracted by murder.

'The Assassins are referred to particularly as the 'Hashishim', as Mick Jagger so nicely pronounces it,' Hollings observes of the dark, pungent atmosphere that sucks Hasan into its hallucinogenic mix. 'In a sense it is *the* Assassins movie. By the very fact that the identities are blurred at the end of the film, through the final shootings, they *all* go to Persia – as it were.'

Earlier in the film, when Turner's lover Pherber (Anita Pallenberg) becomes interested in Chas's secrets and detects the wounds he received from a vicious beating, she suggests they call Dr Burroughs to 'give him a shot'. Bill Burroughs' unseen presence hangs as knowingly over the film as that of Hasan Sabbah – indeed, in the modern imagination, the heretic cult leader and the literary/lifestyle experimenter are one.

There is a certain poisonous miasma which hangs heavy over *Performance*. But there was a more playful side to the psychedelic subculture, and this too touched upon Alamut. In 1975, Robert Shea and Robert Anton Wilson published their bizarre epic *Illuminatus!* trilogy. At the risk of lurching into cliché, the books were very much like Abbe Barruel on acid, stirring sex, drugs and conspiracy theory into a largely non-linear adventure story. At a time when conspiracy paranoia was experiencing a renaissance – with ridiculous theories enjoying serious consideration – the authors wove a saga that explored serious ideas in a satirical fashion. In the era of change-your-life cult books, the trilogy joined Luke Rhinehart's *The Dice Man* and Robert M. Pirsig's *Zen and the Art of Motorcycle Maintenance* on any self-respecting subcultural hipster's bookshelf.

Inevitably, the Assassins merit a role in the trilogy's sprawling frolic through the realms of conspiracy paranoia. While Shea would subsequently concentrate on historical fiction, Wilson went on to become something of an anti-guru, a welcome presence on the fringe offering an open-minded but gently satirical take on the weird and wonderful currents stirred up post-psychedelic era, particularly conspiracy theories.

> 'Robert Anton Wilson's version of Hasan-i-Sabbah is more like a sort of "phantom Sufi", observes Hollings, 'the kind of guy who goes into a shop and says to the guy behind the counter: "Have you ever seen me before?" The guy behind the counter says, "No." So he says, "Well, how do you know it's me?" Or there's that wonderful statement that Wilson liked, "If it ever was true it's probably changed by now."

Bill Burroughs' influence, meanwhile, would outlive his second counterculture – the hippies – and find its third wave in his seventh decade, during the late 1970s/early 1980s, when he was feted by the post-punk generation.

The old man of artistic transgression made it his business to contact British 'industrial music' innovator and nascent occultist Genesis

P-Orridge. Born Neil Megson, Orridge had been a founding member of avant-garde art and music groups the COUM Foundation, Throbbing Gristle, Psychic TV and thee Temple ov Psychick Youth. For him, Burroughs' espousal of the 'Nothing is true, everything is permitted' doctrine held a similar potency to Crowley's 'Do what thou will shall be the whole of the law' – the latter perceived as a purely nihilistic statement by many, though the exigencies of remaking the law by power of the individual's will are oft overlooked.

Burroughs and Orridge gave a joint interview in 1983, at a time when they and Gysin were the subject of one of the influential Re-Search series of alternative coffee-table books. In it, Burroughs maintains the fiction about the last words of Hasan-i-Sabbah, but also sheds light on the enduring appeal of the legend to him:

> ' . . . The whole Assassination method was unique . . . He'd have someone planted; like there was a general about to organise a campaign against Hassan-i-Sabbah. An old gardener who worked in the garden for ten years killed him with a scythe. One of Hassan-i-Sabbah's men. How he got the word to him nobody knows, but he did. Some sort of telepathy perhaps.
>
> 'Well, I found the whole concept of Assassination on that basis . . . very congenial. In other words, to get out of this mess you've got to kill. Remove obstacles.'

As Ken Hollings suggests, in the last few decades of his life Burroughs, who derided all political systems of whatever ideology, had become a cultural anarchist.

But the most potent part of the Assassin legend for Burroughs appears to have been the image of Hasan in his isolation, unseen and locked away from the world but influencing events from a distance: 'Everybody knew who did it but they could not reach him. He had put himself in a no-affect position, where he could affect others but they could not affect him.'

Orridge's activities with the Temple, which he founded, and his 1980s band, Psychic TV, were part of a series of lifelong behavioural and psychological experiments. (Think the Manson Family with arts degrees, more technical acumen and a greater respect for human life.) It was still rare for the Old Man to make his phantom presence felt in Psychic TV's music – although one of Orridge's musical contemporaries, Steve Stapleton, recorded an album entitled *Drunk with the Old Man of the Mountain* in 1987. (Stapleton records under the name Nurse with Wound

– oft-pegged as 'industrial', his experimental electronica tends more towards ambience plus sound samples.) Sans lyrical content, the title is presumably an obscure in-joke about the 'real' Hasan's decapitation of his son for the crime of getting drunk on wine.

Genesis P-Orridge's audio tribute to the Assassin cult would wait until the late 1990s, when he contributed to record producer/musical fusionist Bill Laswell's album *Hashisheen: The End of the Law*. With a title alluding to the Crowleyite interpretation of the 'everything is permitted' maxim, the recording offers a curiously seductive melding of the Hasans of history, the Polo legend and the Burroughs reinterpretation, set against ambient sounds which only occasionally sample the Islamic chanting and Eastern percussion of Arabic music.

'The Houris of Paradise . . . appear in one's essence whenever one desires,' we are told of the Assassin's mnemonic to murder; their private universe is said to be 'an occult space-time continuum consumed by still unimagined liberties,' quite apart from the devout of the Islamic faith. Out of the mostly American narrators (including a breathily didactic Patti Smith and poet/photographer Ira Cohen, a friend of the late Brion Gysin), the English nasality of Orridge stands out. He sounds not unlike Davy Jones of the Monkees as he tells the Assassins, 'Whatever is forbidden for the perverted world is permitted for you,' and also makes the Burroughs-ian inversion, 'Everything is true, nothing is permitted.'

In a track entitled 'The Mongols Destroy Alamut', the Assassins are referred to as 'evil followers of the practice of libertinism', while in 'The Tale of the Caliph Haken' Orridge pronounces, 'he asks me who I worship; I worship no one – for I myself am the one true God'; hashish is described elsewhere as a dissolvable paste in 'an amber-scented drink', as this is clearly the Hasan cult of legend.

In 'A Trip to Alamut' we hear the late Gysin's words linking the subjective reality of Hassan's world with 'the random process of discontinuity [i.e. cut-ups] that Burroughs and I have been working on since 1960.' The final track, 'The Western Lands', is a summation of the last of Burroughs' trilogy which began with *Cities of the Red Night*. We briefly hear the croaky veteran drug fiend himself (who died a few months before the album's release, aged eighty-three) articulating the essence of his fascination: 'Is there a means of confronting death without immediate physical danger? . . . these are the questions of Hassan-i-Sabbah.'

As a counterpoint, the voice of rock 'n' roll idiot-savant Iggy Pop tempers the old literary wild man's words with a greyer historical realism: 'What evidence remains is unreliable . . . There were no women at

Alamut . . .,' no temptresses, no houris of Heaven. We finally leave Hasan to himself on a far more contemporary, far less romantic note: 'One thinks of those evil old mullahs with their harsh, closed faces.'

***

'Be an agent of change. Execute assassinations to impact the world around you.' – *Assassin's Creed* game, Ubisoft 2007.

When the Invisible Brotherhood crept their way into the virtual reality of video games, they went through a cyber-age update. The game's central character is a bartender, kidnapped by a large, shadowy corporation; the dormant mnemonic to murder is awakened in his brain when he is subjected to the Animus, a Jungian piece of computer technology that awakens ancestral memories.

The action moves between near-future and historical past, as our hero finds himself walking in the sandals of Altair Ibn La-Ahad, his Arabic ancestor fighting the Crusaders in the Jerusalem of 1191. Assigned a total of nine assassination targets by Assassin leader Al Mualim (a fictionalised Hasan), Altair finds himself fighting the Knights Templar as mortal enemies. Fictional fantasy still predominates, of course – on his deathbed, Al Mualim reveals that he is in fact a Templar himself, adding new dimensions of subterfuge and compounding the myth which claims that both secret societies were somehow intrinsically linked.

No one expects a history lesson from a video game, and the success of *Assassin's Creed* can be attributed to the stealth the player needs to employ in carrying out spying, theft and assassination missions. All of them are justified by the stated ethos of 'Nothing is true, everything is permitted' – the last words of Hasan Sabbah (or, more likely perhaps, his modern champion, Wild Bill Burroughs).

There have been other 21st century manifestations of the Assassins in the realms of electronic entertainment. In 2002, Firefly Studios released a follow-up to their popular 2001 computer game *Stronghold*, in which players attempt to successfully besiege enemy castles. The sequel was entitled *Crusader*, and in addition to introducing Saladin, Richard the Lionheart and new Arabic combatants, there are a range of new opponents such as the Nizar, who 'may catch you by surprise if you are unprepared for his swift and silent tactics.' The popular *Total War* computer games also feature the Nizaris in their medieval variant, as a unit that can be recruited should you choose to play as the Fatimid faction.

Most colourfully, Hasan Sabbah has manifested in the world of comics. In 1990, Marvel Comics sent their superhero the Black Knight back through time to confront Hasan, billing their villain as 'the 1,000-year-old son of a 1,000-year-old mother!' whose 'power some say is the power of hell itself.' In a story evidently inspired by accounts of the assassination of Conrad of Montferrat, our hero confronts a superhuman sorceror who imprisons hapless Crusaders in a cave, hypnotised into thinking they are in a luxuriant garden.

Marvel's main competitors, DC, have also fielded their own version of Hasan Sabbah as a supervillain. Now known by the geographically-specific name of Khyber, this Hasan is the implacable foe of Superman in one story, a super-powered super-conspirator: 'He has been long thought dead. But in fact, he only grew more ambitious and chose to vanish from the world's gaze . . .'

XIV

THE WRATH OF GOD

Despite Hasan Sabbah's best filicidal efforts, by the late 1100s the role of Grand Master of the Assassins had become firmly established as a legacy passed from father to son. Similarly, Hasan's dogmatic refusal to accept the role of Imam proved futile, as a large element of Hasan II's Resurrection doctrine, as announced in 1164, propagated the idea of the Grand Master as the Nizari Imam. While most of the Assassins calmly accepted this radical announcement, some saw it as a possible excuse to seize power. The first rumbles of the kind of internal strife the sect had previously stirred among their opponents began to shake the foundations of Alamut.

Hasan II was Grand Master for just four years, during which time he appears to have restructured the Assassins, creating a new rank for himself that was a halfway house between Grand Master and the sacred role of Imam. Before he had a chance to complete the transition, or confirm rumours that he was secretly related to the Imam Nizar, he was murdered. It was an inside job, his brother-in-law ambushing Hasan in the Assassin fortress of Lamasar and stabbing him to death in traditional Assassin style.

The conspiracy was ill thought-out. If his killers hoped it would spark a popular revolt, they were to be bitterly disappointed. The mantle of leadership transferred smoothly to Hasan's 19-year-old son, Muhammad II, who rounded up his father's murderers, and a number of their relatives, and had them executed.

If anything the plot strengthened the Resurrection, which Muhammad II immediately reaffirmed. Given the opportunity to join the rebellion against it, the Nizari rank and file had refused. There were now no doubts that the Assassin Grand Master was the divine Imam, descended from the Prophet Muhammad via Nizar. The Resurrection also had other implications. One was that it was a declaration of spiritual victory; that the Imam they had been awaiting so long had finally arrived, signalling ultimate triumph for the Assassins over their benighted rivals. But this could also be interpreted as a concession of defeat, an acknowledgement that Hasan Sabbah's dream of conquering the Islamic world in preparation for the Imam had proven hopelessly overambitious, and that the leadership were now prepared to settle for a mystical form of success.

Certainly, the Assassins under Muhammad II became an inward-looking movement, less concerned with the region's politics, as if they no longer thought that the outside world mattered. Assassins were despatched by Alamut's Grand Master – perhaps even to bring Sinan to heel, who appears to have been operating a more proactive policy in Syria – but the roll of honour, the list of assassinations, was largely allowed to gather dust during Muhammad II's lengthy rule. He was the longest serving of Alamut's Grand Masters, ruling for 44 years, an impressive span for any ruler in such perilous times. But Muhammad may have sunk into a lethargic sense of complacency. Raids by neighbouring kingdoms continued intermittently, proving that the outside world had not forgotten – or forgiven – the Assassins. And changes were afoot that Alamut could not afford to ignore.

During Muhammad II's reign, the Seljuq Sultanate finally collapsed. In 1131, the slippery Sanjar – by turn the most implacable foe and amenable friend of the Assassins – finally made his claim for the crown of Seljuq Sultan after years of plotting and scheming. The post proved very much a double-edged sword, as Sanjar quickly found himself struggling to hold the disintegrating Sultanate together, with a realm too large and unwieldy to allow the rapid U-turns of policy that had been the trademark of his previous career. Being the mercurial maverick of the sultanate had been far easier than being its saviour. In 1141, he marshalled his ranks to face an invasion force descending from the eastern steppes, from a people known in their own region as the Black Chinese. It was a disaster for Sanjar, who only just escaped the carnage with 15 of his best men and was obliged to abandon a whole swathe of the eastern sultanate to the invaders.

The defeat was just the start of the Seljuq Sultan's problems, as a number of his subjects took advantage of Sanjar's distress to assert themselves, while it allowed the Crusader states to his far west to consolidate. The Abbasid Caliph, traditionally a lapdog of the Sultan for around a century, now found the confidence to bare his teeth. A succession of rebellions erupted, most seriously in Khwarazmia, a kingdom that had long been a loyal Seljuq vassal but now began to operate as a sovereign state with ambitious plans. When their shah crossed the line into open revolt, Sanjar was obliged to confront him.

In 1153, Sanjar lost a decisive battle against the fledgling Khwarazmian Empire, and was captured. He was held captive for three years, and died a broken man the year after – a sad end to a long and colourful career. The Seljuq Sultanate effectively died with him.

All of this happened with little response from the introspective Assassin Imam, Muhammad II. In his latter years he was obliged to take an interest, as the expanding Khwarazmian Empire was now on the doorstep. Muhammad made a half-hearted attempt to ingratiate himself with the Khwarazmians by ordering the assassination of a mutual enemy. They were evidently unimpressed; in fact, one of their generals captured and executed a contingent of Nizaris from Alamut three years later.

The Grand Master's son and heir was taking a more proactive approach, secretly sending envoys out to local rulers – including the Abbasid Caliph and the Khwarazmian King – to solicit their friendship, with assurances that, unlike his heretic father, he was a good Muslim, an orthodox Sunni no less. (As was his mother. The issue of an arch-heretic like Muhammad II marrying a devout Sunni is little addressed in most accounts. It must have made for interesting conversations around the breakfast table.)

Once Muhammad II became aware of his son's private diplomatic policy, he was less than enthused. Declaring the leadership of Alamut a sacred hereditary succession had backfired. Muhammad II could not legitimately disinherit his disloyal son any more than his grandfather, Muhammad I, could have disowned Hasan I, however much he hated him. (Though he did make his point by murdering 250 of Hasan's supporters, and forcing another 250 to carry their corpses away on their backs).

If Muhammad II had been planning to discipline his son in any fashion, it never came to pass. In the September of 1210, the Grand Master passed away. Whether it was of natural causes or something more sinister became a controversial topic within the walls of Alamut. In a sense, family history then repeated itself. Just as the death of Muhammad I and the accession of Hasan II resulted in the Resurrection, so the death of Muhammad II and subsequent elevation of Hasan III to the Nizari Imamate triggered another apparent change in direction for the Assassins.

Staying true to his previous promises, Hasan III announced to the Muslim leaders of surrounding regions that not only would the Assassins now renounce Nizari doctrine, they would also forsake Shiite Islam and enter the Sunni fold. The reasons for such a radical shift are just as controversial as Hasan II's Resurrection. Was it a sincere conversion, prompted perhaps by the influence of his mother? Or an example of *taqiyya* – pretending to abandon your beliefs in the face of persecution? Perhaps the trappings of religion were no longer as important to the Assassins as some hidden ulterior political, mystical or philosophical agenda.

Whatever the case, the Assassins appear to have accepted this sharp theological U-turn with the same equanimity that they had greeted the Resurrection nearly 50 years earlier. Whether this tells us that Hasan Sabbah's doctrine held true – that obedience overrode every other virtue – or that something else was going on behind the scenes is difficult to discern from our vantage point, almost a thousand years later.

While Hasan III's embracing of orthodoxy went in his favour, after over a century of dogmatic heresy the sect's neighbours remained suspicious. Their desire to embrace a new convert to the Sunni faith did not easily erase memories of generations of political murder, frequently targeting Sunni theologians including several Abbasid Caliphs. So the new Grand Master suggested that a deputation of local theologians visit Alamut's fabled library, to inspect it. Anything they considered heretical or objectionable would be burnt.

In a scene that would make scholars of any age seethe – particularly modern students of the enigmatic Nizari heresy – numerous sacred texts were cast into the flames, apparently including some penned by the sect's founder himself. Hasan III burned the pages with colourful curses against his predecessors, damning them for straying from the true path. It poses questions to those who claim there was nothing unorthodox about the occult doctrines of the medieval Nizaris, but it also did much to convince the Sunnis of the day of Hasan III's sincerity.

Hasan built mosques and bathhouses in Assassin settlements, a move calculated to make Assassin citadels and villages resemble those of his orthodox neighbours. He began conducting himself in a fashion more akin to a conventional Muslim ruler, riding abroad to survey his lands rather than directing operations from behind castle walls. His mother even went on a pilgrimage to Mecca (though it nearly ended in disaster when her visit coincided with a murder, some locals regarding the Nizari contingent as the obvious suspects).

Hasan III was becoming a regular guy, at least in terms of the medieval Muslim aristocracy. It paid off. The Caliph blessed marriages between the celebrity convert and the daughters of a number of local rulers. As in the old days, he transferred allegiance intermittently between the rival Khwarazmian Shah and Abbasid Caliph, but this time in a more open and conventional manner. (Though old habits do die hard, and there appear to have been an assassination or two.)

It all looked as if the Assassins, medieval Islam's most obstinate prodigal sons, had finally returned to the fold. But what could be so terrifying as to motivate a Grand Master of Alamut to adopt *taqiyya* after his predecessors had refused to compromise their beliefs for over 100 years?

'[The Assassins] said that when the World Emperor Jenghiz Khan set out from Turkestan, before he came to the countries of Islam, Jalal-al-Din [Hasan III] had in secret sent couriers to him and written letters tendering his submission and allegiance,' according to one Islamic source. 'This was alleged by the Heretics and the truth is not clear, but this much is evident, that when the armies of the World-Conquering Emperor Jenghiz Khan entered the countries of Islam, the first ruler on this side of the Oxus to send ambassadors, and present his duty, and accept allegiance was Jalal-al-Din.'

If he had been prescient enough to recognise the terrible threat posed by Genghis Khan at this early stage, then it is easy to see why the Assassin Grand Master might resort to radical measures in order to prepare for the oncoming onslaught.

But Hasan III would never face the growing menace in the east. He died in 1221, after little over a decade on the throne. By this point the leadership of Alamut was very much in the mode of the Nizaris' more orthodox neighbours, vulnerable to the same debilitating intrigues that had embroiled the courts in Cairo and Baghdad. Hasan III's heir, Muhammad III, was only nine when his father died, and so a guardian or tutor was appointed to guide the child king. Under the vizier's guiding hand, the Assassins maintained a very similar course to that set by the young Imam's father. But as the young Muhammad grew older and gained in confidence, the emphasis shifted. The adherence to Sunni orthodoxy – or at least the efforts to maintain the appearance of orthodoxy – were slowly but surely abandoned. According to some accounts, Muhammad III was growing up into a decadent despot of mythic proportions.

In 1967 George C. Brauer published a book entitled *The Young Emperors*, in which he endeavoured to explain how a mighty state like Ancient Rome fell under the rule of a motley crew of disastrous tyrants and psychopaths during the third century. His answer lay much of the blame on the tradition of appointing inexperienced young men, qualified by birth rather than merit and given almost limitless power. Most of us, if offered authority before we have had the chance to develop any powers of reflective wisdom, have the capacity to turn into monsters. All overindulged little children have an element of the tyrant in their character, and the young Muhammad III had all of the qualifications. He was inexperienced, pampered and hailed as divine before he had any chance to develop any sense of proportion or common humanity.

So it was that Muhammad III grew into an increasingly volatile and negligent ruler. Prone to violent mood swings and hallucinations, deaf to good advice, inclined to fly off the handle at anyone who displeased him, the Assassin Grand Master wallowed in perverse pleasures of the flesh. He seems to have become the Middle East's answer to Emperor Nero, who notoriously murdered his mother and fiddled while Rome burnt. But, just as some historians have suggested that Nero's black reputation owes at least as much to unsympathetic commentators – motivated by political hostility and religious prejudice – as the facts, so it is that the unflattering portrait of Muhammad III was created by the pens of Sunni chroniclers, outraged at his gradual return to the heresies of his forefathers. The 34-year length and success of the reign of Muhammad III suggest a man who, while certainly no angel, was probably not a depraved maniac.

Like Nero, who was an enthusiastic patron of the arts, Muhammad appears to have been a cultured man and his reign a minor golden age for Alamut. He restocked the libraries denuded by his predecessor, attracting some of Islam's most celebrated scholars. (Not bad for a supposedly unpredictable madman.) Improved relations with the Abbasid Caliph from the days of Hasan III were maintained, while the first of Genghis Khan's hordes began to eat away at the eastern borders of the Khwarazmian Empire, creating new opportunities for Assassin expansion.

Military expeditions, Assassin agents and missionary delegations all filed out of Alamut and other Nizari strongholds into enemy territory to spread the word. The sect's missionaries were particularly wide-ranging, and it is in this period that Nizari doctrines began making serious inroads into the Indian subcontinent.

The sect's ongoing relations with the Khwarazmians are testament to the dread that many still held of the Assassins, and the curious diplomatic situations that emerged when that unspoken threat was part and parcel of negotiations. After the familiar vicious cycle of massacre and retaliatory assassination had temporarily been arrested by a truce in 1227, Muhammad III despatched an envoy named Badr to discuss matters with the Khwarazmian Shah. On his way, Badr became aware of a recent assassination that might make his journey unusually hazardous, as tempers were likely to be running high in the Khwarazmian court. So he sent a letter ahead to the Khwarazmian vizier, asking if it might be wise to abort his mission.

The Khwarazmian vizier, Sharaf al-Mulk, was in an even greater state of anxiety. The Assassins who had committed the recent murder had made it clear – before they were stoned to death by angry citizens – that Sharaf was their next intended target. The vizier was now haunted by visions of a knife in the gut, delivered when he least expected it. And so he responded to Badr's letter with enthusiasm: not only should the Assassin envoy continue his journey, but Sharaf would join him en route to ensure his safety and offer assistance. The vizier reasoned that only by earning the good favour of the Assassin leaders could he protect himself from their agents. If nothing else, they were unlikely to strike in the presence of one of their superiors. So it was that the Nizari envoy was granted a Khwarazmian escort.

***

Much to Sharaf's surprise, he found that he liked the Assassin. He was agreeable company, learned and a good conversationalist. Every day spent in his company found the dread in the vizier's heart subsiding. Badr found the vizier an amenable companion too, and the extra comforts he provided made the onerous journey pass more quickly. Within a day they spoke like old friends, as their party – accompanied by slaves and soldiers, with camels carrying the supplies – made its way across the plain of Serab. Neither man wished to shatter the air of fellowship that enveloped their caravan, as it slowly progressed toward the setting sun.

That night, they made camp as usual. Sharaf, who knew that alcohol was not forbidden among the disciples of the Assassin Grand Master, had arranged for several skins of fine red wine to be included among the many little luxuries carried by the camels. As the moon rose high in the star-speckled sky, and the fire crackled happily in the circle of tents, laughing voices rose in volume as the two men continued their friendly discourse. But, as the old saying goes, as the skins began to empty the wine began to talk. Topics that had been taboo when their tongues had been more careful started to creep into their conversation, as Sharaf began to unburden himself about the terror he had felt.

Badr did not respond as Sharaf had hoped. He rose unsteadily to his feet, and told the vizier that he did well to be afraid. 'Even here among your own army we have our Assassins,' boasted Badr, all caution forgotten in his cups, 'they are well-established and pass as your own men – some in your stables, some in the service of the Shah's chief herald.'

Sharaf suddenly felt the wine driven from his veins by dread. 'Who are these men?' he demanded to know, struggling to conceal a tremor in his voice. 'Are any of them among us tonight?'

Badr was suddenly aware that he had said too much, but Sharaf was insistent, pressing his question with the fervour of a man who felt his life rested upon the answer. He stood to offer Badr the scarf from around his throat, a strong symbolic token of his personal guarantee of safety for the Assassins.

His courage still buoyed by the evening's drink, the Assassin envoy finally relented and barked five names into the darkness. Five shapes emerged into the light thrown by the fire – each a soldier, fully armed, bowing in turn before Badr as sign of their fealty. Among their number was an Indian, who could not help but smile as he saw the paleness on Sharaf's face. The man who had been issuing him commands for months now stood before him trembling in fear.

'I could have stuck a knife in your belly a dozen times,' the Indian grinned malevolently, 'when you bathed, as you ate, while you slept. You only live because the Lord of Alamut wills it.'

The prospect was too much for the frightened vizier. He cast off his cloak and fell to his knees before the sextet of Assassins. 'Why would you do such a thing?' he entreated, pulling open his shirt to bare his chest. 'What does your master want from me? For what sins or shortcomings on my part does he crave my blood? I am his slave, just as I am the Shah's slave, and I bow before you! I am at your mercy!'

***

When word reached the Khwarazmian Shah of his vizier's craven display, he was contorted with rage. He immediately despatched a messenger to intercept the caravan as it approached his court, with an uncompromising order. All of the Assassins that had been revealed as enemy agents that night were to be executed in the most horrible fashion. Sharaf argued against the directive, but in vain. Caught between the fury of his shah and the prospect of future vengeance from Alamut, he obeyed.

All five of the Assassins agents were bound, and cast onto a mighty pyre built outside his tent, as Badr was obliged to watch. As the men roasted alive in the roaring flames, they shrieked that they gladly sacrificed their lives for their Grand Master and Imam. Sharaf knew it was only a matter of time before he heard from Alamut. Sure enough, an envoy arrived, who the vizier treated with fawning politeness. The envoy demanded 10,000 dinars apiece in compensation for the dead agents, which Sharaf gladly paid, even offering further gifts and financial inducements in the hope of buying his safety.

The other main player in this curious little diplomatic drama, Badr the Assassin ambassador, survived this mission but was not so lucky the following year. His caravan was ambushed by Khwarazmian forces and massacred en route to the court of the Mongol Khan. The official reason was that the caravan included a Mongol diplomat among their number. The Shah needed little excuse to sabotage negotiations between his Nizari rivals to the west and the Mongol threat that lurked on his eastern borders, like ravening wolves.

But those of Muhammad III's deputations that did get through to the Mongols, suggesting alliances, were sent home with a simple message: there would be no negotiations, and no mercy for any that lifted even a finger by way of resistance.

Khwarazmian policy towards the Mongols had been uncompromising from the beginning. Mongol merchants who entered their lands were butchered as spies; the Mongol diplomat who was sent to complain was beheaded; his guards were allowed to live only to bear his severed head home, but not before they had their beards singed. Many historians have condemned the Shah's combative attitude as foolhardy bravado, but it may well have represented his only option in the face of a foe whose brutal ruthlessness was already legendary. Besides, the Khwarazmians were hardly defenceless; with a force that outnumbered any army the eastern Mongols could field against them, the Shah had reason to feel cautious optimism.

Even so, it proved misplaced. The Mongols fielded heavy cavalry superior to the Crusaders and horse-archers superior to the Saracens, in armies supplemented by the best combat engineers that China, the inventor of gunpowder, had to offer. In addition, the Mongols employed terror tactics with an adept brutality that made the Assassins look like amateurs.

The Mongol army swept through Khwarazmia with Genghis Khan at its head, like a consuming storm. The Shah had divided his forces in a defensive strategy, but they were outmanoeuvred and picked off with ease by his swift-moving opponent. The campaign was unusually brutal, even by Mongol standards. In 1220, the ancient city of Bukhara fell. The Khan gathered the survivors in the city's Great Mosque. As copies of the Koran were torn and thrown to the four winds, he addressed the assembled throng: 'I am the Wrath of God,' he announced, 'if you had not been so wicked, I would not be here.' The entire civilian population were ordered to leave, as their city was systematically picked clean and burnt to the ground. Some survivors were deliberately released to spread panic, while others were used as a human shield in front of the Khan's army, to absorb enemy arrow fire.

Samarkand, the jewel in the Khwarazmian crown, held out for just five days. Once within the walls, the Mongol forces butchered the entire garrison of some 30,000 men. Then they turned their attentions to the civilian population. Priests were freed; women were raped, then enslaved; anybody with useful skills was taken as a prisoner to the Mongol territories to the east.

The city whose fate exemplifies the mind-blowing savagery of the Mongols was Nishapur. When his son-in-law was killed by an arrow shot from the city's battlements in 1221, the Khan resolved to make an example of it. Once they had overcome the city's defences, the Mongols set about the systematic massacre of the inhabitants. Men's skulls were neatly stacked into a pyramid, women's into another, with a third for the crania of children. It is said that they even did the same for the citizenry's pets. To complete the job, the city was levelled to the ground. By the time Genghis left, there were some 1.7 million human skulls carefully arranged in the ruins of Nishapur.

It is a sobering image for those who think that recent history has some kind of monopoly on systematic sadism, for the Khan is easily the equal of modern monsters like Hitler or Stalin. Nishapur was not an isolated example. Many once-magnificent ancient cities were turned into smouldering cemeteries by the Mongol hordes. While some of the casualty figures may well have been exaggerated, it is difficult to overstate the impact the Mongols' merciless scorched-earth policy had on their victims. A Persian chronicler reflected a century later that, 'as a result of the eruption of the Mongols and the general massacre of the people which took place in those days . . . there can be no doubt that if for a thousand years to come no evil befalls the country, yet it will not be possible to repair the damage, and bring the land back into the state it was formerly.'

The Khwarazmian Shah fled before the onslaught, dying soon afterwards, leaving his son to fight what was effectively a guerrilla war against the Mongol invaders from the remnants of his father's empire. In 1223, leaving two of his sons to mop up any pockets of Khwarazmian resistance, Genghis Khan headed home at the front of a vast caravan of booty. Any pleasure the Assassin Grand Master or Abbasid Caliph may have taken in the plight of their Khwarazmian rivals must swiftly have evaporated as streams of refugees came westward with tales of Mongol savagery.

In seeking to form anti-Mongol alliances, Assassin and Abbasid envoys were met with polite rebuffs from their new neighbours at best. It was time to try another approach. As far as Muhammad III could see, there was only one thing for it. Assassins were despatched to try and infiltrate the Mongol court. They enjoyed some success, and one of the Khan's sons was killed, but overall they encountered similar problems to those they faced when trying to assassinate the Crusaders, when cultural difference hampered any effective infiltration.

The wisdom of even attempting such a task was questionable. But, like the Khwarazmian Shah, Muhammad III had little option. The Mongols had made it clear that they had no interest in reaching any kind of diplomatic agreement with either the Nizaris or the Abbasid Caliphate. An independent religious figurehead had no place in their plans for world domination, any more than a sect whose name had become a byword for subversion and intrigue. Muslims at the Mongol court had made sure the Khan was well aware of their sinister reputation, and the Assassins had joined the top of his Persian hit list, alongside the Caliph in Baghdad.

In yet another repetition of the generational conflict that had come to characterise the leadership at Alamut, Muhammad III's son and heir, Kwurshah, was vocal in opposing his father's policy. He even went so far as to suggest that the Grand Master's opposition to the Mongols was evidence of his father's insanity. This father-son conflict would open the curtain of the final act. Muhammad III tried to disinherit his son, but rigid conventions relating to the hereditary Imamate thwarted his efforts. Kwurshah complained of his father's unpredictable moods, that he enjoyed scant respect, and charged that the Imam's policy would bring the wrath of the Khan upon them. In short, his father was not fit to rule and leadership should be passed on to him as soon as possible.

Even those who agreed with Kwurshah's proposed policy of appeasement were not willing to contemplate assassinating their Imam. Nonetheless, on 1 December 1255, Muhammad III was found dead – his severed head lying beside his body. According to a hostile Muslim account, making reference to the Assassins' alleged indulgence in alcohol, 'when the Angel of Death met his soul at the time set for its seizing, he complained of the calamitous day. The cupbearers of Hell came to meet him, to shatter the gladness of prosperity in his breast.'

The circumstances of the crime give up a few intriguing details. The victim was found in a shepherd's hut in the Alamut valley. It appears that Muhammad III was interested in farming, and often liked to roam his lands at night. This could be interpreted as another sign of his madness, or else that he shared some of his predecessors' interest in the simpler things in life. At the time of the crime Kwurshah was bedridden with a disease, the perfect alibi for a guilty conspirator. In the wake of the murder, he identified Muhammad's closest companion – too close, according to some gossip – as his assassin. The confidant was quickly executed; two of the accused sons and a daughter were hurled into his funeral pyre after him as alleged accomplices.

Case closed. Any doubts in Alamut about what might really have happened were swiftly eclipsed by events, as the news came that everyone had been dreading. The Mongols were coming!

Genghis Khan had died in 1227, and the ensuing civil war over his legacy gave the world something of a breathing space. His grandson, Mongke Khan, eventually took the throne in 1251. One of his first acts was to send his brother Hulegu to eliminate the Assassins. Some have suggested that the agents Muhammad III sent against the Mongol Khans provoked the move, but it appears that Mongke had decided to wipe them off the map of Persia regardless. Hulegu's vast invasion force set out in 1253, finally reaching the Persian border on the first day of 1256.

Meanwhile, Kwurshah had been indulging in a frenzied round of negotiations with anyone who would listen. He made efforts to return to his father's policy of renouncing heresy, sending messages to the Abbasid Caliph and other Sunni lords assuring them that the Assassins were now, once more, good orthodox Muslims, and offering alliances. He also tried to maintain a friendly dialogue with the approaching Mongol horde, optimistic that Alamut might yet be spared the Wrath of God.

It is easy to see Kwurshah as a kind of Neville Chamberlain figure, the appeasing British Prime Minister of 1939. Sadly, Alamut in 1256 lacked a Churchill waiting in the wings. Hitler's devastating strategy of blitzkrieg would be in part inspired by the highly mobile Mongol method of waging war, and Hulegu's actions in the ensuing campaign sometimes evoke the worst excesses of Hitler's SS.

If Kwurshah had a coherent policy as the enemy drove ever deeper into Assassin territory, it was to delay and procrastinate. As the Mongol war machine began to chew away at the network of fortresses and defensive positions established over generations, the Grand Master endeavoured to find a diplomatic solution. It was an uneven fight between an isolated heretical sect and the most mercilessly efficient military power of the day; between a ruthless, seasoned general and a weak, flawed religious leader whose thoughts were evidently turning from how to save his people to how to save his own skin.

Negotiations were wholly one-sided. Whilst a number of Nizari positions were mounting effective resistance to the Mongol advance, their leader was sending increasingly plaintive messages to the enemy general. Hulegu demanded that Kwurshah come and give his unconditional surrender in person. It was the one demand that the Assassin Grand Master found impossible to meet. But he agreed to begin decommissioning Assassin defences, and sent a succession of his relatives – or at least people who claimed to be his relatives – as hostage to the Mongol commander, as evidence of his good will.

Eventually, inevitably, the Mongol forces that were lapping around the formidable defences of the Assassins reached Maymundiz, the Nizari fortress that stood as the final buffer before Alamut. Hulegu demanded that it be surrendered and destroyed at once. Kwurshah dithered.

> 'As for the mangonels [siege engines] that had been erected it was as though their poles were made of pine trees a hundred years old (as for their fruit, "their fruit is as it were the heads of Satans"): and with the first stone that sprang up from them the enemy's mangonel was broken and many were crushed under it. And great fear of the bolts from the crossbows overcame them so that they were utterly distraught and everyone in the corner of a stone made a shield out of a veil, while some who were standing on a tower crept in their fright like mice into a hole or fled like lizards into crannies in the rocks. Some were left wounded and some lifeless and all that day they struggled but feebly and bestirred themselves like mere women. And when the heavens doffed the cap of the sun and the earth raised the curtain of night from the soil up to the Pleiades, they withdrew from battle.'

This description of the siege of Maymundiz is by Juwayni, the Muslim chronicler who accompanied Hulegu on his campaign, whose accounts of the Assassins are quoted throughout this book. He was no friend of the sect, but there can be little doubt that his eyewitness description of the devastating impact the Mongol war machine had on the Nizari defenders contains much truth. The stones that battered the spirit out of Maymundiz also appear to have pounded Kwurshah into submission. Days later, he surrendered both himself and Alamut.

The sacred birthplace of the Assassin sect was pillaged and destroyed. Juwayni was allowed to pick through anything he thought worthwhile from its legendary library, then the rest was consigned to the flames. With it, many of the secrets of the sect went up in flames, along with the spirit of the Assassins themselves.

Kwurshah doubtless believed he had made the right decision. He was received as an honoured opponent by Hulegu, who indulged the Imam's whims. Kwurshah was a keen camel enthusiast and was given a generous gift of a hundred Bactrian camels. Hulegu even gave the Assassin leader a young Mongol girl he had taken a fancy to, as his bride. But Kwurshah was now his captor's puppet, travelling the Assassin domain, ordering the commanders of each fortress in turn to follow his example, and open their gates to the Mongol invader. Many did but some resisted, revolted by the cowardice of their leader. Lamasar refused to surrender, as did Girdkuh, while Kwurshah's messages instructing his Syrian subjects to send messages of submission to the Khan were ignored. The famed 20th-century travel writer and adventuress Freya Stark believes, 'Alamut might and should have held out.' There were many Assassin leaders who would have preferred to follow the example of Kwurshah's more pugnacious predecessors.

While Hulegu's army was an apparently insurmountable force, it would not have been the first time Alamut had witnessed a miraculous delivery. But they were burdened with an incompetent, cowardly leader. His father was probably right: only an Assassin's knife stuck into Hulegu's belly, or at least left quietly by his pillow as he slept, might have saved them. As it was, Kwurshah headed east, fully expecting a reward from Mongke Khan for the betrayal of his people. The Khan refused to see him, observing that the fortresses of Girdkuh and Lamasar still held out. On his despondent return journey, the last Grand Master of Alamut was kicked to the ground by his Mongol escort, who then finished the job with their swords.

Back in the Assassin territories of Persia, the Nizaris were ordered to present themselves to the nearest towns for a census. It was the pretext for a massacre. Men, women and children were put to the sword in an act of genocide, on a posthumous order dating from the days of Genghis Khan that declared, 'none of that people should be spared, not even the babes in the cradle.'

Lamasar held out until 1258, Girdkuh until 1270, and even Alamut was briefly reoccupied in 1275 – suggesting what might have been if the Assassins had a stronger leader. But it was not to be. 'In that breeding-ground of heresy in the Rudbar of Alamut the home of the wicked adherents of Hasan Sabbah . . . there remains not one stone of the foundations upon another,' relates Juwayni with evident satisfaction. The destruction of Alamut left the Syrian Nizaris wholly isolated.

In truth, since the golden age of Sinan's reign the Syrian Assassins had been stricken by the same creeping apathy that had afflicted their Persian comrades under Muhammad II, withdrawing from the world under the influence of the Resurrection, an occult spiritual victory which negated any need for conquests in the vulgar material world. As in Persia, the activities of the Syrian missionaries and Assassins were never wholly abandoned, but the Grand Masters of Masyaf appear to have slumped into a state of comfortable complacency, devoid of the revolutionary zeal of their early days. Events were overtaking them.

The Crusader states were also suffering from the same gradual drop in combative spirit, as generations of living cheek by jowl with their Muslim neighbours inevitably took the edge off their religious bigotry. The Grand Masters of the Templar and Hospitaller Orders had received annual tributes from the Assassins – much to the dismay of the papacy, who believed these knights of God should have been exterminating unbelievers – just as the Assassins exacted protection money from other local leaders. One lasting legacy of Saladin's campaigns had been an increasing disinterest in the European Crusader ideals. His reputation as a chivalrous leader deflated much of the papal propaganda that portrayed all Muslims as unholy monsters. Crusading was becoming yesterday's news, a feeling exacerbated by a succession of disastrous, farcical and reprehensible Crusades throughout the 13th century.

Events in Persia inevitably had a knock-on effect in the region. The collapse of the Khwarazmian Empire under Mongol assault sent a maverick force of Khwarazmian warriors westward. In 1244, they captured Jerusalem from a skeleton Christian force, encouraged by the Egyptian Sultan. Nobody seemed to care. Crusaders in the region did not rush to the aid of the Holy City, and its capture was greeted with comparative indifference in Europe. One exception was Louis IX of France, who vowed to liberate Jerusalem after surviving a fatal disease, a miracle he attributed to God. The expedition he led to the Middle East – commonly called the Seventh Crusade (1248-54) – failed to make any lasting impact upon the situation, but he did encounter the Assassins. The accounts of his biographer, Jean de Joinville, provide an intriguing insight into the world of the Nizaris in the Syrian sect's twilight years – for King Louis not only employed negotiations with the Nizaris, but also sent envoys to the court of the Mongol Khan – some of the Mongols were Christians and he was prepared to go to any lengths to fulfil his quest of liberating Jerusalem.

The Mongols were heading that way anyway. Fresh from his Persian campaigns, Hulagu came storming southward through Syria in 1260, meeting little real resistance. Then fate took a hand, when news finally reached Hulagu that Mongke had died the previous year. He immediately abandoned the campaign to his subordinates, painfully aware that it was political suicide to be absent when the new Khan was appointed.

It gave the Egyptian Sultanate just enough breathing space to co-ordinate a counterattack. They delivered it on the third of September 1260, at Ain Jalut, locally known as the Spring of Goliath. For the first time a major Mongol force was beaten in pitched battle, changing the balance of power in the region in a single day of bloody conflict. The core of the victorious Egyptian force were the Mamluks – warriors bought as slaves in boyhood to be trained in the arts of war – and the architect of their victory was the Mamluk general Baibars, who had first proven himself against the Crusaders.

In the wake of the battle Baibars seized power and began taking the battle to the Crusaders, determined to complete the job his predecessor Saladin had started a century before in uniting Islam and eradicating the infidel. Throughout the 1260s, he led a merciless advance northward, hammering the Crusader states with a series of shattering victories. In contrast to Saladin, there was little that was chivalrous about this new Muslim champion, as he subjected one captured city after another to ruthless brutality some regard as vengeance for the savagery of the early Christian Crusades.

'If you had been there to see it,' he wrote in one taunting letter to the ruler of Antioch, describing his treatment of its captured subjects, 'you would have wished to have never been born.' The Crusader presence in Palestine and Syria steadily shrunk to a few pockets on the Mediterranean coast. Louis IX attempted to relieve the situation by landing in North Africa in 1270, but this Eighth Crusade proved an even more farcical exercise than its predecessor. He died of dysentery on 25 August that year, in Tunis. His last word was, reportedly, 'Jerusalem.'

The Syrian Assassins were largely spectators to these unfolding events. Alliances with their Christian neighbours were increasingly irrelevant, while the prospect of the triumph of the Mongols, who had exterminated their fellow sectarians in Persia, must have filled them with horror. There was little option but to hope that Baibars would prove more amenable to the Nizari heretics than he had to the Christian infidels. They showered the new Egyptian Sultan with gifts and gave material support to his campaigns. To their immense relief, Baibars seemed well-disposed towards them. But the price of his protection was high.

In return Baibars took the sect's independence. There were attempts to resist his control, acts of rebellion, even reports of Assassins ordered to murder the Sultan, but none of it came to anything. Lacking an Imam, they were in little position to resist and, by around 1270, Baibars in effect became their new Grand Master, appointing and dismissing Assassin leaders, treating their castles as his own property, reducing the fiercely independent sect to mere vassals of the Sultanate. He also apparently began employing Nizari Assassins as his own private Murder Inc.

The Eighth Crusade is also generally regarded as the last. At the behest of Louis IX, Prince Edward of England sailed to the Holy Land, though the French King died before he arrived so he changed course, docking in Acre in 1271. Sensing the desperate situation, Edward began negotiating an alliance with the Mongols against Baibars. A series of inconclusive engagements ensued, as Edward employed his Mongol allies to harass Baibars while Baibars attempted to flank his opponent by building a fleet. In June 1272 the Egyptian Sultan unleashed his secret weapon, sending an Assassin to murder his English foe. The Assassin only wounded his target before Edward overcame and killed his assailant. Legend has it that the dagger was poisoned, and that the prince only survived because his devoted wife Eleanor sucked the venom from the wound.

Such fancies aside, the prince had no time to exact any vengeance as word came from England that his father had died, and he was obliged to sail home to take the throne. As Edward I he was to become one of the nation's greatest monarchs, his successful campaigns against the Welsh and the Scottish laying the groundwork for the United Kingdom and earning him the epithet 'Hammer of the Scots'. He would be unsympathetically portrayed by Patrick McGoohan in the 1995 film *Braveheart*, as the cold-hearted tyrant Longshanks opposed by Mel Gibson's tartan freedom fighter, William Wallace. But it is intriguing to reflect that, had the last recorded Assassin hit before the sect faded from history been a success, British and European history might have looked very different.

Meanwhile, the Crusader kingdoms were living on borrowed time, and the successful capture of Acre by Baibars, in 1291, effectively closed that chapter in history. Which now brings us back full-circle . . .

Conclusion

MASS MURDER IN PARADISE

Assessing the impact and significance of the Assassins poses several basic questions. The first is, to what extent can Hasan Sabbah's revolution be said to have succeeded? In *A Criminal History of Mankind*, Colin Wilson is in little doubt: 'The story of the assassins is a parable in how *not* to go about achieving power.' Wilson cites Hasan's adoption of the assassination policy as his crucial mistake:

> 'For a man who kills by stealth cannot be trusted. He inspires the same kind of exaggerated horror as a poisonous snake or spider. And the comparison establishes precisely why the terrorist method carries the seed of its own downfall . . . Once a man has established himself in this category – labelled "dangerous and untrustworthy" – he can abandon all hope of achieving his aims by normal means.'

But did the Assassins fail in the manner that Wilson suggests? While Hasan surely failed in his ultimate aim of converting the entire Islamic world to his heretical creed – an ambitious aim by any standards – simple survival qualifies as a major achievement under the circumstances. More importantly, from Hasan's point of view, his revolution also survived – both within and without the walls of Alamut – for the best part of two centuries and beyond. The extent to which his doctrines survived unaltered remains debatable. But the fact remains that there are now some 12 to 15 million Nizaris worldwide today, who regard Hasan Sabbah not as a heretic or revolutionary, but as a religious visionary who kept the flame of their creed alive during its darkest days.

The question of how Hasan achieved these ends has taken on a new urgency since an increasing number of commentators started to draw analogies between the Assassins of the Middle Ages and the Islamist terrorists of today. Of course, there is no getting away from the obvious parallel of suicide attacks, but there are also profound differences. In many respects, using targeted murder in order to achieve 'regime change' makes Hasan's field operatives closer to CIA agents than al-Qaeda's indiscriminate angels of death. A lot depends on where you are standing, and the veil of secrecy surrounding the sect has made for a very flexible myth – one employed and exploited in a diverse variety of roles, at every end of the religious and political spectrum.

However, the idea of Osama bin Laden as the spiritual descendant of Hasan Sabbah continues to recur. A 2002 article for *Reason* magazine entitled 'Old School Osama' made such an analogy. While admitting that the 'string of connections is now in bad odour,' its author, Charles Paul Freund, found cause for cautious optimism. 'Hasan Sabbah may have been a puritan ascetic who terrorised his contemporaries in the name of revealed truth,' notes Freund. 'Yet in the end, his career set the stage for the single most dramatic illumination of Islam's modernist potential.' He is referring of course to the modern Ismaili Nizaris, followers of the Aga Khan, whom he describes as 'a remarkably prosperous and well-educated group that exhibits complete religious tolerance, supports liberal politics and economics, and is willing to invest heavily in these principles.'

'Osama bin Laden and the shadow of Hasan Sabbah passed each other recently,' notes the journalist. 'As Al Qaeda was being driven into hiding in Afghanistan, the Aga Khan pledged $75 million in tithed Ismaili wealth for that country's reconstruction . . . Even as Wahabi believers used modernity to multiply the terror of blood that was invented by Hasan, Hasan's distant sectarian descendants were recognising the meaning and opportunity of the modern world.'

Such soberly optimistic views of the legacy of Hasan Sabbah remain in the minority, despite the best efforts of Ismaili academics like Dr Farhad Daftary. Whatever the true impact of the historical Hasan, the mythical version – the Old Man of the Mountain of popular folklore – remains a powerfully sinister and mysterious figure, a cipher for the darkest fringes of political and religious taboo. It seems likely that medieval Europeans concocted the legends of the gardens of Paradise, where Hasan indoctrinated his Assassins, because they found their suicidal behaviour otherwise difficult to comprehend. Recent history has proven that religious fervour represents an intoxicant more than adequate to fuel suicide attacks all on its own. It is a far from reassuring revelation.

On the *Hashisheen* record album, Hakim Bey, a self-styled American orientalist who discerns a mystical alternative to Western sexual puritanism in the theology and folklore of the East, promises the listener,

'Muhammad said that those who had obeyed his will would enter Paradise.'

The album was released in 1999, just two years prior to the most monumental realisation of Muhammad's promise since the days of the Assassins. The perpetrators and their advocates were not a part of any romantically decadent alternative society, nor were they high on anything but piety. But in the hijackings and plane bombings of 9/11, the word 'martyrdom' came back into the modern vocabulary in a manner that implied murder in the name of God/Allah and, as one Wahabi Muslim preacher put it, 'the smell of Paradise . . . I can smell those gardens now!'

***

'O ye who believe, what is the matter with you, that when ye are asked to go forth in the cause of God, ye cling so heavily to the earth? Do you prefer the life of this world to the hereafter? But little is the comfort of this life, as compared with the hereafter.' – Osama bin Laden's February 1998 fatwa against America.

Belief is the most fundamental weapon in the armoury of the modern terrorist (or freedom fighter). Belief can overcome rationality, subvert science and, temporarily perhaps, transform a ragtag grouping of malcontents into a formidable army of Assassins. Such were the events of the morning of 11 September 2001, when nineteen young men of Arab extraction boarded internal flights along the USA's eastern seaboard.

So monumental were the events of that day that its reverberations may still be felt after all of our lifetimes. The images of monolithic New York skyscrapers collapsing are imprinted on our collective consciousness, their repetition by TV and the press eclipsing even the Zapruder footage of JFK's assassination.

In the scale of its terrifyingly surreal spectacle, we may agree with modernist composer Karlheinz Stockhausen that 9/11 was 'the greatest work of art that exists for the whole Cosmos'; we may have sympathy for the jihadists' view that it was a blow struck against the symbols of American plutocracy, or with the consensus view that the approximately 3,000 lives lost that morning were unjustly taken in the worst act of terrorism ever seen on American soil. None of these viewpoints individually contradict each other. (The late Stockhausen would insist he actually called 9/11 'the greatest work of art by Lucifer' – which does not change the meaning of his original statement overmuch.)

To gauge exactly what the day meant to the perpetrators and their fellow conspirators, some small insight is lent by an unlicensed DVD distributed via Islamic charity stores and market stalls in the UK during 2002. (The authors' copy was obtained from a street market in west London.) Entitled *The 19 Martyrs*, it begins with spliced-together footage representing the third attack of the morning, on the Pentagon in Washington DC. Much of this sequence seems to have been culled from unrelated sources, but it culminates in shots of the bombed-out building.

Then Arabic chanting begins, with a subtitled translation from the Koran:

> *'Fight them! Allah will punish them by your hands, disgrace them and give you victory over them and He will heal the breasts of a believing people and remove the anger of their hearts. And Allah turns (in mercy) to whosoever He wills and Allah is All-Knowing, All-Wise.'* (Koran 9: 14-15)

The apocalyptic testimony continues with shots of dark clouds covering the moon, followed by a montage of current affairs footage including clips of the US military prison at Guantanamo Bay, Israeli policing of the Palestinians in Jerusalem and horse riders in Afghanistan:

> *'When layers of darkness cover the horizon, and we are bitten by the sharpest fangs, and our homes overflow with blood, as the aggressor continues his destruction, and the glint of swords and sound of hooves have disappeared from the battlefields and our cries are drowned out by the noise of strings and percussion* [cue footage of Muslims excited by the trivial entertainment of a football match], *suddenly their storms arise* [the Twin Towers of the WTC – the 'World Terror Centre', according to the film's makers] *to demolish their fortresses* [the second tower is hit by a jetliner, less a commercial skyscraper to its attackers than an enemy compound] *and proclaim to them we shall not stop our raids until you abandon our lands* [the massive smoke clouds rise over Manhattan from the collapsed towers].'

The scene changes to humid, dusty desert land in the Middle East, and a calmer narration: *'When we speak about the attacks on New York and Washington, we are speaking about those who changed the course of history and purified the* Ummah [collective Muslim faithful] *from the filth of the treacherous rulers and their followers . . .'*

The first five of the nineteen martyrs are venerated in frame like holy icons: 'Engineer Mohammed Atta's Regiment, Destroyer of the World Terror Centre (North Tower)', with Atta himself framed in the centre in a cameo-like circle:

'We are speaking about men who I do not say merely demolished the Twin Towers and the Pentagon, but rather they destroyed the idol of the times and destroyed his values.' Rather grandiosely, the narrator seems to believe the idolatry of Western capitalism came to an end with the collapse of the towers. The next five martyrs are then brought into frame: 'Marwan Al-Shehhi's Regiment – Destroyers of the World Terror Centre (South Tower).'

News footage of President George W. Bush shaking hands with former Israeli premier and leader of the armed forces Ariel Sharon is labelled 'War Criminals and Child Killers'. As ever, exactly who is the terrorist, who is the freedom fighter and who is the soldier depends on pre-existing beliefs, and whether attacks such as those on the WTC and the Pentagon are perceived as a massive assault on human life and values or as a grand statement *in support of* human life and values.

As the government and military of Israel – understandably locked into a siege mentality, seeing most of their Middle Eastern neighbours as potential nemeses – continue their retaliatory policy of 'smash my windows and I'll carpet bomb your children' in their former occupied territories, All Is Terror to those who remain on the receiving end.

Gruesome footage of bomb-blasted dead children from Afghanistan rams this point home – Palestine, Iraq (where the US was not yet at war, though sanctions were starving Iraqi hospitals of medicines), Lebanon and Kashmir are also cited, as though each individual conflict has the same root cause and the same enemy. In the mind of the modern Mujahideen they are still fighting the West's Crusaders.

'These great men have consolidated faith in the hearts of the believers,' eulogises the narrator as 'Hani Hanjour's Regiment' are brought into the frame, 'Destroyers of the Centre for American Terrorism (the Pentagon).' While there is no praise attached to the mission to aerial-bomb Camp David (the hijacked plane crashing in Pennsylvania instead), each of the nineteen are individually venerated for their earthly sacrifices, with the Koranic promise of reward in the hereafter: *'Paradise is under the shade of swords.'*

One of the younger suicide bombers, Abu al-Abbas, also appears at length in footage from his own 'martyrdom video' — *19 Martyrs* becomes his last will and testament, suggesting that its makers were in contact with those elusive Old Men of the Mountain that the West calls al-Qaeda.

'As I sit down to write this will I do not know how to start,' announces the fresh-faced, longhaired youth, who will shortly take steps to obliterate his existence alongside that of many human beings completely unknown to him. 'So I have chosen to make them letters written by my heart before my pen. I write them while fully conscious of what I am saying.' His address breaks down into a series of twelve aural letters: To You, O Poor Human / To You, O Muslim / To the Practising Muslim / To the Seeker of Knowledge / To You, O Scholar / To You, O Businessman / To You, O Mujahid / To the Parents of the Mujahid / To the Wife of the Mujahid / To My Mujahid Son / To the Men of My Clan and My Tribe / To the Residents of the Arabian Peninsula.

(Al-Abbas claims inspiration from the mother of Khalid al-Islambouli, assassin of Egypt's President Sadat. 'I have to sacrifice a little [her son's life] in the interest of something greater than that,' she testifies in the film. 'This worldly life isn't the best. No, the afterlife is eternal happiness.')

'I write [these words] in the moments before the end – an end like the beginning – with joy and delight and an open heart,' rhapsodises al-Abbas. 'The words are many and the emotions increase. You cannot equal the desirous in his desires until your insides are inside his.'

The Saudi boy al-Abbas is lionised in the film by his mentor, Sheikh Osama bin Laden, as a Koranic scholar as well as a martyr, and the strength of his sincerity shines through disturbingly. The narrator announces in admiration:

> 'He carried both the love of the Ummah and a burning desire for slaughtering the enemy and by the grace of Allah his desire was fulfilled. He was selected to be a part of the ranks of the squadrons [cue Mujahideen undergoing firearms training in the mountain region of Afghanistan] that would carry out the assaults on New York and Washington. He and his brothers soon began taking the exclusive courses that would prepare them for the operations, and all worked studiously to acquire the most knowledge possible and overcome the obstacles before them.'

As a shocked and winded America would discover, it is hard to anticipate the strategy of an enemy Assassin who secretes himself amongst you, working quietly and industriously with both his and your own destruction as the only objective.

Abu al-Abbas's martyrdom testimony continues:

'With this act of mine, I discharge my duty and bring to life the obligation of *Jihad* in the *Ummah*. I have conviction in the duty that this path imposes on me, because the Book of Almighty Allah confirms the compulsory nature of *Jihad* in His Cause to rescue the Muslims from the humiliation that they are suffering and to save the violated lands of Islam.'

In his mind he was akin to an Assassin agent, believing his people under siege and therefore obligated to strike back directly, murderously. And, of course, divine providence would reward him for his actions: '[who] is slain or victorious, on him we shall bestow a vast reward.' (4: 74)

Al-Abbas pre-emptively says of himself,

'When I sacrificed myself cheaply for Allah's Cause, I did not do so in order to escape from a life of hardship, as those whom Allah has disgraced allege . . . when I left home in the prime of my youth, I left in the name of Allah, while enjoying the finest of food and drink, living in a luxurious home, driving a beautiful car and able to find an attractive job . . . And Allah says, "Whosoever desires the life of the world and its adornment, we shall repay them their deeds therein, and therein they will not be wronged. Those are they for whom there is nothing in the Hereafter save the Fire. [All] that they contrive here is vain and [all] that they do is fruitless."' [11: 15-16]

Thus spoke the idealistic tones of absolute world-rejection, and also the voice of righteous fanaticism: 'I embarked upon this path at a time when the grandsons of monkeys and swine from the Jews and Christians have trespassed upon Muslim women, desecrating their honour and violating their dignity.' His ire stoked, al-Abbas shows the viewer a scene of Israeli police beating Muslim women with sticks. The footage is ugly and serves to justify his all-encompassing cause; to the less partisan onlooker, it summons up a world of abuse in which the weaker sex is often still at the mercy of men wielding power – in the Islamic Republic of Iran, for example.

Similarly distressing scenes of the twelve-year-old Mohammed Durra dying under Israeli sniper fire serve to fuel al-Abbas' vengefulness. Besides the removal of the Jews from the Middle East, both al-Abbas and bin Laden speak of the necessity of the West's withdrawal from the Arabian Peninsula – the region of the Saudi oil fields that made the elusive sheikh's family incredibly wealthy. From their viewpoint, the Zionists and the American-dominated West constitute one several-headed beast.

Al-Abbas quotes the Koran 2: 248 – 'How often is it that a small force has vanquished a big one by Allah's will? Allah is with those who steadfastly persevere' – as replayed shots of the hijacked passenger jets fly into the Twin Towers.

> 'I embarked because I long for death and hate this life, and because I have conviction in Allah's promise to us. And I have set out to kill those who love this life and hate death, and I have certainty in Allah's warning to them . . . My objective is this hope inside and out, and my request from the One, the Creator, His Martyrdom in His Path with sincerity, wiping away my sins and saving me from the Fire . . . By this, I hope to receive Allah's reward and the delights that He has prepared in the highest Gardens of Paradise. Their paradise is this world, whereas our Paradise is in the Hereafter, and for us are pleasures and delights which no eyes have seen, no ear has heard and no human has even imagined.'

Except, perhaps, for the legendary Assassins of Alamut. As the young man al-Abbas concludes, 'The price of the Garden is high.' Video shots of desert and tropical sunsets give a low-budget approximation of the Gardens of Jinna. 'The comfort of this world is fleeting, the Hereafter is the best for those who do right . . .' (4: 77)

***

In the immediate aftermath of the 9/11 attacks, President Bush promised, 'The United States will hunt down and punish those responsible for these cowardly acts.' But 'cowardly' always seems a misnomer for Mohammed Atta and his cohorts, infused as they were with the myopic zeal of the ancient Assassins. How can you hunt down and punish the transgressors when (with the exception of one who turned tail and never achieved martyrdom) they have immolated their bodies in the promise of justice on earth, and a divinely erotic afterlife in the hereafter?

The President's promised 'War on Terror', too, was inverted in the actuality – becoming a worldwide escalation of Islamist terror outside of the USA. The Islamic world would perceive the air strikes that preceded

Bush's ground invasion of Iraq, and the war of attrition by Russia against Muslim insurgents in Chechnya, as the modern continuation of a worldwide crusade by the infidel.

Meanwhile, in cyberspace, a cultural war continues to be fought by well-educated guerrillas who will never raise a dagger, fire a gun or detonate explosives. Many Islamist sites have been closed down by American and European security services, though the 'stateless' nature of the worldwide web – and safeguards of free speech such as the US Constitution – makes it naturally difficult to police.

(In the UK, the Birmingham-based Al-Ansaar News Agency sought to release *The 19 Martyrs* as a commercial DVD, almost quaintly unaware that the Al-Qaeda polemic broke domestic laws relating to promotion of terrorism. Doggedly controversial, the Muslim news site that monitors the US War on Terror has been blocked by web servers several times throughout its existence and has been the recipient of a disputed video broadside allegedly recorded by bin Laden. In al-Ansaar's defence, the opening of its unreleased DVD states that the agency 'condemn all forms of terrorism regardless of who the perpetrators are'.)

'The RAND Corporation has a guy called Brian Jenkins, in the seventies he was one of the first people to use the term "international terrorism",' remarks Ken Hollings in the last of his conversations with the authors. 'He's been talking out more and more, saying that, in terms of dealing with the Islamist threat, the one thing we are really rubbish at is policing the Internet. And it's kind of interesting really, the notion that the enemy is already in the system, the enemy is in the network, and, like the Assassin, we are just waiting for him to walk through walls – to walk through firewalls, literally.'

The djinn is in the machine, so it seems. The invisible Assassin who searches and destroys by stealth is now an ancient and unsophisticated archetype. But he persists – without an identifiable form, perhaps without even a corporeal body – in casting his barely discernible shadow across the modern communications media.

SELECT BIBLIOGRAPHY

Baigent, Michael, Leigh, Richard and Lincoln, Henry – *The Holy Blood and the Holy Grail* (Jonathan Cape, 1983)

Barber, Malcolm – *The Trial of the Templars* (Cambridge University Press, 1994)

Bartlett, W. B. – *Assassins: The Story of Medieval Islam's Secret Sect* (Sutton Publishing, 2007)

Belfield, Richard – *The Secret History of Assassination* (Magpie Books, 2008)

Bresler, Fenton – *Who Killed John Lennon?* (St Martin's Press, 1989)

Burman, Edward – *The Assassins: Holy Killers of Islam* (Crucible, 1987)

Burroughs, William S. – *Cities of the Red Night* (John Calder, 1981)

Burroughs, William S. – *The Naked Lunch* (John Calder, 1982)

Burroughs, William S. – *Nova Express* (Jonathan Cape, 1969)

Burroughs, William S. – *The Ticket that Exploded* (Calder and Boyars, 1968)

Burroughs, William S. – *The Wild Boys* (Calder and Boyars, 1972)

Burroughs, William S. – *A William Burroughs Reader* (edited by John Calder, Pan Books, 1982)

Cammell, Donald – *Performance: Classic Screenplay* (Faber & Faber, 2001)

Cole, Dr Jon and Dr Benjamin – *MARTYRDOM: Radicalisation and Terrorist Violence among British Muslims* (Pennant Books, 2009)

Condon, Richard – *The Manchurian Candidate* (Michael Joseph, 1960)

Condon, Richard – *Winter Kills* (Weidenfeld & Nicholson, 1971)

Constantine, Alex – *Psychic Dictatorship in the USA* (Feral House, 1995)

Constantine, Alex – *Virtual Government: CIA Mind Control Operations in America* (Feral House, 1997)

Daftary, Farhad – *The Assassin Legends: Myths of the Isma'ilis* (I. B. Taurus, 2008)

Daftary, Farhad – *A Short History of the Ismailis* (Edinburgh University Press, 1999)

Daraul, Arkon – *Secret Societies* (Tandem, 1965)

Dillon, Martin – *God and the Gun* (Orion, 1997)

Dillon, Martin – *The Shankill Butchers* (Hutchinson, 1989)

Dillon, Martin – *The Trigger Men* (Mainstream, 2003)

Dostoyevsky, Fyodor – *The Devils* (translated by David Magarshack, Penguin Classics, 1953)

Ellroy, James – *American Tabloid* (Arrow, 1995)

Ellroy, James – *The Cold Six Thousand* (Arrow, 2002)

Forsyth, Frederick – *The Day of the Jackal* (Hutchinson, 1971)

Garrison, Jim – *On the Trail of the Assassins* (Sheridan Square Press, 1988)

Grant, R. G. – *Assassinations* (Silverdale Books, 2004)

Hammer-Purgstall, Joseph von, (trans. Oswald Charles Wood) – *The History of the Assassins* (Smith and Elder, Cornhill, 1835)

Hodges, Brian D. – 'Nothing Is True, Everything Is Permitted', Disinformation.com, 6 September 2001

Hollings, Ken – 'Their Hands in Your Life', *Bizarre* #34, June 2000

Hollings, Ken – *Welcome to Mars: Fantasies of Science in the American Century 1947-1959* (Strange Attractor Press, 2008)

Kennedy #1/2 (Morcrim International Publications, 1977)

Knight, Peter (editor) – *Conspiracy Nation* (New York University Press, 2002)

The Koran (translated with notes by N. J. Dawood, Penguin Classics, 1956)

Lewis, Bernard – *The Assassins: A Radical Sect in Islam* (Phoenix, 2003)

Lone, John – *Oswald's Trigger Films:* The Manchurian Candidate, We Were Strangers, Suddenly? (Falcon Books, 2000)

Ludlum, Robert – *The Bourne Identity* (Putnam, 1980)

Mailer, Norman – *Oswald's Tale: An American Mystery* (Little, Brown and Company, 1995)

Maalouf, Armin – *The Crusades through Arab Eyes* (Saqi, 2006)

McKenzie, Norman (ed.) – *Secret Societies* (Crescent Books, 1987)

Marrs, Jim – *Crossfire: The Plot that Killed Kennedy* (Carroll & Graf, 1989)

The 19 Martyrs (unreleased DVD, 2002)

Marshall, Robert – *Storm from the East* (BBC/Penguin Books, 1994)

Nicholson, Helen J. & Nicolle, David – *God's Warriors: Crusaders, Saracens and the Battle for Jerusalem* (Osprey Publishing, 2005)

Nicolle, David – *Acre 1291: Bloody Sunset of the Crusader States* (Osprey, 2005)

Parfrey, Adam (ed.) – *Extreme Islam* (Feral House, 2001)

Posner, Gerald – *Case Closed* (Random House, 1993)

Ross M.D., Colin A. – *Bluebird: Deliberate Creation of Multiple Personality by Psychiatrists* (Manitou Communications, 2000)

Ridley, F. A. – *The Assassins* (Socialist Platform, 1988)

Riley-Smith, Jonathan (ed.) – *The Oxford Illustrated History of the Crusades* (Oxford Paperbacks, 2001)

Runciman, Steven – *A History of the Crusades* (3 vols.) (The Folio Society, 1994)

Sanders, Ed – *The Family* (revised and updated edition, Signet 1990)

Spencer, T. J. B. (ed.) – *Shakespeare's Plutarch* (Penguin, 1964)

Taubin, Amy – *Taxi Driver: BFI Film Classics* (BFI Publications, 2000)

Vale, V. (editor) – *William S. Burroughs, Brion Gysin, Throbbing Gristle* (Re-Search #4/5, 1982)

Wilson, Colin – *A Criminal History of Mankind* (Granada Publishing, 1984)

Wilson, Robert Anton – *Everything is Under Control: Conspiracies, Cults and Cover-Ups* (Harper Perennial, 1998)

Yallop, David – *Tracking the Jackal* (Random House, 1993)

INDEX